Coaching for Martial Artists: The Masterclass Text

Christopher Dewey

Coaching for Martial Artists: The Masterclass Text
Copyright © 2010 By Christopher Dewey

All rights reserved.

Printed in the United States of America. No part of this book may be used or reproduced in any manner whatsoever without written permission except in the case of brief quotations embodied in critical articles and reviews.

For publishing information contact: Fifth Estate, Post Office Box 116, Blountsville, AL 35031.

Cover Designed by An Quigley

Printed on acid-free paper

Library of Congress Control No: 2010940307

ISBN: 9781936533039

Fifth Estate
2010

ABOUT THE AUTHOR

Chris Dewey began martial arts in 1968 and currently holds the ranks of seventh degree Black Belt in Jujutsu, sixth degree Black Belt in Judo, fourth degree Black Belt in Taekwondo and third degree Black Belt in Hapkido.

Chris has been teaching martial arts for more than twenty-five years in community, elementary, high school, university and entrepreneurial settings. He has been the owner and chief instructor of the Starkville Martial Arts Academy since 1996. He currently serves on the Board of Directors of Akayama Ryu Jujutsu.

Chris has a tournament record that spans more than thirty years and has won national Judo championships in both kata (forms) and master's shiai (free fighting). Chris has also been a national level Judo referee, master rank examiner, was the Chair for the United States Judo Association Coach Certification Program from 2000-2005 and the USJA Coach of the Year in 1998. Chris wrote a monthly column for the National Association of Martial Artists MAPro magazine from 2002-2008.

Chris was born in England, lived in Canada for several years and currently makes his home in Mississippi, where he occasionally publishes books of poetry and observes nature through the lens of his camera.

DISCLAIMER

Although every effort has been taken to ensure the accuracy of the information presented herein, neither the author nor the publisher is responsible, in whole or in part, for any liability, loss, or injury that may result, or be alleged to result from reading and/or following the instructions herein. As with all physical activity, it is understood that there is an associated risk of injury or even death. It is recommended that you obtain the advice of a qualified medical professional before beginning or engaging in any physical activity. Studying and teaching martial arts brings with it obvious and not so obvious risks; it is after all, 'martial.' Remember that at the root of what we teach are actions that were derived from, and predicated upon, activities that occur in real combat environments. In combat settings, the runner-up doesn't go home with a silver medal! Do not practice without adequate training and supervision.

ACKNOWLEDGEMENTS

Given that I have been active in the martial arts since 1968, trained in three countries and two continents, and hold Black Belt rank in four different styles, it would be virtually impossible for me to give adequate thanks to all the people to whom I owe a debt of gratitude. I have been blessed to receive instruction from some truly outstanding instructors and mentors over the years, and from their examples I have learned much. Equally, if we are wise teachers we know that at all times we are students and that our students are often our teachers. To my students also then, I owe an enormous debt of gratitude.

So where to begin? I would not be here, writing this were it not for my parents who put me on the martial road all those years ago, with a simple enough question: "Do you want to learn Judo?" Perhaps I should thank all those bullies who led my parents to ask the question in the first place.

Roy Inman is one of the great British Olympic coaches and was my first sensei. He actually came to our house to visit our family, before I joined the Fairholme Judo Club and took my first Judo lesson. How many coaches visit with their potential students before they enroll? Roy, I have never thanked you for opening the door and guiding those first steps. My parents offered the opportunity, but you acted as the catalyst that changed my life completely, physically, mentally and spiritually. I do not know how to thank you enough.

We all stand on the shoulders of giants to see our world. I cannot possibly give my instructors and students the honor due, nor repay the debt that I owe each of you. If this manual helps you, the reader, to improve the martial arts in some small way, or give the opportunity of a new life to a struggling child or an adult looking for direction, then I will have said thank you to my teachers in the only way I know that has real meaning.

Thank you.

PREFACE

The book you are about to read exists for only one reason: to help **you**, the coach. Regardless of your personal coaching mission, it counts for naught if you do not recruit and retain students. My goal is to provide you with the tools necessary and help you to become an effective bridge between your students and the knowledge they seek. As an instructor, coach, sensei, sifu, teacher or whatever you call yourself, you touch the lives of your students. I want to help you perform that task in the most positive, effective and efficient fashion possible.

If you want to be a successful martial arts instructor you will need more than excellent technique and a desire to teach, although these are both indispensable. Being a successful instructor is as much about your personal desire for continuing your own education as it is about what you have to offer your students. Just because you have excellent technical skill or a room full of competition honors, does not necessarily mean that you can convey your knowledge to your students in an effective manner.

Consequently, if you wish to become a truly successful instructor, it is important that you acquire the skills required of a successful teacher; this is where this book can help you. I have taken forty years of my experience as a student, competitor, instructor, coach, and referee in several different martial arts at the club, regional, national and organizational levels, and more than a quarter of a century as a university professor as well as fifteen years as an entrepreneur and distilled them into this book. The fact remains, however, that it is your journey and your path. All that I can do is to hopefully provide some tools to help you along the way.

From a pedagogic perspective, teaching martial arts is no different to teaching any other curriculum. Achieving mastery in any subject requires that each student acquires a set of skills and takes ownership in a process of continual investigation, which together lead to higher levels of understanding. Unlike other areas of teaching, however, which may be predominantly physical or entirely mental, the martial arts teacher has the potential to profoundly affect the student's cognitive awareness, psychomotor abilities, emotional awareness, social skills and can even impact the spiritual aspects of life. When you work with your students you hold the potential to touch all aspects of the learning and growing process.

Thank you for choosing my book, and welcome.

"We are what we repeatedly do. Excellence then, is not an act, but a habit."

Aristotle

TABLE OF CONTENTS

- About the Author — v
- Disclaimer — vi
- Acknowledgements — vii
- Preface — viii
- Table of Contents — x

Content:

- Chapter 1: Introduction — 1
- Chapter 2: Conditions of Learning — 3
- Chapter 3: Communication Skills — 24
- Chapter 4: Pedagogy of Coaching — 30
- Chapter 5: Psychology of Coaching — 82
- Chapter 6: Physiology of Training — 116
- Chapter 7: Physics of Coaching — 171
- Chapter 8: Safety and Legal Considerations — 196
- Chapter 9: Final Thoughts — 215

Bibliography: — 217

Appendices:

- Appendix 1: Sample Eight-Week Progression from White Belt to Yellow Belt — 224
- Appendix 2: Sample Lesson Plan — 225
- Appendix 3: Sample Goals and Progress Questionnaire — 226
- Appendix 4: How can parents help? — 228
- Appendix 5: Sample Warning, Waiver, Release of Liability, Assumption of Risk and Agreement to Participate — 229
- Appendix 6: Sample Risk Agreement — 230
- Appendix 7: Sample Health History Form — 234

Chapter 1

INTRODUCTION

It would probably be a good idea to begin with some sort of idea of how this book came into being. What you are about to read is a distillation, revision and embellishment of three texts that were originally written for the United States Judo Association (Dewey, 2005a, 2005b, 2005c). Admittedly, Judo is a small segment of the martial arts world, so it came as no surprise to me that I was often asked why I didn't write a set of manuals for the larger martial arts community. The more I thought about it, that more I saw the need for a single master-level text that covered all the bases, rather than a series of smaller books.

In reality, this text could just as easily be adapted and applied to any area of learning with relative ease, because, if I'm honest, what I am writing about has little to do with martial arts, even less to do with Judo and a lot more to do with understanding how to create opportunities and environments for learning. We are each unique creatures, so I write from the perspective of a martial artist, a business owner and a college professor, because these are the worlds in which I have lived, and my words, therefore, reflect my experiences.

During our time shared together on these pages, we will cover a variety of topics that build upon each other. Each section could be read as a stand-alone chapter, but I have laid out the book as a progression. We will begin with establishing basic conditions of learning that will form the foundation of everything that is to follow. After building our foundation, we will discuss communication skills, because they will be the medium of knowledge delivery. I'm not talking just about the spoken word, or even our non-verbal communication, although these are obviously critical components of communication. I'm talking about everything that goes into communicating your message and vision as a coach…and that includes the condition of your school, its look, its feel, its smell, everything…all of these things are part of the message and the backdrop upon which you will deliver your classes.

From there we will get into the four P's of coaching: Pedagogy, Psychology, Physiology and Physics. Each of the four P's will contain some information that overlaps with, and is dependent upon, information in one of the other sections. For instance, you can't really talk about age-appropriate teaching methods (pedagogy), without bringing in aspects of physical development (physiology) and mental development (psychology). As such, each section will maintain its primary focus and leave detailed explanations that fall into one of the other areas of interest for the section more suited to their discussion.

By way of introduction then, let's create some broad brush-strokes of what we will be covering in the four P's: Pedagogy is nothing more than how you teach; it deals with the mechanics of the process. In a lot of ways, pedagogy is building a road map of how you will guide your students from novice White Belts to competent Black Belts, and beyond. As such, it will look at a nested set of challenges: lesson plans, syllabus and curriculum.

After understanding how to build a rock-solid curriculum, we will investigate how you will communicate your message to your students and how they, in turn, process the information that you deliver. We will, therefore, look at the all-important area of psychology. Students do not always learn the way you learn, nor are they motivated by the same sorts of carrots and/or sticks. Understanding the reasons why students do the things that they do, will help you successfully overcome the inevitable challenges that you will face along the path to learning and enable you to keep more students for longer.

Having said all of that, we must be willing to engage other disciplines related to: a) the human body and how it maintains a working efficiency (physiology) and b) how human machines interact in the field of combat (physics). In simple terms we need to have some idea how muscles keep working from a chemical perspective (physiology) and how the forces that they generate can be employed (physics). None of this is rocket science, but if you do not have a handle on it, you could be setting yourself up for some pretty frustrating classes…at the very least.

It is one thing to understand what you do, it is quite another to teach someone else how to do the same thing. Personal experience as an instructor of coaches and as a student has shown me that there are many gifted martial artists, who often have the desire to teach, but cannot convey to a willing student how it is that they do what they do with such grace. In order to be effective as a coach, you need to understand how the minds of your student process what you deliver, how their bodies turn it into action and how the resultant forces impact the world of combat.

Remember that teaching, mentoring and coaching is a craft. For sure, there must be some level of aptitude, but excellence is derived from practicing and honing your skills.

Chapter 2

CONDITIONS OF LEARNING

When we teach effectively, we create an environment in which the student is engaged in the learning process. It follows then, that regardless of the subject material, there are particular attributes of the learning environment, which when present, will facilitate the act of learning. As a coach, you are responsible and accountable for both the creation of an effective learning environment and the content of the lessons. To help you develop such an environment, a dozen or so conditions of learning have been described that, in combination, can lead to the creation of a positive learning environment (Gagne, Briggs and Wager, 1992; Martens, 1990; Weers, 1995; Wilen et al, 2000). The level to which you ensure that each of the conditions of learning is met during each class and for each lesson plan, controls the degree to which you will be successful in getting your message across to your students (Figure 2.1).

Figure 2.1: Create an environment in which you can communicate your message so that it is understandable, engage your students and provide training goals that are both meaningful and reachable for your audience. In the example shown, we have a simple blocking drill being shown to a subset of new white belts.

Of all conditions of learning, establishing and meeting goals must rank as the most important. In its simplest form, if you do not know what you want your students to learn, it will be impossible to proceed with the learning process.

Condition of Learning 1: Goal Setting. Goal setting is an integral part of all measured progress. To a greater or lesser extent we all like to have some idea of where we are going and what we are doing. The same is true of your students. Without achieving established goals, your students will become uncertain of where they are going and will lose motivation.

From the educational perspective, goals can be divided into four distinct groups:

Student expectations: First, what are your students' spoken or unspoken expectations of being in your classes? Ask yourself as a coach, why are these players in my class? Do I know? Am I providing what they are seeking? Are they seeking what I am willing and/or able to teach? Helping your students to meet their goals provides meaningful reasons for continuing the process of training. It is therefore important to know why your students are in class in the first place. If the instructor is unaware of the student's goals in training it will be difficult at best to develop a true working relationship. We'll talk a lot more about this aspect of training later when we get into the psychology of coaching.

Specific student performance goals: The second aspect of goal setting is the practical performance goal associated with any given exercise or technique in a lesson plan. Class performance goals are necessarily very specific, short-term goals that lead to overall class satisfaction. On a class-by-class basis, performance goals allow both student and instructor to measure the degree to which a training drill has been successfully executed. Any performance goal must be **specific, challenging but attainable, performance-oriented, time-bounded** and **measurable**. Two of the major keys here are that each goal should be challenging enough to motivate your students and measurable so that the students can see exactly how close they are to achieving the goal. Moreover, a performance goal must be very specific, allowing no room for ambiguity by the student, the coach, or in the ability to measure the goal. Performance goals must be based upon what the student actually does, and not dependent upon an outcome beyond his or her immediate control.

A measurable performance goal for a biomechanical action might include the correct foot or body position. In a tournament situation, an appropriate goal might be to make a specified number of attacks with a specific skill during a given time interval. Obtaining a specific score during a tournament is dependent upon outside factors over which the player has no control, is therefore, outcome related and consequently, not a reasonable goal (Figure 2.2). Whether being used during class or during competition, performance goals must be things that lie within the student's immediate sphere of control.

Figure 2.2: In a tournament setting, a player can control what he does with his body, but cannot fully control whether his throw will be successful or whether the referee will see it from the correct position or give it the appropriate score.

To summarize, and drive home the point for those of you who coach tournament athletes at any level: **A student can control where s/he places his or her body during the application of a skill and the number of times a skill is *attempted* during a tournament match. The student cannot control what score, if any, a referee might award for a successful technique**. By way of example, in the Karate tournament circuits in which I have been both a competitor and a referee, I have had it impressed upon me that if a referee does not see the technique actually impact the surface of the opponent's body, then no score can be awarded, **regardless** of the apparent effectiveness of the technique. Skilled players know this and will always make sure that the maximum number of referees can see their actions, while at the same time controlling the ring so as to actively place the weaker player in blind positions so that even if the weaker player does score, the referees will be unable to see the technique land.

Long-term goals: A third set of goals relates to how your lesson plans fit into a long-term program of study that will lead to higher levels of mastery. Every lesson plan should be a step in the process of getting to a specific goal and presupposes the existence of some sort of long-range plan such as achieving a certain level performance ability (Gleeson, 1967). The ability may be measured by rank promotions, competitive activity, or real-world application. As an example, let us use achieving a Black Belt as our long-term plan. Each requirement for any given rank is an action step within the single goal of obtaining the next rank and should be reflected in your lesson plan sequence. Obviously, each rank is a stair-step of progress and a measurable indicator of how close a student is to his or her goal.

When a White Belt steps onto the mat for the first time, setting a goal of Black Belt may be very commendable, but it is a nebulous goal based on a lack of information. A much more specific and attainable goal as a novice martial artist, is to achieve Yellow Belt and that goal can be broken down into learning the requirements necessary for advancement with an expectation of completing those steps within a specified time window, given regular attendance at class (Appendix 1).

Once the student has achieved the first goal, it becomes easier to establish loftier goals with the assurance of achieving the desired result given dedication and perseverance. If an analogy would be useful, then think of each lesson plan as a section of road and the long-term plan as the road map to a specific destination. If you have no idea what you will be teaching next week, how is the student going to know how useful this week's lesson plan will be to their overall growth and development?

Coaching goals: The last set of goals that affect the conditions of learning are the goals that you have as a coach. Ask yourself: Why are you teaching martial arts? What do you want to achieve? Sometimes, these goals may be competing with each other: For instance if you set the goal of being able to teach only one night a week and also have a personal goal of producing a national champion, I would suggest to you that you have mutually excludible goals. It follows that you must have clear coaching goals, and furthermore, those goals will inevitably affect the types of students that you recruit. Clearly, your teaching goals must be congruent with your philosophical goals (Figure 2.3).

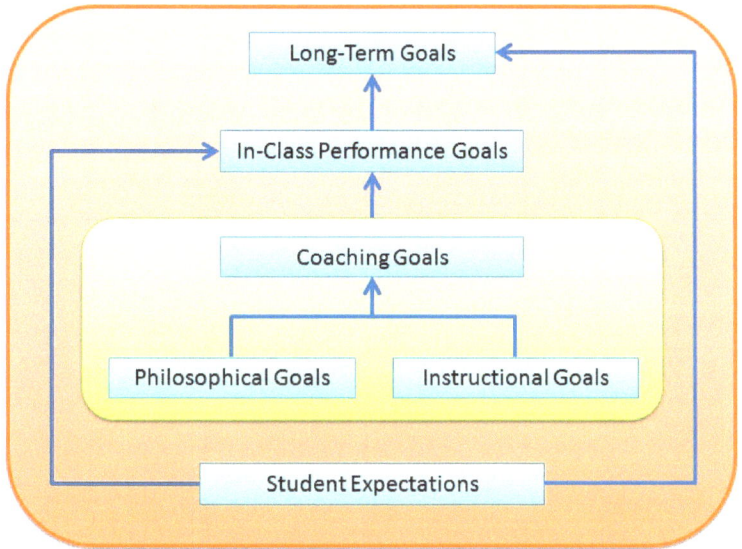

Figure 2.3: Interconnectedness of training goals.

Condition of Learning 2: Movement. It is axiomatic that training in the martial arts is concerned with combat in highly fluid, volatile, dynamic and seemingly unpredictable environments. When martial arts are employed in a real life self-defense scenario or in the highly-charged tournament arena, an ability to maintain mobility is an absolute necessity. It makes sense then, that students need to be aware of the importance of movement from the first moment they step on the mat or the training floor. More importantly, the movements should closely mimic the environment in which they will be used. Static drills that are used to teach a specific body action will, therefore, only have transference to the real world, when they are placed in the context of dynamic action.

At beginning levels of performance it is important that you introduce large body actions and gross motor principles, such as basic posture, keeping the weapon platform balanced, and the ability to produce effective power (Gleeson, 1967). As students become more aware of their movement abilities you can start to refine position and deal with the minor stuff. If you demonstrate correct movement and your students imitate the large actions correctly, the minor aspects will often be self-correcting. Above all, give your students time to experiment with movement and to find the answers themselves before you rush in to correct minor details.

Learning how to move in the martial arts primarily deals with an understanding of four things:

i) How to control your own balance.

ii) How to influence your opponent's balance.

iii) How to generate power and control the delivery of power in your actions.

iv) How to respond to the delivery of your opponent's power.

Every time a student moves an effect is created. Consequently, learning becomes a problem of cause and effect. There is nothing arbitrary when two people are working together in a martial arts class. If one person initiates an action, a response is created in his or her partner and so on (Figure 2.4). Eventually, the successful students will learn to control the effects that they create as a result of their actions. The goal, therefore, is to bring each student to an awareness of the cause and effect relationship between his or her actions and those of his or her opponent. It is this realization that lies at the very heart of excellence in free-fighting performance.

Figure 2.4: Movement as the basis for all martial interactions.

Condition of Learning 3: Activity. A good instructional rule to follow is 85% student activity, 15% instructor explanation. As my colleague, Rob Colasanti, said so often while he was President of the National Association of Professional Martial Artists: *"Send your students home sweaty, smiling and sore."*

He was absolutely right. *Sweaty*: Because they worked on their aerobic stamina. *Smiling*: Because they had a good time. *Sore*: Because they got a full-body workout.

Students come to you to learn and to train, they do not come to hear your war stories or watch you perform. Your students need and want direct experience, so make sure that you let them have as much training time as possible. It is axiomatic that direct, personal experience is the best possible way to learn, which means that students will obtain the maximum benefit from "doing", not from "watching". Active and vibrant classes also serve to maintain student interest, create positive endorphin responses and enhance retention. Make your instructional segments succinct, demonstrate what you need to with precision and brevity, ask for questions, and then let the students practice, practice, practice.

The best thing that you can do for your students is to get out of their way. Let them experiment and learn for themselves. Once you have given a task, together with its performance goal, let your students have as much practice time as possible; let them discover by "doing" and offer guidance only when needed.

Finally, as a safety tip, there is a decreased likelihood of injury if students are warm and stay warm through continued activity.

Condition of Learning 4: Simplicity. Success becomes possible for your students when you give precise direction in the execution of simple drills at the outset and allow plenty of time for practice (Gleeson, 1967). Create clear expectations in the minds of your students and link them to achievable goals. Recurring success in simple drills leads to improvements in student competence combined with a desire for more complex tasks. Competence leads to confidence, and it is the improvement in self-confidence that will enable the student to tackle more complex tasks. Simplicity-based training builds a positive feedback loop in which the student can repeat the cycle with ever-more complex drills as they learn successive parts of their skill set (Figure 2.5). Giving complex tasks before the student is adequately prepared will create confusion and frustration, which leads to a loss of confidence and an erosion of the trust placed in the instructor by the student (Gleeson, 1967). The erosion of trust will lead inevitably to a high attrition rate in your student base.

In summary, keep demonstrations simple, emphasize the key elements several times in the context of application, and ensure understanding by the student (Gleeson, 1967). There are several things that an instructor can do to enhance simplicity:

i) Decide what performance goals should be emphasized for a given class segment.
ii) Be sensitive to how much information the class can handle.
iii) Be willing to repeat your instructions, explain yourself in a different way or alter a lesson plan.
iv) Provide plenty of time for practice.
v) Be prepared to modify tasks according to individual needs.
vi) Provide specific reinforcement of correct execution.
vii) Understand that what one student finds "simple" is not what all students might see as simple.
viii) Build complex drills only after creating a solid foundation with simple tasks that have been successfully completed.

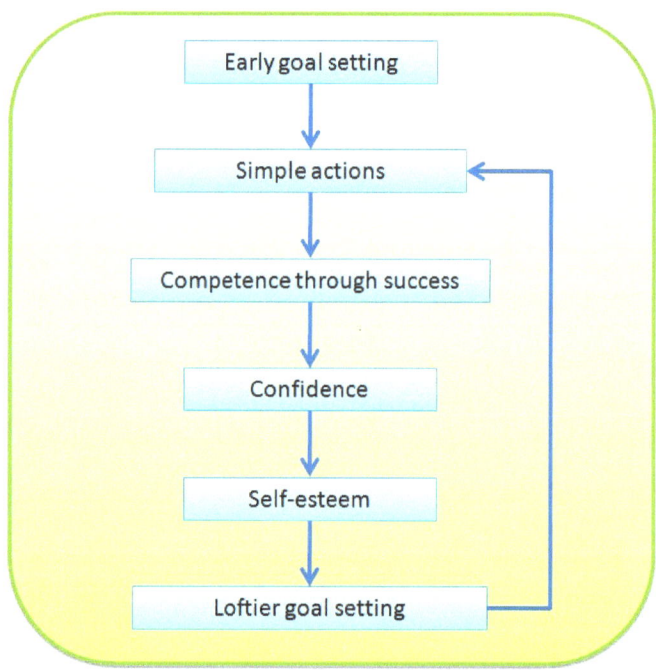

Figure 2.5: Simplicity-based positive feedback loop.

Condition of Learning 5: Foundation. Begin with the simple, and build a solid foundation. In so doing however, do not forget that what you, the coach might consider to be simple, will not necessarily be what your students view as simple.

Since by now it should be clear to you that I like to teach using real examples, try this one: Frequently in Judo and Jujutsu, we may want to teach a leg-sweeping action to our white belts (Figure 2.6). You can tell your beginners to "sweep" their partner's weighted leg from the outside all you want, but many beginners will just put the attack foot down behind their partner's leg and push them over it. There is no sweep! The reason for the difference between the instruction and the resultant action is very simple; a beginning student has the innate abilities to push and to trip, but does not yet have sufficient body control to stand on one leg and sweep the support leg of a mobile opponent.

Figure 2.6: A 'typical' outer sweeping technique. Note how the student changes his driver from the left leg to the right leg in the moment of the throw. In the example shown, the right leg 'should' be the sweeping leg and the left leg 'should' be the driver. In the moment of throw, the right leg is driving and the left leg is actually in the air.

So the point is simple: Teach the principle of what you want as the foundation and don't worry so much about the details. The principles in this case are:

i) Compromise the opponent's balance to the rear corner.

ii) Attack the weighted foot.

iii) Push the opponent into a hole situated behind the support foot (Figure 2.6).

On the basis of the example, it becomes clear that solid foundations are principle-based, rather than technique-based. As such, a principle-based foundation will provide the necessary links from the simple, beginning drills to the more complex, advanced drills (Figure 2.7).

Figure 2.7: An advanced application of the same principles shown in Figure 2.6. In this example, the outer sweeping technique is applied against a knife attack. Note that the right leg is actually sweeping, and that the left leg is in the air as the defender drives through with tight body contact, forcing the attacker to carry the weight of both people on the outside of his left heel.

When you develop a syllabus for your students think more about what biomechanical skills you want them to perform rather than whether they can accomplish a specifically-named technique. If you can build a solid foundational base of biomechanical actions, your students will almost inevitably invent the techniques for themselves. All you then have to give is a set of names, which will act as a common frame of reference in communication.

There is another aspect of this discussion that bears mentioning at this point, which relates to reinforcement and retention: When we attempt to teach students a specific technique **before** they have the biomechanical skill or the kinesthetic awareness to perform the technique, we are setting them up for failure. When we criticize the inability to perform the "required" technique rather than praise our students for successfully mastering a foundation skill, we are throwing away an opportunity for building insight. Moreover, when students do not perceive personal success, we are giving them reasons to quit.

Before I leave foundation, I want to inject a word of caution. Never teach anything that you will have to "unteach" later. If you ask your students to do something that you will ask them not to do later, you are building confusion and frustration.

Let me give you a common example from the world of Judo: A child goes to Judo tournament and in his/her first match; s/he gets thrown by his/her opponent. The child slaps the mat and the referee awards the match to the other player. The child goes to his/her coach. The coach then scolds the child for slapping the mat and says something like "How many times did I tell you not to slap the mat when you get thrown in tournament?" As a Judo referee, it is an interaction I have seen played out countless times. It is an event that will eventually drive the child and his/her parents out of Judo. Why? Again, the answer is simple: In class, the child slaps the mat every time s/he gets thrown, **because that was what s/he was trained to do**. The child's behavior has been conditioned by repetition to a level of instinctive action. What we are dealing with here is called a "Pavlovian response" and involves a conditioned behavioral response (Ormond, 1999). To then give a contradictory command for a similar situation is to ask the child to go against everything his/her body has learned. The new command is doomed to failure from the outset. The best solution is to teach students to use the skills that will be needed (such as turnouts, which will down grade a score in a tournament setting), from the very beginning of their training.

Before I let this go, I'd like to give you another scenario of this principle in action. What follows is modified only slightly from a profoundly educational experience that I witnessed one evening after a class more than twenty-five years ago. A taunting confrontation that began in a parking lot between a college-aged Karate student and a passer-by escalated to the point of physical action. The student dropped back into a fighting stance, and flipped a beautiful round kick to the opponent's head. He then stopped, stepped back and looked around, **waiting for the referee to call for points**! His much bigger, very angry opponent was, however, not point-sparring, and was not about to fight according to tournament sparring rules! Leaving aside all the things that went wrong before the situation got to this point, the student was simply acting on the habituated responses he had learned in class. He may have been far superior in terms of technical skill to his opponent, but had others not intervened and broken up the engagement he would have received a very sudden, and most unwelcome introduction to a real world fight.

The message in both cases is very clear: Training creates instinctive responses, so make very sure that the foundation skills your students acquire have transference to the real world.

Condition of Learning 6: Transference. The foregoing example leads neatly into the condition of learning known as transference. Students like to know that what they are learning has application to how it will be used in the "real world". The skills that our students learn may have transference to any one of a number of areas of their lives, not the least of which includes competition and self-defense.

In the physical domain, it is critical to teach those skills that have transference to the expected environment of performance. In the mental/emotional domain, it is almost as important to practice under conditions that approximate as closely as possible the conditions under which the skill will be used, as soon as possible. Transference brings the technique "home" to our students. If our students can visualize and practice the application of the technique in a "real" situation, then they will be much more willing to learn the technique. Equally, when a situation occurs in which the skill is required, the student will be able to see the opportunity and react appropriately.

Underlying everything that we have been saying so far, lies a recognition that there are principles, which govern the movement of a human body in the fluid settings of all martial arts classes and combat environments. The basic biomechanical principles of balance control, physical co-ordination and control of force lie at the foundation of good martial skill sets. The application of the principles may vary, but the principles themselves do not change. The principles can, therefore, be applied to, and have transference to, all aspects of grappling, throwing, joint-locking, striking, and weapons use. It is incumbent upon the coach to reveal the principles to the students so that they can learn to apply them effectively at the right moments in the execution of their skills.

Be sure, therefore, that you teach your students the correct principles of movement and that the resulting skills have direct transference to the environment in which they will be employed.

Condition of Learning 7: Series and Sequence. Mastery of the subject matter in any learning endeavor is demonstrated by the ability to abstract information from a data set and create meaningful sequences using the available data. By way of example, we may teach a student the words of a language, but it is only by putting the words together to create a meaningful communication in an effective fashion that a mastery of the language is demonstrated. In general, we tend to recognize that the more fluid the communication, the greater the degree of mastery. We can apply this analogy to the extent that the practice of any martial art is a form of communication. As students demonstrate increasing levels of grace and efficiency in manipulating the elements of the language of a specific martial art, they are demonstrating higher levels of mastery. Continuing the analogy, no informational component of a language stands on its own. Consequently, the techniques that we teach in martial arts must be part of a series, not a syllabus of isolated movements that share no connectivity to one another. Don't just teach words, teach how to use them!

By way of example, a series as used in a throwing drill could consist of the individual parts of a single technique such as: movement, gripping exchange, balance control, entry to the throw, moment of throw and finish to a pin or a joint lock (Figure 2.8). Before we can do anything useful in a throw though, we must move and we create an off-balance in our partners. Our training partners and competition opponents, however, are dynamic people who will not stand still and wait for us to enter the throw, once they find themselves off-balanced. For sure, when we teach a throw, we can isolate movements within the drill, yet in the dynamic training environment actions are not discrete and isolated. A technique standing alone, serves little purpose. It is only when a technique is added to others that the language of the martial art comes to life. Series-based teaching, therefore, requires that we do not teach our skills in isolation, but rather show how the pieces of the language fit together as a meaningful whole.

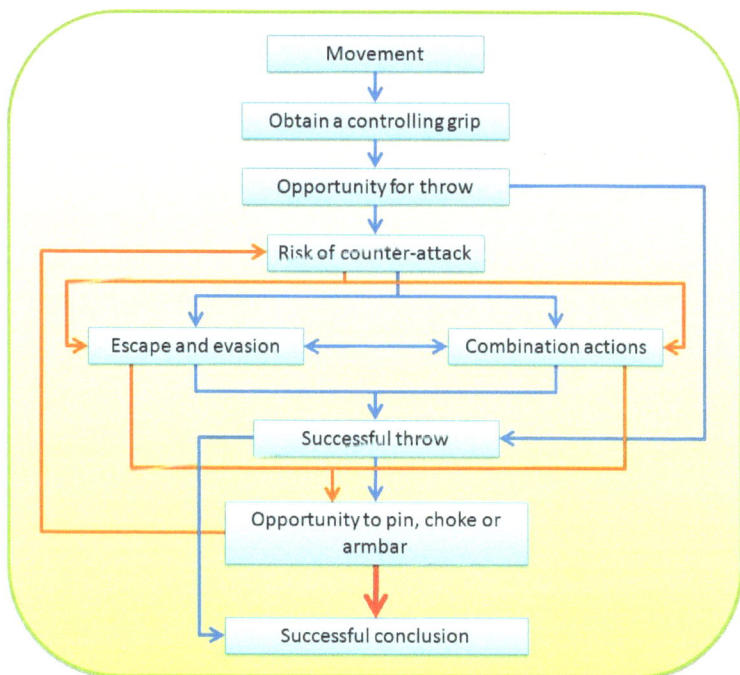

Figure 2.8: Series and sequence as a modification of Figure 2.4 and applied to Judo. Note the possibility of having the pin, choke or armbar countered and therefore the possibility of repeating part of the sequence.

It is only your imagination, your willingness to experiment and the degree to which you encourage your students to do likewise that limit the possibilities for the creation of effective sequences.

Lastly, teaching by series and sequence presupposes that there are some elements of the syllabus that need to be taught prior to other elements. Consequently, we should begin with simple drills and work up to more complex drills. Teaching by series and sequence also ensures that we will build a solid foundation and also create meaning in our classes.

Condition of Learning 8: Value, Meaning and Benefit. If we teach principles that build a strong foundation and create viable skill sets that have transference to real situations **as perceived by the students**, then it follows that what the students are learning will have value and meaning to them.

For instance: If you are very excited about competition but a student of yours couldn't care less about competition, then all your encouragement about how this or that drill will help your student in tournament is falling on deaf ears. The drill may have all sorts of application to your view of the world, but to the student in question, it has no meaning. Students will always learn more quickly if **they** believe that what you are teaching has value to **them**. When students have a sense of meaning and perceive value in what they are learning they will remain motivated and want to learn more. The reverse is also true: If there is no meaning in what the students are asked to do, they will lose interest and quit.

When you teach, encourage questions that establish an understanding of value. Ask questions to find out whether your students actually understand what they are doing and whether or not they understand why they are doing it. Find out if what they are learning has meaning to them.

There is a second aspect to meaning, which relates to the intrinsic versus the extrinsic benefits that your students derive from the activities that you ask of them. Intrinsic benefits are those which the students create for themselves whereas extrinsic benefits are those that the students earn such as rank, competition honors, approval of parents, coaches, peers, etc..

In the final analysis, students take martial arts classes to improve how they feel about themselves. The non-stated goal is to improve self-worth and self-confidence. If what we teach does not feed that goal, or the stated goals (personal fitness, personal security, competition honors etc.), then the students will lose interest and quit. As an instructor, it is important for you to know what motivates your students to come back to class and to perform at their best. By continually pushing our students' "hot buttons" we keep them invested in the process of learning. Don't just take it for granted that your students will keep coming back. Find out what it is that motivates them to come back and ensure that you continue to provide that level of meaning or those perceived benefits.

Condition of Learning 9: Satisfaction and Enjoyment. There is an adage, which says that success occurs when preparation meets opportunity. In the martial arts, opportunities include things like rank tests, demonstrations, tournaments, and real self-defense situations. In all the preceding cases, appropriate kinds of preparation will prevent the delivery of a disappointing performance. Having effectively prepared your students, they will feel good about themselves when they successfully use that preparation in the context of an opportunity-based situation.

In terms of teaching, your students will feel success when they have practiced a drill and can then use it effectively. Satisfaction and success create a win-win situation for the player and the coach as well as creating positive synergy in the class as a whole. If your students do not have success then they will experience frustration. In almost all instances, a lack of success is because you have asked your students to do something (modified from Martens, 1990):

i) That is beyond their current level of physical, mental or emotional development.

ii) Without emphasizing the key elements.

iii) Without adequate preparation.

iv) That is too complex and needs to be broken down further.

When your students do not experience success, do not lay the blame at their feet. Take personal responsibility and look to yourself and your expectations. Are you being too rigid in your demands, or have you missed a key ingredient necessary for the students to learn? In the final analysis, enjoyment leads to high levels of motivation and an increased desire to learn more. If your students aren't enjoying themselves, why should they come back to the next class?

Condition of Learning 10: Reinforcement and Feedback. As coaches, we often tend to think of reinforcement as giving praise for things we like, but there is much more to it than that. Reinforcement is associated with Operant Conditioning as described by B.F. Skinner (Klein, 2002; Ormond, 1999) and creates an increase in a behavior as a function of the consequences associated with an event. It stands to reason that something, which reinforces behavior in one player, may have no effect on another player. Reinforcement events will, therefore, be specific to each player.

There are two types of reinforcement: Positive and negative. Positive reinforcement involves any event that increases the occurrence of a specific behavior; negative reinforcement removes something aversive and results in an increase in a specific behavior that was occurring before the aversive event occurred (Klein, 2002). We'll talk more about the reinforcement later, but for now, the critical point when using feedback is that it must be immediate, specific and should create a positive outcome.

Giving immediate, positive reinforcement when you see something you like creates an association between the behavior and the reward. It follows then, that it is important to praise exactly what you liked about what you saw. Saying "Nice kick!" doesn't cut it...the student has no idea just exactly what was good about it. Tell the student that the kick had great hip rotation, a really tight chamber, or precise weapon formation, targeting, something.....but be specific and link it to the outcome, so that the student will know what to do again and what result will be achieved by repeating the action. When you reinforce in this way, you are in a better position to offer specific performance corrections that allow you to explain **how** something can be improved and **why** it can be improved.

When you make corrections to technical performance avoid the "Don't, don't, don't" formula, which is so prevalent in our societal interactions. I prefer to use the "Do this, don't do this, do this" formula. People tend to remember the first and last things you tell them. In correction, show and tell your students what you want, then show or tell what they are doing and then repeat what you want. Always explain why you want the change. When you correct technique, sandwich correction between rewards. For instance: "Great hip position, now bring your front foot back to here, you'll get more body rotation, which will add power to the throw, great hip position though". You will notice that in the example we used positive reinforcement to do two things: Reinforce what we liked (the hip position) and to correct an action that would improve performance (moving the front foot back further).

I'd like to leave you with an example of negative reinforcement as well, mostly because it is often misunderstood and confused with punishment. Let's say that a student is practicing falling skills. Once the learning escalates to rolling and falling, the student starts falling on his/her shoulder and becomes less willing to do the rolling drill. In this case the coach could use negative reinforcement to remove the aversive element (pain associated with landing on the shoulder) by introducing a crash pad, or moving the student back to a lower level of falling, until he/she feels more comfortable and is creating smoother, rounder rolls without landing on the point of the shoulder (Figure 2.9).

Figure 2.9: Falling on a crash pad.

When reinforcement is used correctly, it always creates a positive outcome. Consequently when we use reinforcement in appropriate ways, we are encouraging our students to develop positive self-expectancy. When they are given positive feedback (in the form of positive or negative reinforcement), students will tend to respond with an increase in their own expectations of personal success. With continuous, specific reinforcements, which create positive outcomes, students will internalize the notion that they are capable of success and they will expect to be successful.

Negative feedback, however, tends to undermine self-belief and does nothing to enhance the learning environment. Unfortunately we use lines like "Don't do that" all too frequently. These sorts of phrases are coded into almost all of us from an early age, and it is easy to fall into using them when we coach our students. Before you say "I don't do that", have someone record all your classes for a week and then watch them and see how you reinforce your students…you might just surprise yourself.

Condition of Learning 11: Cooperation. Learning any martial art skill set requires varying levels of cooperation at different times during training. It is a critical factor of retention that the student and the instructor both be aware of what is appropriate for any given drill.

Obviously, when first learning a technique complete cooperation between partners is an essential requirement for ensuring safety and for learning the technique effectively. Conversely, when students are practicing free-fighting, greater levels of resistance, noncompliance and competition are appropriate. Practice however, is not tournament, and tournaments have rules, unlike the real world of combat. When your students are engaged in free-fighting drills in class, there is an opportunity to experiment and learn how to improve skills in a free flowing, volatile and highly dynamic, but essentially non-competitive environment. It is not a license for your best student to continually blast everyone in the class with his/her best tournament skill. There is a time and place for intense practice, but class practice may not be the right time. It is the instructor who must monitor and enforce the appropriate levels of cooperation in order to protect the safety of the students, maintain value in training, prevent frustration and minimize risk of injury. There is a fine line between competitive spirit and the loss of control in a class. The instructor carries the responsibility for ensuring that both cooperation and competitive spirit remain within specified limits.

Condition of Learning 12: Creativity. George Weers, one of my Judo mentors, is fond of saying "*Creativity lives on the edge of chaos*". Students will find much more meaning in what they are learning when they have the opportunity to experiment and discover martial arts for themselves.

In the world of pedagogy we talk in terms of inquiry-based learning, and discovery-based learning, but in essence what we are attempting to do is to get the student to invest in their own learning process, to ask questions as well as seek their own answers. At this point, instructors become facilitators more than teachers in the traditional sense of the word.

If you teach the principles early on, then the students will tend to invent moves that demonstrate the application of a given principle. I consider this to be creativity at its best. In any learning process, the freedom to employ **creativity** is what makes the experience unique to each student: It is therefore important to encourage appropriate levels of experimentation within the limits of the lesson plan. Be aware though, that allowing creativity is "risky" teaching! Risky, because you do not have total control of what is going to emerge from the minds and bodies of your students. Each student will make any action fit his or her own body and develop a "personalized form". So, the goal here is to avoid forcing our students into exact replicas of who we think they should be. Our students will make many mistakes along the way to creating the skills which work well for them and that is as it should be.

Given that you, as a coach, provide appropriate reinforcement, your students will succeed through their failures. Every mistake is a precious lesson that brings us closer to the performance goal we are working to attain. Creativity then, is part of learning how to master our mistakes and turn them into success. Such moments of creativity can be called "Edison moments" after the famous inventor. There is a well-known story about Edison concerning a time when a young journalist interviewed him. The journalist asked Edison why he didn't quit after so many failures at attempting to invent the light bulb. Edison explained that he hadn't experienced 5000 failures, he had in fact successfully discovered 5000 ways that would not work and was precisely 5000 ways closer to the way that would work. This is not mere semantics. It is a critical ingredient in understanding the difference between those who will succeed in life and those who will quit.

As instructors, it is our duty to promote creativity, to nurture it and to foster its use in our classes. Failure to do so will stifle your students. It will also limit your own potential and prevent you from seeing innovative ways of doing things.

In closing this segment, I want to share with you a story about creativity: I am always on the lookout for novel ways to teach old skills…after all, all the gifted teachers that I have known were (or are) magicians who disguise the basics and the obvious to make them appear new and different…all the while honing simple skills that build rock-solid foundations for quality martial artists…or students and performers of any subject for that matter.

My story begins in the international departure lounge at Atlanta airport several years ago where my six-year-old son was playing with another boy (we'll call him Ryan) who he'd just met, and I was reading a book. It turned out that Ryan had recently started taking "Karate" and was eager to demonstrate what he knew to my son. Most of it, (as you might expect from an excited young boy getting ready to fly to a new country for the holidays) was merely throwing his arms and legs around and yelling, but then all of a sudden he dropped into an amazingly deep, well-practiced horse-riding stance and called out a blocking drill sequence that I had not seen before. Ryan went through his blocking routine, calling out the moves as he did so. As quickly as it began, the moment was over. All of us who teach striking arts, have blocking drills of one kind or another. Ryan had just added a new drill to my teaching repertoire. I filed the drill in my mind for later and looked down at my book. A few lines further on in my book, synchronicity smacked me between the eyes as I read: *"Meaning is essential. If this moment truly matters to you, you will experience it fully."* The opportunity for creativity that occurred in those few, brief moments was produced because, as both students and teachers, we learn best when we are willing to see the world in new ways, using the eyes of a child. Seeing the world in a new way can be an extraordinarily difficult thing to do as an instructor, especially if you have a lot of experience and/or rank in a particular style. What made the Atlanta airport moment work for me was that I was able to step outside of my shell and see something new in the performance of a drill that did not come directly from my particular striking art. I was not bound by the fetters of a style-based form, because I saw value in function.

Condition of Learning 13: Form and Function. Form can be defined as the shape of something, or the manner in which an action occurs. It is normal to expect that form follows function, insofar as changes in form will occur to meet the specific demands of a given function.

For aspiring martial artists, form and function are intimately tied to the creation of an arsenal of defensive and offensive skills that will be both effective and efficient should tactical situations occur requiring their use. When we teach martial arts, we tend to offer techniques by names such as shoulder throw, or roundhouse kick, but every student will develop a personalized form of the techniques we teach. The essential elements of the technique will still be there, but the form will be necessarily altered to fit the age, physique, fitness and experience level of the student as well as the tactical situations in which each student finds him or herself.

Additionally, a tactical situation is one in which an opportunity exists to employ a learned skill. In combat settings, the size, shape, speed, and direction of travel, available weapons, fitness and/or fatigue level and relative skill levels of the combatants will all affect tactical situations. Form then, is an individual thing, and if an instructor wishes to be successful, it is necessary to recognize that within the prescribed limits of a technique there is a lot of room for students to evolve their own form as the needs of their bodies and the tactical situations dictate.

In its essential truth, good form gets the job done. It may not always look very pretty, but if it is an appropriate tactical solution and does the job effectively then it has good form. So the main point is that "good form" is biomechanically sound, tactically effective **and** functionally efficient.

As coaches, it is also important for us to recognize that "form" changes over time. Often changes over time are associated with proximity to a qualified instructor and with an individual's interpretation of perceived meaning. A simple example can be found by examining the pre-arranged Judo or Karate kata (form). Different instructors will have different insights into a given "kata" and, therefore, teach it in their own way. As a matter of course, the form of the kata will evolve over time as successive generations of instructors get further removed from the originator of the kata. In essence, successive re-interpretation of the kata will lead to subtle changes, which will magnify over time. By way of illustration, anyone who has competed in kata competitions in either Judo or Karate knows that there is a "standard accepted" form of any specific kata. We also know that scores given at different tournaments for essentially the same "form" can vary widely according to the judges' interpretation of what constitutes the accepted standard on that day.

If you stop and think about it, the old how-many-black-belts-does-it-take-to-change-a-light-bulb joke holds a lot of meaning here. So what's the answer? All of them. One to change the light bulb and all the others to say *"Yes, but that's not the way we do it in my dojo."*

It is easy to get trapped by form and lose sight of the more important functional meaning of the skills that we are intending to impart: Good form gets the job done!

Final Comment: Hopefully, you can see that the conditions of learning are an inter-related set of conditions that create the best possible learning environment. It is our responsibility as instructors to create the learning environment and to foster the ability of our students to acquire the best possible experience from their learning opportunities. The conditions of learning should never be far from your mind when you teach class, develop lesson plans or build a curriculum.

Chapter 3

COMMUNICATION SKILLS

When you decide to teach, it is imperative that you develop an appropriate communication skill set, if you wish to be effective. You must have credibility, be able to control an entire class with a single word, and motivate each student through understanding and example. An effective instructor in any arena is respected, commands loyalty and is trusted. Without respect, loyalty and trust you will never produce and keep students of any caliber. You may be able to recruit, but you will not retain your students.

We attribute levels of credibility to all those with whom we communicate. High levels of credibility are associated with those who:

i) Are knowledgeable about what they say.

ii) Make what they say relevant to their audience.

iii) Are consistently honest.

iv) Speak positively and do not use negative communication.

v) Treat you like an equal.

vi) Pay attention and truly listen to what people say.

vii) Maintain conformity between their body language and their verbal language.

There are several components of, and strategies for, learning effective communication skills (Alessandra, 1990; Carnegie, 1936; Corcoran and Graden, 1998; Dimitrius and Mazzarella, 1999; Faber and Mazlish, 2002; Le Boeuf, 1987; Thompson and Jenkins, 1993). Effective communicators understand that their job is to captivate, illustrate and motivate. All successful communicators captivate their audience, which is, in essence showing the value of their message to the audience, regardless of the age of the audience. The implication here is that a person who is dramatically successful at communicating with adults, may not possess the talents to be as successful when attempting to communicate with younger people. As a direct consequence it is entirely possible that you can be very effective teaching adult classes, but less effective at teaching children's classes. When you offer martial arts classes, it makes sense to find assistant instructors who have strengths in the coaching areas in which you are less talented.

Again, regardless of the age of the audience, effective communicators illustrate their messages in ways that members of the audience perceive as being specifically designed for them and directly applicable to their lives. Moreover, effective communicators can motivate their audience to take action, and to keep on taking action until a successful conclusion is reached and new goals need to be set.

In a nutshell, motivation and captivation are the keys to recruitment and of students. Captivation begins when a student enrolls at your school and motivation in class ensures retention. Captivation opens the front door, and motivation locks the back door. Captivation, illustration and motivation, therefore, need to be integral parts of every lesson plan and effective instructors understand that they must continually captivate their audience with the value inherent in what they offer, exceed student expectations, illustrate with examples that provide meaning, and motivate their students on a daily basis. These then, are the bedrock principles for effective marketing and communication. If you want to know what your students are buying, seek understanding from your students. Ask questions, listen to the answers your students give you and be aware of, and responsive to, their concerns. Make no mistake about it; in every class you are marketing your product and your students are either buying in, or walking out.

Figure 3.1: When you work with your students, make sure that you take the time to really listen and check for understanding, especially when you offer correction.

Communication is integral to every event that happens in your school, but perhaps it is nowhere easier to lose a student than in the moments when we offer correction to performance (Figure 3.1). When you correct your students, leave them to practice for a while (Gleeson, 1967) then go back and check to see how the correction has improved performance and whether they understand the reason for the change and can feel the difference that the correction makes.

Instructors who are effective in their critiques always critique the action and never the person. Statements like "*I've got Yellow Belts who can do better than that*", or "*You should be better than that by now*" are both direct attacks on the person performing the technique and have zero content concerning the technique that needs to be improved or how to improve it. Effective instructors ensure that they draw a clear distinction between a critique of the technique and a criticism of the person. As a direct result of critiquing only the technique and not the person, instructors are capable of effecting positive change in their students by leaving the person's self worth intact and yet demonstrating where improvements can be made in technical performance. Something else to remember about critiques and communication in general, is the fact that the way in which you praise, reinforce and/or punish one student will be registered by everyone else in the class and they will assume that if you treat one student in a particular way, that is how you will treat all students. This is particularly true in the children's classes. If you truly listen to one student or take a little extra time to help them with a specific challenge, the other students will register your actions, and be more likely to make the assumption that this is how you are likely to behave toward them, especially if your actions are consistent and habituated.

One of the most underrated skills of effective communicators is that they **really** listen: They make eye contact with people, they pay attention, they do not get distracted, they do not interrupt, they respect the views of those who are speaking. Active listeners will make sure that they truly understand by paraphrasing what they are being told and by using feedback questions to clarify meaning. Active listening is not a mere technique; it will only work from a true motivation for deep understanding of your students. Truly listening to your students will result in a more open communication pattern in which your students are not afraid to seek clarification about things they do not understand. People who know that they are being truly valued will also be more apt to reveal how they feel, which will lead to stronger relationships between instructor and student.

Dale Carnegie (1936) emphasizes the point that to be truly effective communicators, we need to not only listen, but must be sincerely interested in what is being said to us. Feigned interest will not suffice. When a student tells you about his or her goals and/or concerns, you, as the coach must be sincerely interested in what is being said. The teacher-student relationship (or coach-athlete relationship, if you prefer) is based on the notion that the student believes that you care about his or her training. If you act, or seem, disinterested in the student's concerns, then you convey a sense that you are not interested in them as a person and are, therefore, less likely to be concerned about their growth and development.

Effective communicators make sure that their verbal communication is congruent with their non-verbal communication. As an instructor, you will become aware very quickly that your students will pick up on your non-verbal cues almost immediately...sometimes to your own frustration and embarrassment. If you tell them to do one thing in a technique but you are doing something different, they will copy your actions, not your words (Figure 3.2).

Figure 3.2: Offering correction using the '**show**-*tell*-**show**' and '**do this**-*don't do this*-**do this**' formulae. In the example, the student was having difficulty making her throw work, because of a poor foot placement. So we let her see what we wanted, what she was doing, how to fix it and then watched her perform with the correction made. The image shows the '*tell*' and '*don't do this*' portion of the correction. In this case the non-verbal communication was far more useful than the words used.

Another aspect of "communication copying" is the instructor's level of enthusiasm and their mood. If the instructor is excited about what s/he is teaching, then the excitement will be contagious. It is a recognized phenomenon that individuals "catch the mood" of the people with whom they interact

(Goleman, 1995). A martial arts instructor has the ability to affect deeply the mood of his or her audience; consequently, it is important for instructors to be positive about their classes and to generate enthusiasm for what they are teaching. Sometimes this can be a real challenge, but personal discipline can prevent you from ruining a martial arts class because you had a "bad day at the office". We tell our students to leave the stresses of the day at the edge of the mat, it is only reasonable that as coaches we should do the same. A few moments of reflection before teaching a class can make a huge difference in the quality of your teaching. Remember also, that your students will be picking up on all your non-verbal communication, so it is imperative that you control your mood when you enter class to begin teaching.

Non-verbal communication may constitute as much as 70% of total message. The non-verbal communications are expressed through what we call "body language". Since martial arts training is also about learning to perceive an attack, we teach a lot of non-verbal body language skills without realizing it. For instance, in free-fighting scenarios we learn to pick up subtle cues in facial expression and muscular tension that occur immediately prior to the launching of an attack. The majority of these cues are "out of awareness" signals sent by your partner and are received equally "out of awareness" by you as you respond to the dynamic interchanges of free-practice. It is the precision with which we receive, interpret and act upon these signals that governs the efficiency and effectiveness of our response.

Although the foregoing may seem like a digression, I use it to illustrate an important point. If we are instructing our students in threat assessment through repeated exposure to free fighting scenarios, then it is also a sure thing that our students will become more adept at reading our moods and body language in the overall framework of the class environment.

Be aware then, that body language, includes several different parameters including (Dimitrius and Mazzarella, 1999; Goleman, 1995, Thompson and Jenkins, 1993):

i) Body motions such as gestures, nervous habits and similar actions. Included here would be all your habitual head, hand, foot and body movements.

ii) Physical characteristics such as size, shape, age, sex, odor, physique.

iii) Touching behaviors that act as either positive reinforcements or as negative infringement of a touch boundary.

iv) Voice characteristics that include tone, pace, modulation, rhythm, inflection, pitch, and also include all the ways in which meaning and intent is audibly inferred by the listener as separate from the actual words.

v) Almost imperceptible facial expressions that are "out of awareness" signals concerning emotional state.

vi) Body positioning skills that relate to your personal security and space boundaries. Body position also communicates the level of desire to communicate.

In summary then, communication is a critical component of your ability to influence, educate, and inspire your students, but even great communication skills will do you no good if you have nothing to teach or lack the skills necessary to present the information. In the next chapter then, we will investigate the nuts and bolts of how to teach and develop great lesson plans.

Chapter 4

PEDAGOGY OF COACHING

Introduction: A **curriculum** is nothing more than a body of knowledge that we wish to impart to our students. Recall from Chapter 1, that there will be foundational components of the curriculum that must be acquired by the student before more advanced materials can be presented. The existence of a curriculum also implies that a time-line exists for its presentation and that each lesson is part of a journey in the presentation of the curricular information. All of which brings us to a **syllabus**, which simply represents the order in which the required information and/or skills will be presented. The functional unit of both the curriculum and the syllabus is the **lesson plan**, without which, it is very difficult to guide your students towards any meaningful set of goals. A lesson plan is a step on a journey, and the journey will reveal the syllabus in its entirety. Operational units within each lesson plan define the learning expectations for the class. The operational units are the teaching segments and **drills** (Figure 4.1).

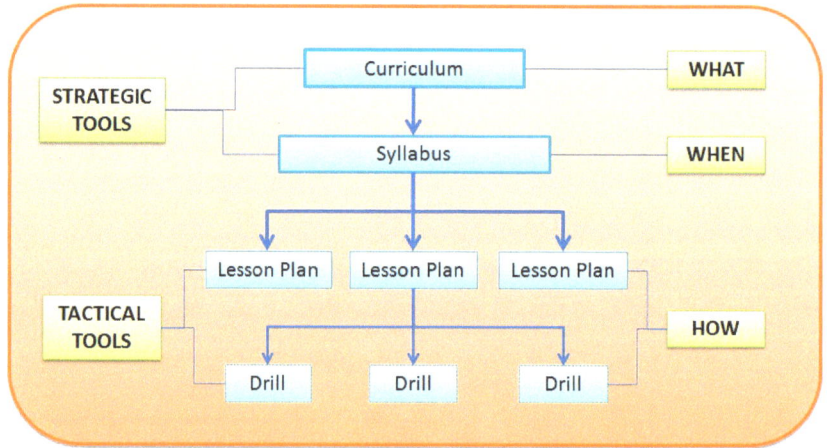

Figure 4.1: Instructional components and their dependent subsets. Notice that there are both strategic and tactical elements to the teaching process and that the curriculum tells us "what" to teach, the syllabus provides us with an order of "when" to teach and the lesson plans and drills tell us "how" to teach the material components of the curriculum.

One of the standard models for teaching in almost any environment, is the Hunter Method (Wilen et al, 2000), which involves several elements:

i) A review of previous material.

ii) Introduction of new materials.

    iii) Explanation and demonstration of new materials.

    iv) Clarification and checking for understanding.

    v) Individual study.

Before we get immersed in building lesson plans, however, we should pause for a minute to consider what it is we wish to accomplish with a lesson plan. Do we want our students to learn a collection of named techniques, which they can repeat back to us on a test, or do we want our students to be able to abstract information and build for themselves solutions to situational problems in which they might find themselves? The answer to this question says a lot about the nature of the curriculum you will develop, the way in which you present your information and the teaching goals you set.

Teaching a Technique: Due to the influences to which I have been exposed over the years as field geologist, a martial artist, and a business owner, there is a very clear distinction in my mind between technique and skill. At this point in my life, I tend to view technical knowledge as theoretical and I view skill development as the practical application of learning (Figure 4.2). From the martial arts perspective, technique is a thing we learn; it is a tactical tool. Skill, on the other hand, represents the strategic ability to use techniques in a seamless, efficient and effortless fashion. Skill is the outcome of untold numbers of repetition. I like the view that technique is a tool of teaching and skill is a testament to the quality of a learning experience (Gleeson, 1967, 1983). Each time we repeat a technique we make small adjustments as we evaluate our ability to produce the desired outcome. By constantly monitoring practice performance, improving the quality of our repetitions and performing the technique in the setting in which it will be required, the technique evolves into a skill (Gleeson, 1967, 1983; Scott, 2005).

Mastery in any field of endeavor comes from only one place: Repetition in the crucible of learning. Great performers do not necessarily have very flamboyant techniques, but they do perform the basics with an astounding mastery. Thus, skill becomes the external demonstration of an internalized technique (Figure 4.2). You can see this on the tournament circuit: skillful competitors have refined their actions to such a level that people of lesser experience are totally outmatched.

We can all aspire to be great technicians given the time, desire, repetition and sweat. Eventually, some of us might even become skillful.

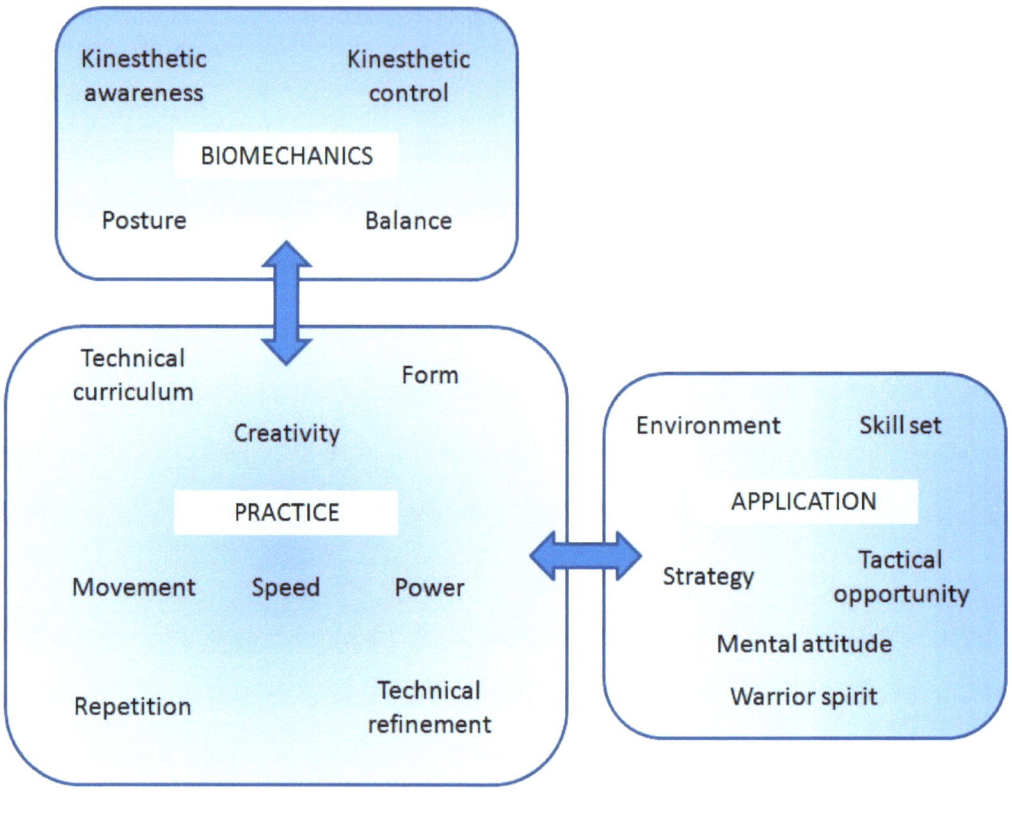

Figure 4.2: The components of, and interplay between, technique and skill.

I believe, however, that there is another level, which is attainable: The level of "mindless ability". In these very, very rare circumstances you meet a student who has practiced for so many years that the movement of energy, which defines the execution of a skill, is so efficient that you do not see the person performing, you simply see an effortless performance. The action becomes a thing of beauty.

Setting this level of attainment as your overarching coaching goal will keep you forever on the path. "Good enough" will never be acceptable and excellence is always a beginning point. Setting this level of ability will keep you humble; it will keep you training in times of doubt and through the plateaus of frustration. Setting this level of skill as your goal will help you keep an open mind and an empty cup. Every time you step on the deck you will know that you are still a beginner, still learning, still climbing the mountain. It will keep you mindful of what it is to be a student. One of the greatest things that I have learned from the martial arts is that the well of knowledge is infinitely deep and that no matter what I learn; it is miniscule in comparison to what I have yet to learn.

Technical ability is, therefore, a commodity that can always be refined, it is not a fixed quality; there is always room for more practice. Consequently, mastery in any field of endeavor knows only one teacher....experience. Everything else is rhetoric. There are no short cuts, no substitutes and no quitting.

If our students can take techniques and turn them into skills then we have successfully used a tool (technique) to build a tactical weapon (skill) that our students will be able to use in an opportunity-based environment (competition, self-defense etc).

From this perspective a specific technique may be offered such as "Ahp Chaki (front kick in Taekwondo)" "Harai Goshi (sweeping hip throw in Judo)" or "passing the guard (in Brazilian Jujitsu)". The point is that a technique is a building block of something larger than itself, and serves little purpose if it stands alone (recall if you will, Figures 2.4 & 2.8). Offering up techniques as isolated strikes, throws, joint locks or hold-downs is little more than stamp collecting. One of our coaching goals is to develop integrated patterns of movement for our students that bear resemblance to the performance-based environment of the real world in which the skills our students learn will receive actual use. **Our primary teaching goal, therefore, is to build lesson plans that present the style of martial art we teach, in the manner in which it will be used.** Having trained in this way, whenever your players meet the specific situation for which they have trained, they will automatically use the learned programmed skill (Figures 2.8, 4.2).

Teaching a technique can be broken down into a variably-numbered stepwise process (Corcoran and Graden, 1998; Gagne, Briggs and Wager, 1992; Martens, 1990; NCCP, 1979). In this manual I will use a ten step process:

i) Demonstrate the technique, if possible in a dynamic situational-based scenario.

ii) Explain its significance and purpose.

iii) Break the technique down into its functional components.

iv) Highlight the key points. Set the key points as performance goals for the students.

v) Demonstrate the technique again, from various angles.

vi) Relate the technique to what the student already knows and again emphasize the key points.

vii) Check for understanding, ask for questions, clarify and give a final demonstration.

viii) Allow the students to practice. Let them discover for themselves. Stand back and let them to experiment and to work on their own before you intervene (Figure 4.3).

ix) Practice the technique under "real" conditions as soon as possible.

x) Review the progress, re-emphasize the key points, and renew performance goals.

Figure 4.3: Sometimes the biggest favor that we can do for our students is to stand back and let them figure things out on their own. In this gripping drill there is only one performance goal, but a lot of different ways to achieve a controlling grip.

You will notice that this method of teaching is similar to Hunter's method described earlier, and can be used as a template upon which individual demonstrations can be built.

Remember also, that it is important to keep your demonstration/talk time down to 15% of class time and allow 85% for practice, so each demonstration, complete with analogies, should **only** take two or three minutes at the most. An easy test to see whether your students are getting the training time they need or whether you are talking and demonstrating too much, is to give a stop watch to one of your assistant instructors and every time you call stop the class to talk have the student record the time used. At the end of the class subtract off the amount of time you spent talking from the actual class time and then recalculate the figure as a percentage. If you do this for several classes you will soon see how much time you **give** to your players and how much time you **take** from your students.

The next trap to avoid is correcting your players too soon. Providing the answer too soon, removes the possibility of discovery-based learning. Discovery-based learning is always more effective in long-term acquisition of knowledge. Allow your students to make their own mistakes, give them the opportunity to be self-correcting and guide them towards making personal observations of their own body actions and finding their own solutions by asking questions like:

"Why do you think your partner was able to step over your leg during that throw?"

"What could you do to adjust your body that would generate more power in the kick?"

"Do you see what you do with your right elbow when you punch?"

"Can you find a way to improve your control and energy efficiency in that hold?"

These sorts of questions give your students an opportunity to discover their own answers, which will have much greater impact on the gradient of the learning curve, than if you provide the answers automatically. Remember, **a steep learning curve is a good thing**. It means that your students are learning a lot, quickly. Learning is a partnership and you, as the coach are a facilitator of the process. Consequently, there is a fine balance here, between:

i)   Allowing the students to find their own answers.

ii) Guiding them towards the answers they need.

iii) Recognizing that more information is needed before frustration sets in.

Moving from the process used to create a demonstration to the actual method of presentation, there are at least six ways in which you can present a technique:

i)   Whole method.

ii) Whole-part-whole method.

iii) Part method.

iv) Chaining.

v)   Active problem solving.

vi) Shaping or successive approximation.

Each of these methods may be of use at different times, depending upon the nature of the technique that you wish to present and the learning styles of your students.

In the whole method, you demonstrate the drill and let the students practice it as a unit. The whole method works well for relatively simple actions, or for techniques that do not readily subdivide themselves into workable portions, like making a jab punch.

In the whole-part-whole method, you show the technique, break it down into pieces and then build it up again (Gleeson, 1967). The method can be used for complex motor actions where a student might learn a competition drill, a Karate kata, or a throwing-to-ground hold sequence in Judo. Whole-part-whole methodologies appeal to both global and analytical thinkers because the global thinkers get to see the whole skill and the analytical thinkers get to break it down into pieces as they practice.

In the part method, you teach part of the technique and then add to it as the students gain mastery over each portion, until the technique is complete. The part method is useful for very complex techniques or series that require many discrete actions. Again, the examples given above work well in the part method, but be aware that the part method can be frustrating to global thinkers while inherently appealing to analytical thinkers.

The term "chaining" is used in the training of athletes when building desirable body mechanics and evolved from the work of B.F. Skinner on Operant Conditioning (Le Unes and Nation, 2002; Ormond, 1999). Forward chaining is similar to the part method insofar as it breaks a complex set of actions down and then builds them up. In this instance, however, new elements are introduced to the sequence as the drill progresses. Chaining is rather like running up and down a set of stairs and adding one extra step each time you run up the stairs. Forward chaining starts with a basic action and then adds to it in incremental units. Each time a new element is added, the student goes back to the beginning, completes the sequence and adds the new element. As new elements are added, the potential number of possible outcomes increases dramatically. It is possible that by the time you get to the end of the drill sequence your students may have arrived at quite different end points, **despite having followed all the steps**. Forward chaining differs from the part method because although it presents a series of steps that build upon the earlier steps; **your student are encouraged to experiment and are not given a predetermined end point**. In the field of sports science, chaining is the preferred term (Le Unes and Nation, 2002), but you may also run into terms such as forward framing and direct engineering, which are essentially the same thing.

In backwards chaining, you start with the end point of a process and work backwards to find out how to arrive at a destination. Backwards chaining can be a very powerful way to present information, and if you do not prescribe too many limits, your players will become very creative in finding ways to get from the end point back to the starting point. By backwards chaining, your students will figure out the most efficient way to get to where they want to end up. As an example, suppose you want to end up in a classic grappling hold down, Kesa Gatame (scarf hold) from a standing position with the minimum number of actions (Figure 4.4). If you have your players start at the end point and work backwards to the beginning they will very quickly discover that the answer might be as simple as move, grip, sit!

Figure 4.4: Sometimes the simplest way to get an opponent to the ground is to wrap an arm around the head and sit into the scarf hold.

Backwards chaining, therefore, will often lead your players to cut out a lot of unnecessary actions. Another good example of where reverse engineering works, is using a goose-neck come-along used in Hapkido and Jujutsu. The biomechanics of the action might be quite simple, **once mastered**, but getting from the initial grip to the final come-along can be very frustrating in the early stages of learning. The frustration is easily avoided when students reverse-engineer the lock (Figure 4.5).

Figure 4.5: The Goose Neck come-along. The sequence runs from A to D, but if students start with the lock and work backwards, it is often easier to learn the transition move from B to C.

In the active problem-solving method, the coach provides a problem for the students and then steps back to allow them time to find their own solutions. In pedagogic circles, this sort of teaching is referred to as inquiry-based learning and can offer several benefits. Firstly, one of the beauties of this particular method is that it exposes innate talent in the student population. Secondly, it rapidly becomes apparent to the class as a whole, when the review of solutions occurs, that several viable solutions to the problem may exist and that there is not a one-size-fits-all answer. The trick to making the method work is in the coach's ability to let the students figure things out for themselves, but also be able to recognize when more information is needed *before* frustration sets in (Gleeson, 1967). By carefully framing the problem and setting the parameters that safety require, it is possible to generate some really creative answers and then share them amongst the class.

Shaping, or successive approximations of desired behavior, is another method of learning that has been derived from the work of B.F. Skinner on Operant Conditioning, that can be applied to each of the examples given above (Klein, 2002; Le Unes and Nation 2002). In shaping, a skill can be rewarded when it is even marginally successful for a player in the early stages of learning, but rewards are only given for more precise activities as the player improves. In this way, the coach is able to "shape" the skill by reinforcing gross actions early in the training process and precise actions, later in the process. Shaping also encourages a novice player to focus on large, gross actions first and focus on the detailed, fine motor skills, later. Combined with correction of undesirable elements of the action, shaping can be a very powerful tool for enhancing learning.

Teaching Models: The next step in the process of presenting new information is to understand the instructional model or paradigm from which you are teaching. There are essentially three models for teaching martial arts, each of which we can still see as operational at various martial arts schools and clubs.

The first model is the **Technical Paradigm**. In the technical paradigm, the instructor teaches by technique, using repetition and rote memorization. There is little discussion of why a particular technique works, or is executed in any particular way. The emphasis is upon the traditional interpretation of form and learning the technical components of the curriculum. The technical paradigm was an outgrowth of the notion that technical purity is the practical basis of skill. Many of the older instructors taught using the technique paradigm; students were not encouraged to ask questions, we were encouraged to copy *ad nauseum* and learn through repetition, eventually discovering the meaning behind why we did things for ourselves. In some ways, the technical paradigm is a distortion of discovery-based learning. Examples of the technical paradigm would be:

i) Solo repetitive kicking and punching drills, from a specified stance.

ii) Practicing isolated techniques, without inserting them into some sort of combat strategy.

iii) Practicing rank requirement, purely for the sake of rank advancement.

In the **Principle-based Paradigm**, the instructor uses technique as the servant of principle and teaches students what principles apply and how to use biomechanical principles to obtain maximum effect from the techniques. In this model, there is less emphasis placed upon the technique as such, and more emphasis placed upon understanding the mechanical principles that make the techniques work. Examples of the teaching using the principle paradigm might include:

i) Working on the application of force lines as they apply to controlling a hold in a grappling environment.

ii) Examining the position of the support foot for creating an effectively balanced weapons platform and controlling power delivery during kicking of multiple-level targets.

iii) Discovery of the "hole" in throwing actions (see Chapter 7).

The third model is the **Situational Paradigm**. In the situational paradigm, the instructor creates situations, which serve as a medium for learning both the application of principles and the selection of appropriate (biomechanically efficient and effective) technical solutions to the tactical problem at hand.

i) Examining the throwing potential of driving the sleeve end down whenever you get a grip.

ii) Examining the striking potential whenever you get outside and behind your opponent's weapons.

iii) Examining the reversal potential of the legs-around bottom (guard position) in a grappling environment.

By working at a situational level from the beginning, students learn to use their skills in "real life" settings as an integral part of their training. The situational paradigm is preferable to being taught a set of techniques and then leaving the student to figure things out once s/he is faced with a situational challenge such as a free-practice environment or worse yet, a tournament or self-defense event (Graden, 1997, Weers, 2003).

The premise behind the situational paradigm is to enable students to see the opportunities inherent in any given situation from the beginning of the training process. Very often during free-practice, whether in the striking, grappling or throwing arts, students completely miss attacking opportunities **because they have not been trained to see them**. The situational teaching scenario fosters the sort of student development in which players are taught to recognize and respond to specific situations (Figures 2.8, 4.2, 4.5). The goal of situational-based teaching methodologies is, therefore, to lead each student towards developing conditioned responses to specific tactical situations (Le Unes and Nation, 2002). Thus, the key to effective training (Figure 4.6) is the depth to which the conditioned response has been internalized.

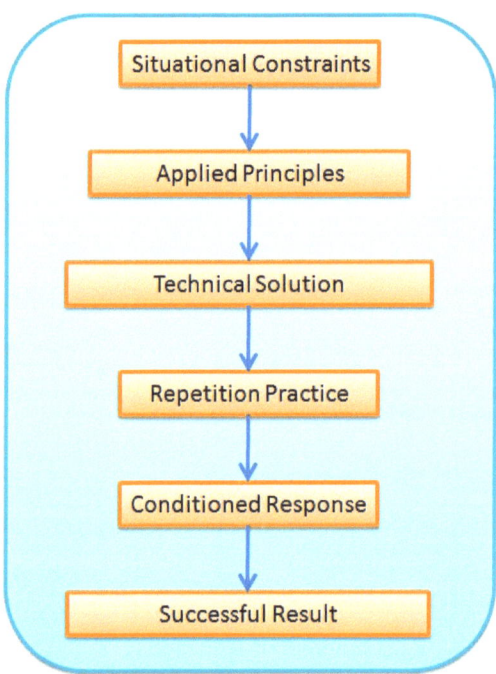

Figure 4.6: A flow diagram for the situational paradigm clearly demonstrates the value of a process-based learning environment that provides the student with knowledge of an applied environmental setting, biomechanical principles needed and viable technical solutions.

The idea of the Conditioned Response was first studied by Pavlov (Klein, 2002; Le Unes and Nation, 2002) and is often referred to as "Classical Conditioning." In a combat environment, there is little time consideration of alternatives, the conditioned response must occur from a deeply embedded muscle memory and result in a reflexive action given the correct stimulus, no matter how slight that stimulus might be. A good example of a conditioned response in Judo or Karate is learning the correct timing of combination actions. In the early stages of training, players doing free-practice often create openings for combination actions for their partners, but those openings are missed because they are neither seen, nor felt. The stimuli are present, but have no effect. A window of opportunity may be parts of a second in duration and can be easily missed when a player has to consciously recognize and the react to a potential moment to throw or strike.

As players learn to feel the responses of their partners, the use of combination actions becomes the more common. Eventually, very subtle body motions by one player can elicit highly effective combination or countering actions by his or her partner. **It is all a matter of feeling and timing**. There is no time for thinking; the combination must be a conditioned response to the stimulus provided by a player's body motions in response to the original attack. The ultimate result is that players learn to practice by "feeling" rather than being so dependent upon "thinking." As such, the practice moves from being a left-brained analytical process to a right-brained intuitive endeavor. To quote from David Hawkins (2002, p.138):

"...after all, we don't dance from logic, we dance from feeling patterns."

Building Skills: Remember that *"repetition is the mother of skill"*, which implies that **everything** your players learn, if practiced often enough, will become a skill. Unfortunately then, our students can become exceptionally skillful **at the wrong things**, unless we monitor performance. It is, therefore, part of the instructor's job to make sure that the skills are developed upon a stable postural platform, are biomechanically sound and can produce appropriate amounts of power and control. Some of the main principles we want to develop are:

i) Using all the muscles and joints that can be used.
ii) Using the joints in the right order.
iii) Allowing the non-involved muscles to remain relaxed.

Each joint action generates a force and when all the joints are used together in the right order there is a compounding effect to the joint forces (summation of forces) and a continuity of action through the joint series (Hamill and Knutzen, 1995; NCCP, 1979). Beginning players often have too much tension in their actions because they have not learned to relax the non-involved muscles. As a result their actions are jerky, tight and do not reach their maximum potential power output. As your students become kinesthetically aware and respond to appropriate reinforcement, they learn to use only those joints and muscles that contribute to any desired action.

As the quality of the skill improves, it becomes possible to examine other elements of the action, which impact the effectiveness of the skill. The first of the associated elements might be postural or operational base stability. The instructor needs to help the student discover the most stable configuration of his or her body that will permit the maximum generation of force in the preferred direction.

By way of example, let us take the "classical" application of the side-straddling hold down, (Yoko Shiho Gatame, in Judo). The key elements of this action that make it effective as a grappling move involve the correct position of chest-to-chest, maintaining the "T", keeping the hips down, head up, chin tucked, knees off the mat, toes dug in and feet spread (Figure 4.7).

Figure 4.7: The elements of postural stability in the side-straddle hold

There are a lot of elements here, but which ones create the postural stability that permits the **maximum** application of force? The toes dug into the mat provide a driving line, so they provide a force. The force is delivered through the hips, so here is one of the key postural elements. The second main postural element is the chest-to-chest contact, which is where the force is delivered into the opponent. In this example, therefore, the main thing to emphasize to your players is to keep the hips down, head up and to drive through the chest. What is significant here, is that hand position is a function of opponent size and situational application. Consequently, adjusting gripping position in the absence of a well-developed power base and driving line is meaningless.

Until a player has developed the basic components of the action, tweaking minor aspects of position will not create the desired improvements in skill performance. The reason for this is that if the larger joints are not being used correctly or the postural base is out of alignment, the delivery of power will be compromised. It is best to work on the gross motor skills first and then refine the minor aspects of the action as the skill matures.

The reason that we have mentioned all of this is because as our players develop skills we can find common elements to different skills that, when corrected, will create a cascade reaction through all aspects of the player's performance. Skill refinement must, therefore, be an integral part of every lesson plan, but needs to be presented in such a way that the player can see the benefit to doing the drills and making the repetitions. Learn to disguise the repetitions, so that the students feel as though they are learning something new, but at the same time they are working on core skills that form part of their foundational base.

Using Drills: Drills are repetitive tools that create habitual responses and from the building blocks of a lesson plan. Consequently, every drill you use in class should have some objective. For instance:

i) Drills can be written for simple things like improving endurance, strength, speed or posture.

ii) Tactical drills can also be developed that emphasize a particular tool, such as learning a new kick, hold down, joint lock or throw or perhaps taking a single attacking action and following it through a series of transitional skills from a standing combat environment into a grappling environment.

iii) Drills can also allow our players to turn techniques into reflexive skills that will be used in the environment for which they were intended. For instance: If you are training law enforcement officers to maintain ground control of a prone suspect, then it is possible to develop a series of drills combined with verbal commands, which can be developed and used to take the suspect from standing to ground and which expose the officer to minimal risk.

iv) Drills may also be strategic; an example of which might be building competition strategies for a player who has developed as a skilled left-sided kicker when facing a lighter, faster predominantly right-sided opponent who likes to close range and use hands.

Using these vastly different examples, I want to stress that drills need to have a purpose, and that the development of drills is only limited by your imagination as an instructor or your ability to network with other coaches and "borrow" their ideas! You should also be aware that the goal of developing and using drills is to create a more or less permanent change in behavior of your students. When practiced sufficiently often, the drills that you employ will create what we can call "muscle memory." Under these circumstances, drill repetition passes into the automatic stage of learning. Drills should, therefore, have three elements (Weers, 1996):

i) An objective.

ii) Transference.

iii) A training effect.

The objective of the drill is to build an effective combination skill. The transference is that the drill can be added to the player's personal combat system and the training effect is that the player will recognize the throwing opportunity when it occurs and attack accordingly. The story does not end here though, because we have only examined one aspect of the possibilities inherent in the range of tactical situations that might be encountered in a combat environment. The next logical places to go might include looking at possible defense opportunities and/or follow-up possibilities in a grappling environment.

The point here is that drills, just like warm-up games, have something strategic or something tactical to teach the players. Drill practice allows the players to develop skills by repeating actions. Drills, therefore, provide the coach an opportunity to refine the habitual actions of his or her players and reinforce the use of actions that improve the effectiveness and efficiency of the desired skill. Slowly but surely, drill practice permits conscious incompetence to evolve into unconscious competence, by which stage the desired action is automatic and the player completes the practiced drill without really thinking about it when the opportunity presents itself in the environment for which the drills were designed. You will note two things here:

i) Automatic completion.

ii) Environment for which the drills were designed.

In summary, drills must lead to the development of effective and efficient skills that will find employment in a specific environment of performance. It is important, therefore, that our players be given:

i) Techniques (tools).

ii) Time to practice well-designed drills.

iii) Time to build skills through repetition and refinement of action.

Having thus laid a foundational framework for our lesson plans, we can use drills as components of a series of integrated lesson plans (Nishiyama and Brown, 1960; Scott, 2005; Weers, 1996). Every lesson plan should be built upon a teaching objective and may involve the use of several different drills according to the needs of the lesson.

The teaching objective of any given drill can be expressed in terms of "student outcomes" such as: "At the end of the drill the student will understand/demonstrate _____." It is important to recognize, however, that drills may not be uniformly effective in a single class period for all students in the class, but will create a training effect over time. Consequently, it is important not to expect all students to perform the drill with the same level of finesse at the end of the practice session. Drill practice must allow for individuality of the learning process. Individual student performance goals, such as percentage success rates can therefore be used to measure progress of learning during specific drills. As an example, a sparring drill that emphasizes keeping the hands up to protect the face and the elbows down and in to protect the chest can be measured for a novice player versus an advanced player by using a rubric of different expected percentile success rates for each player.

Lesson Plans: Making lesson plans is possibly the easiest, and yet most overlooked part of teaching martial arts. Writing lesson plans simply requires setting a goal: Know what you want to achieve, set a time-line, develop a plan of action, implement the plan, assess your progress and review the plan. As instructors, we already know that there is a progression to learning. You start with simple drills and build upon them according to the syllabus from which you are teaching. We can develop a syllabus to do any number of jobs for us from preparing a player to compete at an international competitive event, to preparing a law enforcement officer for the occupational hazards s/he might meet on the streets. Regardless of the purpose of the syllabus, there will be a time-line during which you must prepare your student to meet the challenge for which training is being undertaken.

For the sake of simplicity, let us say that our syllabus will prepare a student to train to Black Belt. If each rank advancement is a stepping-stone to the achievement of Black Belt, then the syllabus can be broken down into a series of requirements for each rank and tied to a time-line. The time-line gives you some idea of how many lessons you have to cover the required material in a timely fashion (Gleeson, 1967; Graden, 1997; Martens, 1990; Nishiyama and Brown, 1960). Equally, if each drill in your lesson plans helps to build the set of skills that a student will need to perform with any degree of confidence in their chosen environment of application (tournament, self-defense, law enforcement), then the same rules apply.

So, the ingredients of building each lesson plan are inherent in the nature of the syllabus itself, because you already know:

i) What you have to teach.

ii) The operational teaching window.

iii) How many lessons in which you have to do it.

Despite the obvious prompts given to us by the material we teach, building lesson plans is one of the first places that martial arts instructors lose control of student retention. We tend to teach whatever comes to mind at the moment we begin teaching each class and, therefore, have not thought seriously about the needs of our student population. A mitigating factor is that often we teach mixed rank classes and frequently do so without the benefit of assistant instructors. In an effort to offer something to all, we often end up giving frustration to the lower ranks and boredom to the upper ranks. Despite what organized educational programs dictate, many martial arts instructors continue to teach classes of mixed ranks and ages. When instructors are forced by circumstance to teach children at the same time as adults, or teach classes of mixed rank, it is important that the students be grouped according to ability and age. It is equally important that each group is assigned an assistant instructor in order to create a quality learning experience for everyone involved.

In a similar fashion, children need to be taught in an age-specific manner that will differ from the way in which you teach your adult population. We will visit age-specificity in a moment, for now, let us return to the idea of creating a set of lesson plans, which will enable us to help our students meet their objectives.

Obviously your lesson content must be appropriate to the developmental level of the student body and, therefore, you will have more to draw on as you get into the more advanced class groups. Going back to basics is not a bad thing in the advanced class, but doing advanced techniques in a beginner class is asking for confusion, frustration and possible injury because the appropriate foundation has not been laid. Another aspect of our eagerness to teach too much, too soon, is that students will get bored in the later "advanced" classes when they are upper ranks because there is nothing "new" for them to learn. Knowing how many ranks your system has from White to Black, combined with a time-line of how long the process of ranking to Black Belt should take, provides a clear framework for equitable division of the required material across all the ranks. Don't forget though, Black Belt is not the end of the learning process, so it makes sense that there will be some techniques that will not be exposed to your students until after they have reached Black Belt. Moreover, we tend to forget that the color belt system was developed for the Occidental culture and in very traditional systems, Black Belt was considered the first of the true "student" ranks and that often the teaching ranks did not begin until fourth degree Black Belt and higher.

At this stage you should have the following information:

i) Number of ranks from White to Black inclusive (6 to 9 belts depending upon your specific martial arts system, counting the Black Belt promotion).

ii) Time-line to reach Black Belt (about four years).

iii) Time-line for each rank leading to Black (two to three months each for the early ranks, longer for the advanced ranks).

iv) Number of available lessons per rank (e.g. two lessons per week x two months for White to Yellow = 16 lessons).

v) Material that needs to be covered before Black Belt (dictated by your syllabus requirements).

vi) Equitable distribution of requirements across the rank system, so that no rank is overloaded with requirement.

Now, it is a simple matter of taking a calendar and working out the order of the material you need to cover and then writing it into lesson plan outlines for all the classes at that rank (Appendix 1). The process of spread-sheeting your lessons will force you to prioritize the information that you must teach and organize it into a specific order according to the needs of the syllabus and the developmental level of your students. It will also force you to consider what situations your students are most likely to face, what principles you should be teaching and what technical solutions might be appropriate for the level of development of the class.

As an example, the process may entail outlining all the lesson plans for advancement in Jujutsu from White to Yellow Belt in two months of classes at the rate of two classes per week (Appendix 1). It is important to recognize that many of the elements that are introduced as distinct classes will have been introduced within the framework of previous classes. By way of illustration, at the end of Week 1, Month 2, (Appendix 1) there is a class devoted to the transitions from standing to ground play. Do not imply however, that the students have not been doing this sort of work in previous lessons; the outline merely serves notice that there is a class in which the principles that apply to transitional play will be investigated in detail.

Once you have an outline of the classes you need to teach, write the actual lesson plans. To help in this process, the first time you teach from a schedule of lesson plans, write each lesson plan in skeletal form before class, and then rewrite it in more detail after class, because you can use the class experience to see what elements needed to be changed. When writing a lesson plan, you can use a standard and modify the details, but there should be some basic components that are common to all your lesson plans (Appendix 2).

Make the warm-up appropriate to the drill portion of the class, and build the class to a peak of performance, then slowly cool the class down again. There are not a lot of books devoted to specific martial arts warm-up drills, but if you don't own one, get a copy of Gleeson (1989) and a copy of Byl (2004). Although Gleeson was writing from the perspective of Judo, his book is a little gem with a wealth of "games" that can easily be adapted and used as warm-up drills to increase awareness of tactical play, biomechanics, mobility, balance, flexibility, as well as building speed and stamina, regardless of your style of martial art. There are some drills that are specific to Judo, but I have successfully modified a lot of the drills to fit the Taekwondo classes that I teach. Many of the "games" can be used in children's classes to great effect because they disguise repetition. "Games" also work in adult classes because they inject a spirit of levity into the class. Byl (2004) was writing a general text for warm-up drills, but again, many of his games and exercises can be modified to fit your specific needs. The internet is a great source of warm-up drills and 'YouTube' has any number of ideas in the form of short video clips that you can use to add variety to your own warm-up. We will talk a lot more about warm-ups, later.

Schedule a lot of time for individual practice. Keep technical material to a reasonable amount, so that you do not overload the students with information that they cannot process. Remember that students will be able to concentrate for about fifty minutes, which means that the material you offer in any single class period should be congruent and make a useful teaching unit if you want your students to gain the most benefit from the class.

Each lesson should have a specific teaching goal, which will be attached to the performance of a technique/drill or series of techniques/drills (Gagne, Briggs and Wager, 1992; Scott, 2005). In short, if there was one thing you want your students to leave with at the end of a particular class, what would it be? The answer to that question is the pedagogic goal for the lesson plan (Appendix 2).

Your lesson plans should leave your students motivated and wanting more. They should leave your class with an endorphin rush, feeling excited about the next class. We will talk more about this in the chapter on psychology when we talk about the flow experience. It is also important that the lesson plan be flexible enough for you to adapt the lesson to any side roads that it might take as a result of a student's question. Never be afraid to digress from a lesson plan if the class could benefit from some unexpected development, question or insight.

There is also a liability side to lesson plans. If you are ever sued for negligence and can produce a collection of lesson plans, it gives a more favorable impression that you know what you are doing and not simply making it up as you go along. Having said this, lesson plans are not things to be carved in stone and used over and over again. As you learn more, and as your class demographics change, you will find it expedient to revise your lesson plans. What is important, however, is that:

i) You have a clear idea of where you are going from class to class.

ii) You know how long it will take your students to progress from one stage of development to the next (assuming regular class attendance).

iii) Your students are adequately equipped to perform in the environment in which the skills they are acquiring will be used.

iv) You are adequately preparing your students to rank on schedule.

Ultimately, the performance goal for a lesson plan is to keep a student on track for rank advancement and/or opportunity-based performance at the correct time. If your students are attending class regularly, then there is no excuse for not having them ready for rank advancement in the prescribed time if you have a series of well thought out lesson plans. Equally, if you are training a competitor and have a clear set of lesson plans to prepare your athlete for competition at a specific tournament, then the same applies. Of course this means that you must be monitoring:

i) Student progress.

ii) The time-line.

iii) The lesson plans.

iv) The training goals.

By monitoring time in grade and having predetermined rank dates, you will be able to track each student's progress toward rank advancement. Students who are aware that their instructor knows when they should advance in rank, are apt to have a lot more confidence in the instructor and the lessons they are given. In much the same way, students are more likely to trust their instructors when they know that s/he is aware that there are specific skills, which must be acquired in order to participate at a specific level of tournament by a given date.

Testing: The nature of martial arts training presupposes that there will be tests of ability along the way. Such testing may come as a rank test or it may come when a student steps up to the line at a tournament, or meets a self-defense challenge.

If we continue the theme from the last section and use rank advancement as an example, then provided that the instructor is teaching from a syllabus, with a clearly defined set of lesson plans and an expected time-in-grade procedure, then the following items will be known by both the student and the instructor:

i) How long it should take to get from White Belt to Black Belt.

ii) How much time should be spent in grade at each rank.

iii) The material necessary for promotion to each rank.

To teach in such a way as to keep the students unaware of what they are supposed to know or when they will see their next promotion, is asking for a high attrition rate. When a student enrolls, s/he should know the expected rank date for promotion from White Belt to Yellow Belt (Graden, 1997). It is the student's responsibility to learn the information presented and to show up to class. It is the instructor's responsibility to make sure that the correct information is being presented to the student and that the ranking event happens during the expected time frame. When the instructor makes sure that the event happens on schedule, a win/win situation is being created for everyone:

i) The student's trust account with the coach receives a significant deposit.
ii) The student becomes more motivated to progress.
iii) The coach feels the reward of seeing the student making progress.
iv) Other students in the class acquire confidence that they too shall receive the same rewards for their investment of time, money and effort.

Moreover, nothing needs to change about the process or its outcomes as your students move through the ranks. In fact, if you are consistently providing quality learning experiences that lead to demonstrably successful performance-based testing (in whatever venue – be it tournament, rank test or other setting), the relationship of coach and athlete will invariably get stronger.

Since it is axiomatic that preparation prevents poor performance and that success occurs when preparation meets opportunity, it follows that a rank test should be a positive experience. If the student has lived up to his or her end of the agreement and has made the commitment of being in class for the requisite number of classes and has learned the requisite amount of material, then it is up to the instructor to honor his or her end of the agreement and provide a ranking opportunity for the student on schedule (as explained in the syllabus). In this way, both the player and the instructor each take a share of personal responsibility to ensure a positive outcome. Remember that rank promotion is a goal itself and that goal setting requires an objective, a plan of attack and a deadline for completion.

There are some important points to be made here: A rank test is a known entity, predicated upon the acquisition of specific knowledge. The outcome is something that the student can control, if you, as the instructor are providing the correct information, test the required information and if the student has honored his or her end of the learning equation.

Although the foregoing emphasized the rank test scenario, many of the same comments apply when we are preparing our players for competition. If we coach of competition athletes, we have a duty to adequately prepare our players for competition at any given level on the tournament circuit, which means that our curriculum, syllabus and lesson plans will need to reflect the stated goal of competition. The instructor can provide the drills and the tools and the athlete can acquire the knowledge, the skills and the physical and psychological fortitude to stay the course. There is one big difference however: **Neither the coach nor the player can control the outcome of a match** (Figure 4.8). Certainly, the well-prepared player may have the stacked cards as fully in his or her favor as possible, but in every match, there are events and circumstances over which the player has no control. Under these circumstances a successful outcome for the coach, the athlete and the coach/athlete relationship will be based not on tournament wins, but on meeting pre-determined tournament goals such as making some specified number of attacks using a particular tactical weapon. By focusing upon controllable outcomes, the athlete is more likely to remain motivated and continue to improve regardless of the tournament win : loss ratio.

Figure 4.8: The only thing that a player can control in a tournament match is how s/he uses his or her body. Neither the outcome of any action, nor any scores that might be awarded, nor the final outcome of the match are things that the player can directly control.

As an aside, when a player is consistently winning 85% of his or her matches at a given level, let's say the State level, it is time to move up to a bigger challenge, like a big regional tournament, or maybe the national level. At the new level, new lesson plans will be needed to build new competitive skills. During this new level of skill acquisition, it would be unreasonable to expect that same student to continue winning at the 85% level in the tougher competitive arena. It is, however, reasonable to set performance goals for each match and build the new skills needed to improve the win : loss ratio. The implications of this approach are that if you move a student up to a tougher competitive environment too soon, s/he will become discouraged and may lose faith in your insight as a coach; but if you leave a student in a competitive environment that is no longer a challenge, s/he may lose motivation.

Going back to the example of rank testing, the next questions are: What, when and how to test. Obviously, the students need to be evaluated upon the material necessary for rank promotion, but that is not a license to administer ten-hour rank tests that test the boundaries of human endurance. In so far as what to test is concerned, it is a good policy to show your students more than you will require on a rank test, so that you actually test a small portion of their knowledge base. Again, this does not mean rank test are not challenging, but they should demonstrate to the students that they have learned the required material. It is also a good idea to test all ranks up to Black Belt **in class**.

Taken in total, this approach to testing demonstrates that you have confidence in your ability to prepare your students for the test and your students know that they will pass when they are asked to test. Moreover, it means that we are preparing our students for success, not some chance based upon the whim of the instructor on the day of the test. It also means that the student body gets to continually see successful promotion exams, which will give motivation to the under-ranking students, and underscores the principle of positive self-expectancy.

I tend to adopt the adage of "*over-teach and under-test*", which means that I do not feel obliged to test all the material that I presented at a given rank. A syllabus explains to the student what is required for advancement to the next rank. The syllabus does not however, restrict what must be taught at any given rank. There is always the freedom to teach **more** if you wish. When the student ranks, require only what is on the syllabus, but make sure the student is aware that s/he knows more than will be demonstrated. A direct result of this methodology is that the students feel very confident of their abilities when they test for their next rank. If you teach more than your will require on a test, your students may see material that will either complement their rank requirements, or not be required until later in the rank system, thereby giving them longer to prepare. This is especially true in the upper ranks, when there is a longer time in grade between ranks.

There must be a balance that fosters the growth of the students, motivates and inspires them to set challenging goals and which doesn't swamp them with material at the low ranks and leave them nothing new to learn at the upper ranks. A cautionary note here: If you have enough time in grade to be able to fill classes with material that is not required, then perhaps an artificial time in grade standard has been established. If your students can perform all the required material at an appropriate level of competence, within a shorter time frame than is currently required, perhaps it is a sign that time in grade should be shortened, not necessarily that you do not require enough material.

Long-term Planning: The key to student retention involves learning how to build a long-range training plan with your players and help them to reach their potential. Long-term planning is, therefore, by necessity, is a collaborative project, heavily based in the notion of teamwork. Our overriding goal then, is to understand and employ the steps necessary to keep our players coming back for years, regardless of their original motivation for starting martial arts training. Remember that the two most important aspects of building a successful program are:

i) Recruiting qualified people.
ii) Retaining them.

Before you can build long-term relationships with your students, however, you must know your own goals and the path upon which you have set your program. You must have a detailed vision of your school. It is also important to have some kind of notion of the sorts of people you want to train. Since the emphasis of this section is upon building long-term relationships with your students/clients/athletes, it is worthwhile considering what qualities you would want your students/clients to have. Obviously you cannot be all things to all people; there are some things that as an instructor you do better than others, and some things that you have no real desire to do. That's fine. All I ask is that you be honest with yourself and be clear about it in your marketing.

Equally, your students will come to you with some ideas about what they are looking for. If you are clear about what you offer in your program, it will be much easier for you to attract and retain the right types of students for **you** (Hall and Brogniez 2001). If you are attracting the right sorts of students for your program, then it is also probable that you and your students will share similar values, goals and priorities. Ultimately, attracting people who share similar values, goals and priorities will help you to create mutually beneficial long-term plans.

Consequently, before you move on with this manual, please take some time to complete the following exercise:

You are going to need two hours to complete all four parts of the exercise, but you don't need to do it all in one go. Take at least thirty **uninterrupted** minutes to answer each part. Put each component of the exercise aside for a few days and come back to your answers later to see if they really reflect your core desires or simply represented the feelings of the moment.

i) **Draw the vision of your ideal program**. What does your ideal school look like? Get graphic. Describe the colors, the shape, the layout, the size, the pictures…all of it. Where is your school located? Do you own it? Who is training there? Why are they training? What activities are going on? How many staff do you need to run the school, outside of instructors? What ancillary programs do you offer (after-school programs, tutoring programs)? How many instructors are there? How many students? How many classes are going on at the same time? How big are the classes? Why are you teaching? What things do you emphasize?

ii) **List the characteristics of your ideal student/client**. In your list be detailed and specific. Think about all aspects of the student. Do you want them to be punctual to class? Do you want them to keep regular attendance and let you know if they will be missing class? Do you want them to trust, respect and/or admire you? Do you want them to be aggressive, determined, competitive, eager, analytical, practical and/or creative? What is the ideal age of your students? Do you work better with children or adults? Do you want your students to be goal-oriented, positive, happy, considerate, reliable and/or have a sense of humor? Do you want your perfect students to have a healthy lifestyle? Do you want them to bring you more students through personal referrals? What values and priorities does your ideal student have?

iii) **What should your students expect from you**? What are you willing to provide? The task is a little easier because you are simply setting a series of guidelines for yourself. What are you willing to do to help your students? Are you able and/or willing to coach them at every tournament they attend? Do you have other responsibilities like refereeing or tournament hosting that may conflict with your ability to coach your players? Are you willing to provide private training when needed? Are you willing or able to supervise supplementary training? Are you willing to seek extra training for yourself to meet your students' needs? Are you willing or able to teach form (kata or poomse), self-defense for women or children, law enforcement skills, competition skills? Do you have the ability to work with at-risk populations? How big are you willing to let your dojo get? When will you have enough students? What are you willing to sacrifice to get there? How much extra work are you willing to do? How far do you want to go outside your comfort area?

iv) **What makes your perfect clients tick**? It is very important to know what your clients value. If you know what makes you tick, and you know what makes your players tick, it will be much easier to come up with a long-term training plan that meets your needs **and** the needs of your students. Conversely, if you don't know what makes your students tick, how can you provide what they are looking for, except through trial and error? In this question it is important to recognize the priority order of the values set. For instance: You may have two students who both value family, education and martial arts. One player values martial arts above all else, and then family next and lastly his or her education. In this instance a player will sacrifice his or her education for family needs and family needs will be placed after the needs of his or her martial arts training. The second player with exactly the same values creates a different priority ordering and places family above education and education above martial arts. In this instance the player will sacrifice martial arts for schoolwork and schoolwork for family issues. I'm not asking you to judge whether either scenario is right or wrong. I am asking you to see that a player who is willing to sacrifice family and school for his or her martial arts training, is going to have a completely different view of training when compared to the student who places martial arts after his or her education and family. An athlete who is seeking an international competition career may have to make very difficult choices about delaying education to take advantage of their opportunities in the competitive arena. Are you capable of helping them to do that? Are you **willing** to do that? As the coach, are you aware of the implications for your student's future, should s/he have the ability and desire to walk such a path?

The questions that you have just answered will have significant ramifications in the development of the long-term relationships with your players. Think very carefully about the implications of your answers: Remember the old Chinese adage *"Be careful what you wish for, you might just get it!"*

Team-building: Team-building is going to be an important part of creating a successful program that keeps your players coming back year after year. In the section on psychology we will discuss how different students respond to intrinsic and extrinsic motivators. Ideally, we want our players to be intrinsically motivated to return to class. We want them to feel the internal drive to set goals, meet challenges and overcome setbacks and obstacles on their way to success. As instructors, however, it is our job to support the intrinsic motivators with a series of extrinsic motivators, such as providing exciting, educational, inspiring and motivating lesson plans. Communication and coaching style will also impact the effectiveness of the external motivators that we might use. In order for our players to feel a sense of ownership of their training there must also be a collaborative relationship between student and instructor. In this context such collaboration will create a team consisting of the instructor and an individual student. If you run a business there will almost certainly be larger teams, such as the school management team and the instructional staff team. It is therefore important to understand the role of the team-building process in the development of your long-term plan. First and foremost in any team-building process there must be a sense of vision-based leadership. It is here that the exercise that I just asked you to complete comes home to roost. Your team must believe in the vision and wish to see it come into reality. First you must use your imagination to create the vision, next you must believe, only then you can achieve.

There are specific aspects to building a team that are crucial for the team to be successful:

i) Goals: The team must have a clear sense of where it is going (Figure 4.9).

ii) Ownership: The team members must have a sense of ownership in the process and the goals.

iii) Power: The team must have a sense that it has control over its own destiny; that each member of the team is empowered in some way to contribute the team project.

iv) Commitment: All members of the team must be willing to commit to both the team goals and each other.

v) Involvement: Each member of the team must be actively involved and participate fully in the project goals.

vi) Support: Team members must be willing to support each other and although differences of opinion and approach will undoubtedly arise, team members must not degenerate into open competition against each other.

vii) Adaptability: The team must accept change as an inevitable consequence of setting out on a journey.

viii) Coaching: A team will need a team leader, who will act as the primary authority figure. The team leader is not there simply to dictate policy; a team leader is a facilitator, ensures that the team maintains its vision, maintains control over its own destiny and reviews its progress towards the intended goal.

ix) Trust: As a direct result of continually meeting and/or exceeding goals the team will develop trust in itself and its members. Trust will result in the creation of a synergetic partnership in which the team members achieve more together than would be possible if they were working alone.

x) Accountability: Teams must be working toward some sort of deadline or performance date, at which time the work of the team is put to the test (Figure 4.9).

Teams work best when they believe in the mission of the organization to which they belong. The consequence of an organizational mission will be that it will influence the types of team goals that are generated. In a reciprocal fashion, the team-building process must also enhance the overall organizational mission if both the team and the organization are to be successful.

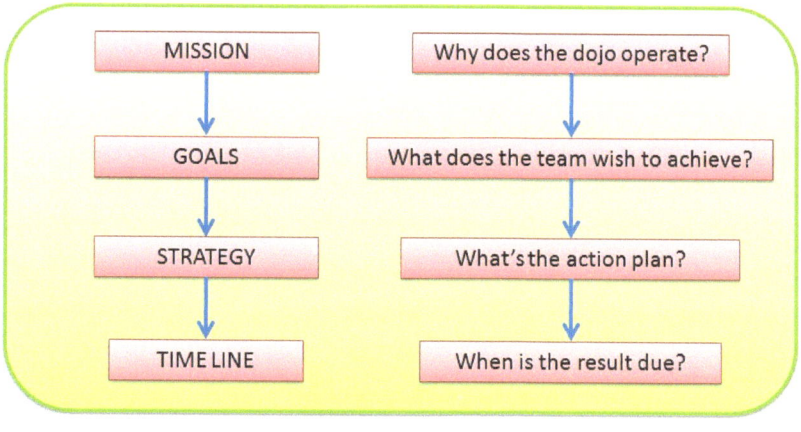

Figure 4.9: Team-building activity profile.

As we learned earlier in this section, the curriculum for a martial arts program defines the skill set that will be given to the students. Often the students see the curriculum in terms of their rank syllabus (strategic teaching elements). The individual lesson plans (tactical teaching tools) that are offered from class-to-class represent pieces of a jigsaw or sections of road on a route map.

When you build long-term relationships with your students, it is therefore critical that your students agree with the overall programmatic mission. In simple terms: If you want to run a recreational facility (organizational mission) and one of your students wants to become a serious contender for a full-contact championship title (player vision), then the mission of the school and the vision of the player are at odds with each other.

Conversely, if your school has been consistently training athletes for National-level tournaments, then the arrival of a student with his or her sights set on an Olympic berth might be just the challenge that you as a coach need to motivate your entire student base to strive for higher levels of performance (Figure 4.10). In this case, the programmatic mission, the training teams and the long-term training plans would all have a high probability of creating synergy and mutual benefit for everyone involved. The synergistic result would be that the members of the school would achieve more than they did striving for the previous set of goals, purely and simply because an appropriate catalyst had been added to an already functional system.

Figure 4.10: Setting mutually supportive goals and deadline that serve the mission of the school.

During the team-building process, there will be several steps that lead to success (Temme, 1996). Assuming a team has been created and they have agreed upon a goal, one of the first things that will happen is that ideas must be forthcoming that can then be crafted into a series of actionable tasks. Differences of opinion will inevitably occur at this juncture, which will generate the need for resolution and the development of a win/win consensus. The application of excellent coaching skills in the areas of communication, negotiation and facilitation cannot be underestimated during this stage. The next step will involve taking action and then examining the results of the action taken, prior to refining or modifying the goals, if necessary.

You will probably discover that informal as well as formal teams will develop within your school. A formal team might include you as the instructor and an individual student when you develop an individualized long-term training plan tailored to the specific needs of the student. Implied within this statement is the notion that not all students will share the same goal set within your program and it will be important to create specific training programs that motivate each student, so long as the student goals are coincident with the mission of the school. It is also possible that informal groups will develop to train together or develop a supplementary training regime together. Two places I see this happen a lot is when we are approaching a school-wide Black Belt rank testing event, or when a group of students want to get some extra training time in prior to a tournament.

To summarize then, during the course of developing long-term training plans with your students you will find it necessary to enter synergistic, collaborative relationships with your students that require team work for a successful outcome to occur. There is a key point here that we sometimes miss: Long-term planning, that employs team-building processes will lead to **transformation of the student <u>and</u> the instructor**. It is a win/win scenario.

Long-term training plans will therefore:

i) Keep your students motivated, inspired and educated.

ii) Develop the full potential of your students.

iii) Create individualized training plans for your students that are appropriate for their physical and psychological level of development as athletes.

iv) Create desire for more learning and/or progress in your students.

v) Create extraordinarily high levels of retention.

vi) Create a sense that "this is the place to train if you want to get _____", which in turn will raise your recruitment levels and place a filter at the front end that filters out people who do not embrace the overall mission of the school.

vii) Create a highly focused program, with a clear sense of mission.

viii) Lead to transformational changes for your players, and for you, the instructor.

As we showed earlier in this section on pedagogy it is important to use a curriculum, syllabus, lesson plans and predictable testing dates, so that your students will recognize that you have developed an over-arching long-term plan for their growth and are not simply using some haphazard set of notions about rank and progress. Building a long-term plan for your students lies at the heart of a long-term relationship and has a direct effect upon trust and respect. It is not enough, however, for the instructor to rely on the syllabus, lesson plans and testing dates, although these do provide a solid framework upon which to build.

Since the syllabus, lesson plans and testing dates are developed for the whole class, each student also needs to know that the instructor cares about individually personalized development. Putting a new colored belt on a student every time it is due, does not necessarily communicate a sense of understanding the personal needs and goals of the student on the part of the instructor, there needs to be much more. Your students need to be continually informed of their progress and what they need to do to continue their development. Each student is also more than a cog in a machine that needs oiling every once in a while. Students have opinions about what course their training should take and the sorts of goals that they might want to achieve. It is at this point that the personalized long-range plan enters the picture.

Long-range planning is about planning for success. It is about helping your students develop skills that they can take to the peak of their potential. Long-term planning is about developing skills that are built around each student's own unique talents and abilities, needs and goals (Gleeson, 1967). Long-range planning can take many forms and will be affected by your programmatic focus. There are, however, some common elements to all long-range plans:

i) They will be collaborative projects. The plan will result from a dialogue between the student and the instructor, who together plan, monitor and evaluate the student's progress towards his or her stated goals.

ii) They will be personal and idiosyncratic, specifically designed to meet specific needs and help your students to reach their stated goals.

iii) The plan may include written, discussion and video components.

iv) The plan will include both physical and mental skill set development goals, action plans and target dates. The plan must help the student to develop physical skills that include tactical weapons as well as strategies for the employment of the tactical weapons. It is important that the training environment and training drills mimic the environment and conditions of use as much as possible, as soon as possible (Gleeson, 1967; Weers, 2003), especially where competition or self-defense is the focus of the training plan (Siddle, 1995). For students who train for self-defense or competition, this item will become the Personal Combat Training System (PCTS) and will ultimately form the focus and core of the training plan. Once a student has developed a PCTS there will never be a situation where s/he enters the environment for which the skills were developed without some sense of purpose.

v) The plan will include personal and mental fitness/growth/performance goals, action plans and target dates. You will want to include such things as:

a. Supplementary physical training **in addition to** the martial arts training and measurements of improvements in physical conditioning over time.

b. Mental training including visualization, relaxation drills, focus drills.

vi) The plan will be used to develop an individual training plan that will reinforce strong skills and enhance weaker areas of development through the use of training drills and periodic evaluation of abilities over time.

vii) The plan will include a record of progress over time.

viii) The plans will use video media to help the student develop skills and strategies and serve as a basis for demonstrating development over time. As an example here, it is possible to record a student performing a particular Karate form and discuss the high and low points of the form, then set specific goals for improvement, develop action plans that will lead to improvement in those areas, set a target date, review and assess the improvement at the target date by making another recording and comparing it with the first. Equally, video comparisons might be made between the student's performance and the video performances of known kata specialists. Additionally, if the player wishes to compete at tournament, then video comparisons can be made with performance videos in the training environment and performance videos in the competition environment.

ix) Lastly, the plan must include an accurate assessment and understanding of the rules of engagement for the environment in which the skills set will be employed.

The very first step in building a long-range plan for your students, is to understand what your students need from their training. You may think you know, but it is important for your students to explain to you what their needs and goals are and how they visualize their long-term development within your program. A good way to **begin** this process with the student is to have every student update a "Progress and Goals Questionnaire" each time they move up in rank (Appendix 3). Over time, the students will see that their goals and objectives within the program have changed and become more refined and focused. The questionnaire is a first-level entry into the long-range plan. Nothing however, replaces the face-to-face discussion with a discerning instructor who truly wants to help his or her students to excel. It is only when you take personal interest in the desires of your students and begin to develop detailed training plans that the process of long-term building really begins. In the early stages of development, the relationship you develop with an individual student will be much like that of a teacher and student, but as you both learn, grow and mature, the relationship may evolve into a mentorship, rather than a straight forward coaching relationship.

Once you know what your students want from your program, you can begin to build a long-range plan that will get them to their desired destinations. A mutual awareness of the student goals within your program is absolutely essential. Just because **you** want a national champion, and you think that your student has the natural talent to make it, does not mean that it is the student's desire to compete on the national scene. A failure to recognize and accept the student's desires will ultimately cost you the student. Likewise the reverse is true. If you have students who itch to compete and you do not train them so that they will be able to compete effectively, you will ultimately lose them as well. Again, this is not a matter to be judged as right or wrong. It simply underscores that all actions and relationships within your school must be congruent with the overarching vision of the school, if they are to have any chance of being successful. The degree to which you can recognize, understand **and** meet the needs of your students (whether the needs have been fully verbalized or not) and the degree to which they fit within the overarching vision of the school is the degree to which you will be successful at retaining your students.

So, let us assume that we have reached a level of mutual understanding, and have some stated goals; we can now begin to plan how to get there. In the second step of long-term planning, you need to set a training regimen upon which to build the details of the actual plan:

i) How many times per week does the student train?

ii) What types of supplementary training does the student need?

iii) How often does this sort of training need to be done and at what level of intensity?

iv) How will training need to be modified over the training year? It is especially important to modify training during the year if you are dealing with a competitor and a tournament calendar. You will want your students to be at their peak when tournament season arrives.

v) How will training need to be modified as the student develops increased levels of:

a. Mental commitment,

b. Physical fitness,

c. Skill?

vi) How will the training change as the student moves up the ladder of success?

Although this is the second stage in developing the long-range plan, it is still a fairly general framework.

The third stage of planning is to meet the specific needs of your students at their current level of development. Let us assume for the moment that we are dealing with an adolescent male Orange belt student who has some basic sparring skills, about six months of training experience in Taekwondo and who has decided that he wants to go to tournament. How do you as a coach deal with the student? You could say, *"Great, there's one next weekend."* You then convoy all your players to tournament the following weekend and your player enters the fray along with everyone else. After all, this is how you learned and it worked for you. Obviously this approach will not help to build the kind of relationship that the student was seeking, so it is incumbent upon us as coaches to make sure that we adequately prepare each student for his or her first tournament.

Assuming that you make this commitment you could approach the problem by telling would-be competitors to come to the competition classes that you hold in the pre-tournament season. Duly excited, your students show up with their new sparring gear and lots of enthusiasm. Your student is pumped and ready to learn how to compete. What actually happens is that the students finds themselves faced off against students who have been coming to this class for months, or years, and who have, by trail and error, figured out how to survive. Needless to say the new student gets pummeled by those with more experience and frustrated by their own seeming lack of ability. Only the tough students survive in this kind of environment, all the others will quit. Throwing unprepared students into a free-fighting environment is asking for attrition in your student base and could, under some circumstances, be considered as negligent. So this approach is also clearly inadequate but is still, unfortunately all too common.

If we have done our job right in the early classes, our students should have a reasonable array of weapons and skills and have learned some of the principles of movement. Our students should have an awareness of situations in which the skills they have been learning will be applied. Equally, our students will have been training with drills that mimic the environment in which they expect to use their skills. The task of the instructor now becomes to demonstrate how those weapons and skills can be used for attack and defense in a dynamic and initially unpredictable environment (for the student at least), and mold the weapons and skills into an effective fighting arsenal, built around the notion of an integrated combat system.

Building a Person Combat Training System (PCTS): To negotiate any combat environment effectively, there are skills, which must be developed (Gleeson, 1967; Siddle, 1995; Weers, 2003). There are, in fact, two distinct sets of skills: Tactical skills and strategic skills. The flexibility of the latter is going to be dependent upon the breadth of the former. So what are the tactical skills of combat? Adapting from Gleeson (1967), Ames (1993) and Weers (2003) we can list twelve of them:

    i) Ability to maintain your mobility.

    ii) Ability to restrict your opponent's mobility.

    iii) Ability to maintain a balanced, stable weapon platform (postural base).

    iv) Ability to destabilize your opponent (mentally and/or physically).

    v) Ability to generate powerful techniques that use all joints and muscles at the correct time, in the correct order.

    vi) Ability to effectively apply power, ensuring that your opponent is carrying your weight on the ground or feeling the full force of your strike, joint lock or throw.

    vii) Ability to build combination skills that support your primary attacking weapons.

    viii) Ability to minimize your own potential target areas, reducing the chances for your opponent to use his/her primary and secondary weapon systems.

    ix) Ability to defend against, and counter your opponent's attacks with techniques of your own and/or avoid being struck, thrown, joint-locked, choked or pinned when attacked, through the use of escape and evasion skills.

    x) Ability to control personal space at close range and prevent or remove any of your opponent's grips, or to turn them to your advantage.

    xi) Ability to use transitional skills as you move from one combat range to another (for instance moving from striking range into grappling-throwing range, and finally into groundwork-grappling range).

xii) Ability to end an engagement with the skillful use of appropriate closing techniques when the opportunities arise.

You will notice that we have not listed any specific techniques or talked about your student's favorite skills. The twelve tactical abilities are the defining aspects of combat, and a weakness in any one of these areas will limit the ability to control the strategy of an engagement. Strategic skills relate to the manner in which your students employ their tactical skills. If you are the coach of a competition-based player you remember from what we have said earlier that your player cannot control the outcome of the match. Your players can, however, strongly **influence** the way each match is played. **Your players can control their own actions and choices, but they cannot control their opponents or the referees or everything that could potentially happen during a match. Strategy in competition is consequently concerned with exerting the maximum amount of influence on the way the match is played to create the greatest possible chance of a favorable outcome for your player.** We can list six major strategic elements:

i) Be prepared ahead of time mentally and physically.

ii) Develop a psychological advantage early.

iii) Understand and use the rules of engagement to advantage.

iv) Control the use of combat environment.

v) Increase the number of attacks per unit time.

vi) Make opponents regret launching an attack; it will make them wary of anything but their major skills, for fear of getting punished or caught in an untenable position.

When we build integrated combat systems for our students we must ensure that all the tactical elements are supported by a clear knowledge of where, and when, they should be used. Think of it like human chess! Remember also, that because you are building a learned, practiced and studied combat system, what begins as an unpredictable combat environment inevitably turns into a highly organized and predictable encounter. At the outset, and from the inexperienced player's perspective, it's a case of *"What just happened? I never saw it coming."* Experienced players, however, know the game and can see the impending attack long before it materializes. From the experienced player's perspective it's very much a case of *"Been there, done that. Seen it before."* It is precisely because the combat environment has become predictable that highly experienced, skillful players in free-fighting environments frequently end up exerting less effort.

A personal combat system will be a strategy that draws on the strengths of each student and protects his or her weaker areas. Your primary job at this stage is building specific training drills for attack and defense patterns that emphasize the most natural skills that each student has thus far developed. Regardless of the intended environment of use, questions that will need to be answered include:

i) What is the student's dominant side/leg/hand/eye?

ii) What are the best offensive skills currently? What drills can be developed to enhance those same skills and build them into an integrated pattern of attack skills using effective offensive weaponry?

iii) What are the optimal moments for the student to use the primary offensive skills in the environment of use? Is there a preferred moment to attack?

iv) What should the student do if the attack fails and s/he is counter attacked? Which way should s/he move? What is most likely to happen next? What weapons do the opponents generally have available with which to counter attack?

v) Does the student have adequate defensive skills for varying targets? What drills need to be developed to enhance defensive capabilities?

vi) What sorts of movement skills does the student need to practice to complement the primary offensive weaponry and safeguard the vulnerable targets?

vii) What are the weakest areas as they pertain to the environment of use? What drills can be developed to reduce the student's vulnerability?

viii) Are there habits that need to be modified, such as bending over, poor foot placement or becoming immobile and rigid in the face of an oncoming attack?

ix) Are there telltale habits (pre-incident indicators) that precede the execution of an offensive technique?

These are all questions that you can begin to answer on a class-by-class basis as you teach the fundamentals of situational encounters for the environment in which the PCTS will be used. In this way the "real" environment becomes more predictable for your students and they will begin to see patterns of movement both in themselves and their partners. Once you have answers to these questions you can develop individualized training drills and a time-line, which together, will enable your student to develop the skills necessary to build a personal combat training program. The sorts of drills you use will be specific movement drills that run through a pre-ordained series of actions aimed at improving specific aspects of the skills being used such as: Foot, hand and body position, posture, footwork, turning directions, speed, commitment to the attack, follow through, agility, combination actions, transitions to other combat ranges etc.. The instructor will need to evaluate and modify these drills as the student's skill level improves. The player needs to keep a class-by-class training record of:

i) What did you do? What did you learn? What did you focus on?

ii) Details of training drills used.

iii) Number of repetitions done.

iv) Aspects of training that need attention (such as fitness level, mental concentration etc) and plans for working on them.

v) Summary details. What looks good? Why? What needs work? Why? What pieces of the PCTS are missing or weak?

When you have prepared your student adequately with a rudimentary attack system it will need to be tested. In the case of a competitor, the testing arena is the tournament. So you go to tournament. Set specific goals for each match such as:

i) Attacking whenever the opponent changes to his or her non-dominant side.

ii) Making a specific number of attacks per unit time.

Set one or two very specific goals that you can measure at the end of each match. Work on the major goals first: For instance there's not much point worrying about getting a submission if your player has difficulty controlling his or her balance and position in a grappling environment. You should record video of the match and not worry overly much about the outcome. The important point at this stage is that the set goals were met, which can be easily seen by watching the video. Once you see how effective the player was at meeting his or her match goals against an unknown opponent, you can begin to refine the system and modify it according to the nature of the tournament experiences. You can also begin to integrate new elements into the attack system to take advantage of other opportunities that appeared in the match for which the student was not so well prepared. Again, at the end of the tournament, you and your student should get in the habit of building a log of what happened during each match and set new goals and target dates of what to work on next. Over time you and your students will build a very comprehensive written and video record of the tournament activities, which includes performance related information such as: What attack patterns were used, on what side of the body, after what specific pre-incident indicator by the opponent and so on. In this way your students will develop a very clear picture of what they need to do to improve in this area of performance, and, what is perhaps more important, they will have a mechanism in place to do so.

The long-term plan is always a work in progress; it is always in need of modification. Goals and objectives will change for your students over time as their skill levels improve. The mark of a really great motivator and a truly caring instructor is the ability to understand the changing needs of his or her players and to continually help the students to develop long-range plans, to sense when the plans need modification and to be ready with the next stage of the evolution.

Training Cycles or Periodization: The next component of long-term training involves an understanding of training cycles and the training calendar as it pertains to your specific martial art. Periodization allows us to plan the training for our students by creating training cycles that may span weeks, months or even years (Bompa, 1999; Corcoran and Graden, 1998; Cochran, 2001). During our discussion we will need to refer to several aspects of training, including:

i) **Duration**: Generally, duration refers to a single training event, such as a single class. Duration can also refer to a series of sessions, but for our purposes we will tend to restrict the definition to the length of individual training components.

ii) **Frequency**: Frequency is simply the number of times a training module is repeated per unit time. For instance if your student comes to class twice a week, you have established a training frequency for that component of training. A novice martial artist may only need to work out twice a week (frequency), however an elite competitor will need to work at a much higher frequency to obtain the training effects necessary to compete effectively. Frequency of training can be recorded for each type of activity in which the athlete is involved such as the specific number of martial arts classes each week, supported by the number of sessions of supplementary training.

iii) **Intensity**: Intensity is normally concerned with the physiological difficulty of training, or put another way, how much effort the athlete has to expend to do the work. As an approximation, we could also equate the intensity of any given training episode to a number of heart beats per minute as an indicator of work being performed by the athlete. Intensity can be changed in a number of ways. Using martial arts training as our example, intensity can be manipulated by varying the frequency, number and length of practice sessions during the week, rest and work periods within each practice session and numbers of repetitions of each drill within the work periods. In another case an athlete may be engaged in a weight training activity twice a week. If the frequency is increased to three times a week, the intensity has also increased. Equally, we could leave the frequency at two times per week, but increase the amount of work done in each session, thereby increasing the intensity. The amount of work done in each session could be altered by manipulating the number of drills, the number of required repetitions per drill, and the number and/or length of rest periods (lower intensity work being performed) between drills.

iv) **Load**: Load can be visualized as an external component that affects intensity. For instance a 156-pound student throwing a 200-pound student in a repetitive throwing drill is experiencing a higher load than if the same student was throwing a 120-pound student with the same throw for the same number of repetitions. The relationship is that when load increases intensity will also increase.

v) **Specificity**: Relates to the creation of drills that simulate specific types of martial arts actions. Specific drills and exercises that simulate an action will lead to similar neuromuscular responses that would be used during the execution of the specific martial arts skill. The goal of specificity in training is to make the athlete's body more efficient. For instance: We might want to work on plyometric leg actions to help a student build a powerful jumping kick or shoulder throw.

vi) **Volume**: Volume is the **quantity** of a training component. For instance total number of front kick or throwing repetitions per class would constitute a quantity of training. Remember this though: quantity of repetitions does not necessarily equate to higher levels of intensity (work done).

In the development of a program of training that involves periodization we will need to balance each of the elements defined above. Therefore, by making good use of these elements we will be able to use periodization to:

i) Prevent overtraining.

ii) Reduce risk of fatigue injuries.

iii) Maintain optimal psychological arousal during the training interval.

iv) Create the opportunity for continuous gains in strength, speed, endurance and flexibility.

v) Promote a long-term perspective of skill development.

vi) Prepare your students so that that they peak at the right time for competition, and

vii) Provide adequate recovery time.

The training idea is really very simple, and can be related to the Goldilocks Problem. For every player there is an optimal training window where there is a positive training benefit (porridge is just right). If the training is too light or too sporadic (porridge is too cold) there is no effect and if the training is too intense or too long (porridge is too hot) then the athlete will be a candidate for burnout (Figure 4.11). In essence the Principle of Diminishing Returns indicates that ever-increasing amounts of training will not create greater benefits, and may in fact, lead to burn-out and /or injury.

In simple terms, periodization allows a coach to vary the frequency, intensity, load, volume and type of the activity over time. The two main variables that coaches manipulate during training cycles are intensity and volume. Although it should be obvious that a student will generally be obtaining a training effect when both volume and intensity increase, there are other times when an athlete will be training "hard" even though intensity has increased and volume has decreased.

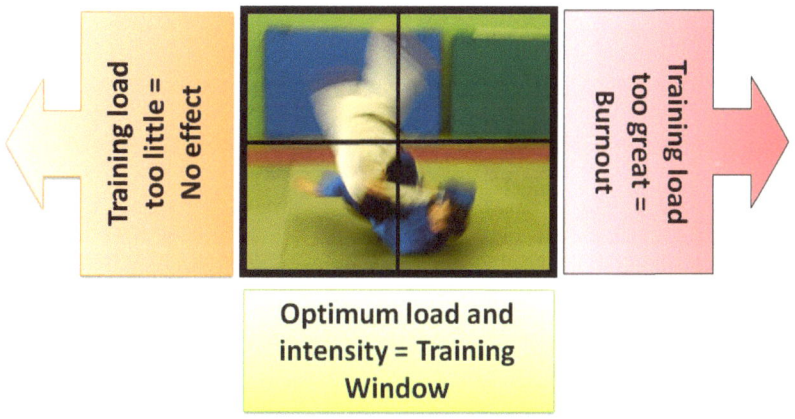

Figure 4.11: The Goldilocks Principle applied to athlete training.

The total amount of training time can be broken down into macro-, meso-, and microcycles. Macrocycles generally last for a year or more, whereas mesocycles would be better correlated with a specific training season, such as the off-season, the pre-season and the tournament season (Bompa, 1999; Cochran, 2001; Martens, 1990). Microcycles might be as small as one week or as long as one month in a long tournament season. Consequently, if you are developing a long-term plan for a tournament athlete, it is important to know the major tournament(s) for which your athlete needs to peak and which tournaments are less important.

Periodization works because it achieves an optimal level of training. Training can be viewed as a form of stress, which can be defined as any externally applied force or demand. In this case the training is an externally applied demand upon the body of the athlete, who ideally, adapts to the training both physiologically (body changes) and psychologically (mental changes). In 1936, Hans Selye developed a theory called the General Adaptation Syndrome (GAS), which can be divided into three stages (Powers and Howley, 1990; Selye, 1978):

i) Alarm.

ii) Resistance.

iii) Exhaustion.

When training begins, a student is confronted with the "Alarm" stage. The alarm stage is related to the fight or flight response. A student will either work through the initial lack of physical fitness or stop training. In the second stage the student enters the resistance stage where s/he begins to see an adaptation to the workload. The more often the player chooses the "fight" response during the Alarm stage, the easier will be the adaptation to the "Resistance" stage, over time. When the athlete continues to work under increasing amounts of applied stress (training demands), the player enters the third stage of GAS, which is the "Exhaustion" stage. At this stage the athlete ceases to obtain any benefits and performance levels diminish. Rest is mandatory at this point if overtraining is to be prevented (Bompa, 1999; Corcoran and Graden, 1998).

When you develop a plan, which involves periodization, it is important to consider the age, skill-level and fitness-level of your athletes. Each plan should be individualized for each player, although all plans will share several common elements. One of the first things to do is to decide how many hours are going to be dedicated to training during the year and how those hours will be subdivided for the off-season, pre-season and tournament season. Next it will be important to decide what training results you want to achieve and then decide what training elements will be used to obtain the desired results. According to Bompa (1999), in martial arts the limiting factors are starting power, reactive power, and endurance. It is clear then, that training objectives will be to enhance both the anaerobic and aerobic energy systems, develop starting and reactive power and develop muscular endurance (see chapter on physiology). Purely as an example, the training elements might include:

i) Three classes of martial arts per week, each lasting one hour.

ii) Running for aerobic endurance.

iii) Weight-lifting for strength and plyometric power.

Once you have decided what the training activities will be, the next stage is to establish supplementary training frequencies and goals (such as number of times per week, duration of training interval, distances to be run per unit time, weights to be lifted and numbers of reps etc.). Finally, set limits on the increases in work that you will require during each meso-cycle as appropriate for each athlete.

Given that you have established a total number of workout hours for the entire period (let's say, one year); and since you have established three martial arts training blocks per week, you can then subtract this total block of time from the yearly total to arrive at how much time you have available for supplementary training.

During the pre-tournament season, a typical meso-cycle might be to progressively overload the athlete during a four-week cycle (Figure 4.12) increasing the load (amount of work done) and/or intensity (difficulty of training) of running and weight lifting, but keep the duration (amount of time for each session) and frequency (number of training times) stable. Using weight training as an example; the first week (microcycle one) might emphasize building muscle mass, the second microcycle might emphasize muscular endurance and the third microcycle might emphasize power (force per unit time), whereas the fourth microcycle could focus on maintaining a muscle balance (Cochran, 2001). Like all training protocols, it is important to develop correct technique, start light and build up gradually in terms of both frequency and intensity.

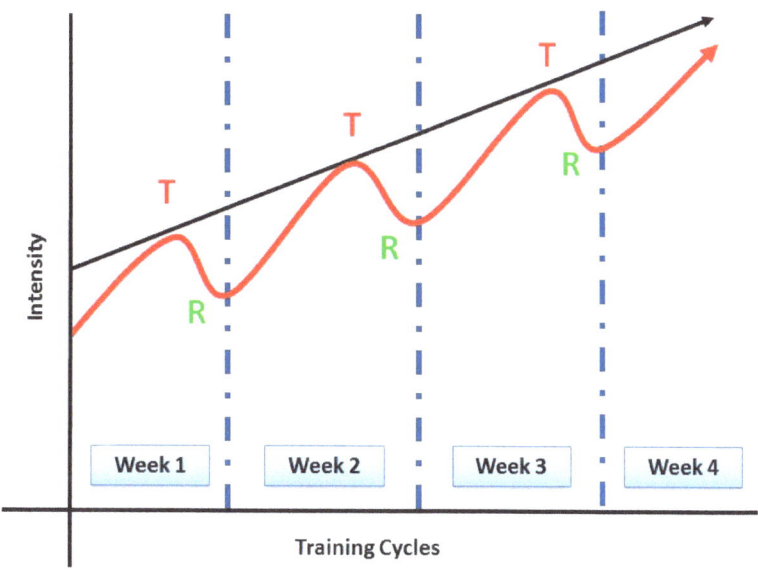

Figure 4.12: A month-long meso-cycle.

At the end of the four-week period, there would be a recovery time built into the program that would allow your athlete to prepare for the next cycle. Bompa (1999), Corcoran and Graden (1998), and Kreider et al (1998) all emphasize that driving a player to higher levels of performance without allowing for recovery time will lead to overtraining and fatigue, and ultimately defeat the purpose of the training load. If load is systematically applied without adequate recovery time, a player will cease to show improvement and enter the exhaustion phase, which can lead to increased likelihood of injury and will only be overcome by forced rest. Conversely, given adequate recovery time, a player will be ready to undertake the next cycle and show continued improvements in performance with increasing training demands.

In an effort to keep your players engaged and motivated, it is better to give a variable prescription, rather than a specific "must do" list of activities (Martens, 1990). For instance, if improvements in aerobic endurance running is a component part of the training for then you might want to offer a couple of training choices, such as running a longer distance over flat ground or a lesser distance over an incline in the same amount of time.

To summarize thus far:

i) **Macrocycles** represent long periods of time involving several training seasons. Although macrocycles are frequently one year in length, there is no reason why a coach and player cannot set out much longer macrocycles.

ii) **Mesocycles** Typically mesocycles are several months in duration and represent an individual training season. For instance, the pre-season would represent a mesocycle.

iii) **Microcycles** represent the weekly components of a mesocycle. Each microcycle will progressively increase the training load and conclude with a rest period (Figures 4.12, 4.13). Successive microcycles will add progressively more training load and together form a mesocycle.

In a general way, each scale of cycle will show a progressive increase in the training load associated with a recovery period **regardless of the amount of time that they encompass** (Figure 4.13). Consequently, in the simplest form, each type of cycle will tend to demonstrate three parts:

i) An increasing level of training that heightens the training intensity, adds to the training load, and which leads to a maximum training effect.

ii) A fatigue phase, during which improvements in performance are compromised.

iii) A recovery phase, which allows the body to repair and the mind to prepare for the next cycle of training.

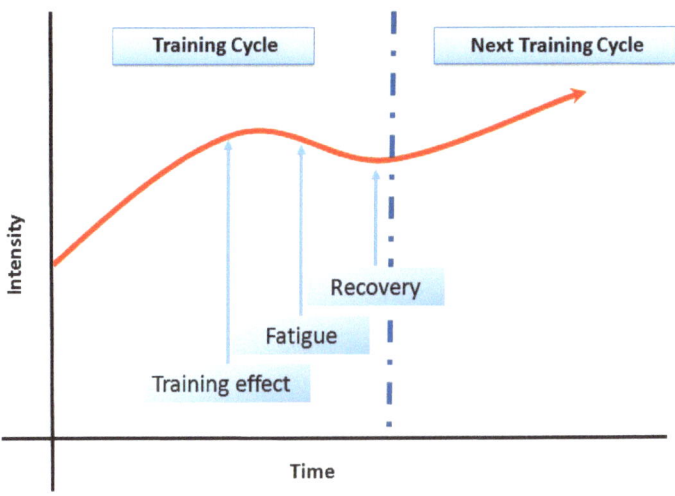

Figure 4.13: Components of a typical periodization cycle.

In the earlier example we used martial arts, running and weight lifting as the training elements, the off-season is when we would emphasize running and the pre-tournament season is when we will load the weight lifting to make the gains we are seeking in each area of fitness (Figure 4.14). An appropriate training cycle, therefore, means that our player would be working hardest during the pre-tournament season, work to maintain fitness levels during the tournament season and stay on a lower intensity maintenance schedule during the off-season.

During the off-season, our player would be learning new skills and developing the PCTS, while maintaining the aerobic fitness level. The off-season is the ideal time to go back and look at the effectiveness of the PCTS during the preceding tournament season and make adjustments to the training plan, add new elements to the PCTS and adjust elements that need work. The pre-tournament season would, therefore, be used to develop greater levels of strength, endurance and other specific aspects of fitness as necessary. The pre-season would also be used to practice the PCTS skills, so that they are ready for use when the tournament season arrives. The tournament season would be used to work on the active tournament skills (those skills being used as part of the current PCTS) and maintain levels of fitness. The tournament season is **NOT**, however, the time to give your player a whole new set of skills and expect the player to use them in his or her next tournament. The tournament season is the time to refine and polish what our player already knows.

Figure 4.14: Seasonality as it affects athlete fitness, preparedness and the Personal Combat Training System.

So again, to summarize thus far:

i) **Off-season**: Build the PCTS, add new skills, review previous tournament season performances and effectiveness. Maintain aerobic levels of fitness (Bompa, 1999). Work on low intensity activities. Work on the mental learning process for both tactical and strategic elements of play.

ii) **Pre-Tournament season**: Practice the elements of the PCTS, emphasize repetition and build in plenty of time for drill practice. At the beginning of the Pre-tournament season, after the off season, there will be a period of anatomical adaptation as your player's body gets used to higher demands and intensity of training. It is important in this stage to make sure that you work on adaptations in the right order and do not increase the demands too quickly. Anatomical adaptations will include building lean muscle mass (hypertrophy) and if the aerobic foundation has been maintained, then improvements in anaerobic endurance will be necessary. If aerobic endurance was compromised during the off-season, then the aerobic system will have to be developed prior to the anaerobic system. (Chapter 6) Build strength, speed and stamina (Bompa, 1999). Cut weight if necessary. Increase intensity and load of training using four-week cycles with a recovery period at the end of each cycle. Work on the mental game of concentration, focus, determination, and persistence.

iii) **Tournament season**: Refine the PCTS as a function of tournament performance, but do not attempt to develop new skill sets. Work on the details of the current PCTS skill set and emphasize repetition. Maintain levels of fitness (Bompa, 1999), slack off in volume to a lighter training regimen emphasizing the aerobic energy system more than anaerobic system, but maintain strength. Allow for post-tournament recovery time. Maintain fighting weight. Emphasize mental discipline.

Monitoring Your Athletes: Performance monitoring should be an integral component of long-term training plans, and will necessarily be a collaborative process involving both the instructor and the student. You should encourage your students to develop daily training diaries, which could be as simple as a training log or as elaborate as a detailed account of all activities and their impact. Gilbert and Beatie (2003) refer to these as "reflective tools" because they permit a student to consider the implications of the nature and effects of the training in which s/he is involved. Reflective logbooks allow a player to discover more about what works as a part of the tactical tool box and what tools will help to build a strategic game by studying and restudying the notes made on each class over time. Reflective notebooks also allow the players to recognize for themselves the onset of training stress. Obviously, notebooks are only useful if the player is willing to commit to the discipline of keeping up with the entries and the instructor is consistent in regularly discussing the notebook with the player.

Additionally, computer technology affords each coach and athlete the possibility of creating coaching organizers that prompt both player and coach to input data as a record of activity or a measure of performance. Whatever method of monitoring you choose, it is critical that you track performance over time and watch for signs of overtraining and burnout.

The notion that you get more benefit from continually pushing your players is erroneous (Moran and McGlynn, 1997), so be on the lookout for both physical and mental signs of overtraining, and remember that it is better to prevent overtraining by careful attention to training management than it is to repair the damage done by overtraining (Kreider, et al, 1998). As an instructor, you should be sensitive signs of overtraining in your athletes that include:

i) Apparent boredom.

ii) Lack of concentration.

iii) Loss of interest and motivation to attend practice.

iv) Deterioration in performance.

v) Sleep disturbance.

vi) Loss of appetite and other digestive problems.

vii) Mood swings.

viii) Susceptibility to minor injuries (musculoskeletal failure).

ix) Susceptibility to minor illnesses (suppression of immune system efficiency).

x) Feelings of chronic fatigue.

xi) General chronic joint aches and headaches.

Don't forget though, that what may constitute overtraining for one student may not be overtraining to another student. Additionally, don't lose sight of the fact that what constitutes overtraining for a novice student, might be perceived as a mild workout for a highly trained and active Black Belt.

The bottom line is that training too hard can lead to increased risk of injury, and reverse many of the benefits that your students have worked so hard to achieve. Some factors that can contribute to increasing the likelihood of overtraining (Moran and McGlynn, 1997) include:

i) Length of the training season may be too long.

ii) Limited social support structure.

iii) Lack of training variety leading to boredom.

iv) The instructor, the student or the training may be too demanding.

v) Lack of self-belief and weak mental skills.

vi) Competition pressures.

vii) Unrealistic training and/or performance goals.

A wise instructor helps to develop a training plan that will maximize his or her player's training opportunities but which will not lead to burnout. It is the responsibility of both the instructor and the student to be sensitive to the early signs of burnout and be prepared to modify the training plan accordingly.

Putting it all together: From what we have said thusfar, when you train your students, regardless of where they will use the skills that they acquire, there are four things that you will need to do for them:

i) Build tactical skills.

ii) Build strategic skills.

iii) Enhance physical fitness.

iv) Build mental skills.

Ultimately, therefore, the purpose of your long-term training plan training **inclusive of cross-training opportunities** will be to help your students to improve their level of fitness and by extension, also improve their martial arts performance in some way. Specifically, you will want to:

i) Increase levels of fitness in the areas of energy and power production:

    a. Aerobic endurance.

    b. Anaerobic endurance.

    c. Muscular strength.

    d. Muscular endurance.

ii) Increase levels of fitness in the areas of agility, balance and flexibility.

iii) Provide both mental and physical variety.

iv) Increase the tactical tools available, which may in turn increase the strategic possibilities.

v) Increase mental toughness, concentration and focus.

vi) Reduce risk of overtraining and over-use injuries.

vii) Provide opportunities for training during injury rehabilitation and recovery.

Chapter 5

PSYCHOLOGY OF COACHING

An interest in intellectual development, personality and understanding of personality types, can help you to understand some of what you do as an instructor and some of what your clients do as students (Hirsh and Kummerow, 1989; Keirsey and Bates, 1984; Riso and Hudson, 1996, 1999; Sternberg, 1997). Understanding the various personality types and forms of intelligence goes a long way to explaining how we learn, how we teach, how we are motivated and why some things we do as coaches work for some of our students, but not for others.

As a starting point for this chapter let's start with the statement that we tend to teach in one of two ways: We either teach the way we were taught, or the way that best fits our learning style.

If we wish to be effective, however, it is clear that a good instructor must learn how to present the same information in differing ways to different groups of students, so that they can **all** learn effectively. One of the teaching goals of the martial arts instructor should be to assist and encourage students to step outside of their normal learning or processing modes. When we do this, we can often create opportunities for periods of insight and rapid growth. Seeing from a new perspective can often lead to moments of insight that have large-scale trickle down effects throughout the student's awareness. We can only create such opportunities if we know how our students learn and are able to tailor our teaching methodologies to maximize the learning potential.

According to the Gallop Organization (Buckingham and Clifton, 2001), there are 34 "signature themes" to the talents that people demonstrate in the areas of thinking, striving and relating and each of us is unique in the ways in which those talents are manifest. At the same time, educational books tell us that there are seven distinct types or forms of intelligence (Wiley, 1995; Tracy and Rose, 1995):

i) Logical/mathematical, which involves inductive and deductive reasoning, scientific thinking and recognizing patterns.

ii) Visual/spatial, which relates to our ability to create mental images and notice details.

iii) Kinesthetic, which relates to our ability to understand how the body moves and remember what we have done.

iv) Verbal/linguistic, which relates to how the brain processes words and develops explanations. It is the dominant pattern for most western educational processes, regardless of student pre-disposition.

v) Rhythmic, which relates to awareness of tonality and music.

vi) Interpersonal, which relates to the development of social skills involving empathy, sensitivity and the awareness of other people's moods and feelings.

vii) Intrapersonal, which relates to the development of introspective skills and spiritual awareness.

There are, however, few empirical data to support this compartmentalized view of intelligence (Sternberg, 1997). In fact, emerging ideas (Dispenza, 2007; Doidge 2007; Sternberg, 1997) suggest that the brain is much more plastic and non-localized in its functioning than previously thought and it may be unreasonable to assume that any specific part of the brain is the source of particular sorts of intelligence. I mention this because in Sternberg's view of intelligence there are fewer types of intelligence:

i) Creative.

ii) Analytical.

iii) Practical.

iv) Reflective.

The significance of this statement becomes clearer when you consider the often-heard claim that martial arts are radically different to many sporting activities because they work on so many levels, simultaneously. When we teach martial arts, we are providing a tool with which our students can use all aspects of their "intelligence." To paraphrase Sternberg (1997, p.128) and to recast his statements in the light of teaching martial arts:

> "*Effective* [martial artists] *balance analytical, creative and practical abilities during their training. What is perhaps more important, especially with regard to the development of competitive* [martial artists]*, is that to be truly successful our students need to use the quality of reflection to know how and when to use analytical, creative and/or practical abilities effectively.*"

Having said all of that, let's think about what happens as a student moves from Novice to Expert player. When your students begin training they have no real knowledge of the nature of the task they are undertaking. Conversely, at much higher levels of training there are moments in which they will act instinctively without thinking consciously about the actions being performed. The progression from beginner to expert passes through four very distinct phases of mastery, and this is pretty much true for any field of endeavor. Curiously though, if you ask your students where they are on the four levels of mastery, they will tend to rate themselves higher than their abilities actually show them to be. Be that as it may, we can recognize the four levels of mastery as being:

i) **Uninformed Incompetence**. At this stage of development we don't know that we don't know anything. We do what feels normal or seems right or natural. We work mostly on instinct rather than using learned facts.

ii) **Informed Incompetence**. At this stage we are aware that we don't know anything. We also know that we have just begun to learn and that there is so much we don't know. We make frequent errors, have momentary flashes of insight and are definitely on the steep end of the learning curve.

iii) **Conscious Competence**. At this level we are pretty good at what we do. We know a high percentage of the curriculum; can perform the required techniques with some degree of proficiency and feel pretty good about what we have achieved. We can be relied upon to get things right and can be left alone to figure out a problem based on the information that we have already been given. Everyone who embarks on a learning journey of any kind should be able to reach this level of mastery.

iv) **Unconscious Competence**. At this level we act on instinct once again. Our knowledge is so much a part of us that we act instinctively and with a high degree of accuracy. In the Japanese martial arts, performance at this level is often referred to as "mushin" or "mind of no mind." Mushin occurs when the expert performs a skill without consciously planning the skill ahead of time. Early in our training, moments of mushin are sporadic and unpredictable events, but as our mastery increases so does our ability to act appropriately without conscious thought (Figure 5.1).

Figure 5.1: Pat Burris, Olympic Athlete and National Judo Coach is giving a demonstration of a skill that is so much a part of him, that he is almost in a meditative state of complete relaxation as he teaches.

The journey through the four levels of mastery is controlled by many factors, but from the perspective of psychology, the early stages of learning at the level of the Unconscious Incompetent involves acquiring gross motor actions, which instructors deliver through **techniques**. As we discussed in the section on pedagogy, as your students progress through the four levels of mastery, they will turn the techniques into skills (Gleeson, 1967, 1983).

The keys that turn techniques into skills are setting, practice and performance. Skill development, therefore, is the litmus test of true learning. It is axiomatic that repetition in the correct setting is the mother of skill. We repeat the technique over and over, making small adjustments in the technique as we evaluate our ability to produce a desired result. By constantly monitoring practice performance, improving the quality of our repetitions and performing the technique in the setting in which it will be required, the technique evolves into a skill.

A skill, therefore, is the external demonstration of an internalized technique. In terms of body movements, techniques tend to be choppy whereas skills are executed with grace and efficiency of movement. Consistent improvements will, therefore, lead to skill (Martens, 1990, NCCP, 1979). The process of learning a given technique will create a more or less permanent improvement in ability, not just in the technique being taught, but by extension, in other areas of the student's experience. There is behavioral change, which is demonstrated by the improvement in ability, but underlying that, there is also a cognitive change. Cognitive change is a change in the student's abilities with respect to his or her powers of mental association (Ormond, 1999).

So, from the perspective of psychology we need to understand how our students acquire the information that will lead them through the four levels of mastery.

In the psychological realm, when learning a physical action, a student can blueprint a simple action, but the complex world of the martial artist requires that our students develop highly adaptable motor programs in order to successfully complete the assigned task of learning to become skillful.

We can envision a blueprint of a simple action as something that could be transferred from the instructor to the student by visual example, and verbal instruction, followed by physical imitation (Martens, 1990). An old teaching adage states that students will remember nothing of what you say and only half of what they see. It is critical, therefore, that what we say, as instructors must be congruent with what we show. When you teach, give a good visual image backed up by a few precise words as pointers for the student to copy. The teaching method is a stimulus to the student, from which the student will derive the necessary information to build a blueprint of a simple action.

There are a few simple whole actions in martial arts that can be blueprinted, without first breaking them down to smaller parts. An example of a simple action that can be blueprinted is the action of standing on one leg and sweeping or flexing the other, using a wall to help maintain balance. Standing on one leg is a simple action that can be abstracted later into any number of possible scenarios from throwing to kicking. Once the mechanics have been blueprinted and are understood, it is easier to introduce unassisted balance back into the equation and then to add a partner.

Complex actions, which constitute the bulk of martial arts-related activities, require motor programs (Martens, 1990), which are produced when the student abstracts information from other areas of knowledge that pertain to the drill being taught. There are many "combat-like" actions that children do with innate understanding, such a tripping over a playmate in the playground, or wrestling with siblings. Innate understanding can be the base from which a beginning student in the martial arts can abstract the data necessary to build a complex motor program.

By way of creating an analogy: You can be given a blueprint of how to write the alphabet, you can also be taught to read and write words, but you could not possibly be taught every single word combination that is possible using the words that you have learned. To follow through the analogy, the techniques we use are the letters, the striking, throwing, locking and ground fighting combinations and counters are the words and sentences, whereas the effective free-practice or tournament performance is the skillful use of the language. Obviously, by this stage in the development of our students, behavioral modification has been dramatic and their patterns of mental association have also changed. The changes may have been so profound in fact, that when they step on the tournament mat, your students may be capable of completely novel mental associations, which you as their instructor might not have predicted.

It is clear, therefore, that students will take the information that they have been given, modify it, abstract it and recombine it with other data to make it useful for any situation in which they will use the skill. Any time that students use a skill they will need five pieces of information (modified from Martens, 1990):

i) The environmental conditions in which the skill will be applied.
ii) The kinetic demands of the skill such as speed, force, direction, etc..
iii) The actual consequences of the action.
iv) A comparison of the actual outcome with the intended outcome.
v) An awareness of how to modify the motor program to achieve the desired result.

You will notice that much of this information has little to do with the actual technique so much as the environment and situation in which it is being used.

The next step in our investigation of the psychology of learning is to realize that as our students progress through the four levels of mastery, they will also go through three stages of learning, which involve a mental stage, a physical stage and an automatic stage for each technique that evolves into a skill.

In the early stages of learning, students will use their mental capabilities to understand what is required to perform the desired technique. In the middle stage, students will spend time with physical practice, learning the fundamental movements and refining the motor program according to the mistakes that define the boundaries of successful execution. The quality of feedback during the practice stage is critical. Students gain sensory feedback from each performance as well as verbal and non-verbal feedback from their instructors. The rate of progress at this stage is, therefore, often dependent upon the quality of the communication between instructor and student. In the later stages of learning, the performance becomes automatic. At this stage students will tend to correct errors almost instinctively and thinking about what they are doing will actually hurt their performance (Martens, 1990).

The question now becomes, how exactly do your students learn? We do not all learn things in the same way so we need to understand that apart from the stages of learning, there are also ways of learning.

In general, students are predominantly visual, auditory or kinesthetic learners. Visually oriented students like to see lots of technical demonstrations, whereas auditory learners prefer to hear explanations and talk things out. Kinesthetically motivated students will understand by doing repetitions of the technique and will often try to physically follow along as the instructor demonstrates a new technique. It becomes important for the instructor to touch all the learning styles during the teaching presentation and to understand the differences between the three approaches to learning and the specific needs that each type of student will have in order to learn effectively (Martens, 1990).

As well as differing ways of acquiring information, students also have different ways of processing the data they receive. There are at least four ways in which students respond to, and process data:

i) **Global thinkers or Analytical thinkers**. Global thinkers will see the big picture and like to be shown the application of what they do to other areas of their knowledge. Analytic thinkers will break things down to understand how they work. If you use kata (practice of form) as an example, global thinkers will want to be shown the whole thing, whereas analytical thinkers will tend to process each part of a form separately until they can build a cohesive whole. Global thinkers will get the whole form and then work on perfecting it. It terms of brain dominance, analytical thinkers are primarily left-brained, whereas global thinkers tend to be more right-sided.

ii) **Similarity-based thinkers versus Difference-based thinkers**. Similarity-based thinkers will tend to process information according to how closely it matches what they already know, whereas difference-based thinkers will tend to see the differences between what they know and what you are teaching. Similarity-based thinkers will see the common elements between techniques and difference-based thinkers will see what separates the techniques into categories. Similarity versus difference-based thinking is more a matter of degree to which your students demonstrate a tendency, rather than a black and white process.

iii) **Pleasure seekers versus Pain evaders**. According to Rifkin (2009), the notion that humans are primarily pleasure seekers is facile and a good deal more complex than the early psychologists and philosophers like Jeremy Bentham suggested. According to the premise that first appeared in the Age of Enlightenment, people respond to social stimuli in terms of self-interest by either seeking pleasure or avoiding pain (Rifkin, 2009). Pleasure seekers will be motivated to perform because of what they stand to gain from doing something, whereas pain evaders will be motivated by what they stand to lose if they don't do something. As an example of this, pleasure-seeking tournament players will be motivated to perform repetitions of a drill because they might be better to able to win a match. In contrast, pain-avoiders will be motivated to perform the repetitions because if they don't acquire the skill, they might lose more matches.

iv) **Internally referenced versus Externally referenced thinkers**. Internally referenced thinkers have a very strong self-image and belief system and will monitor their performance according to the progress that they have made over time. Externally referenced people will tend to compare themselves to those around them and seek outside approval that what they are doing meets the established criteria of performance. Internally referenced people will tend to get frustrated if they do not feel that they are making the progress that they believe they should be making. Conversely, externally referenced people will tend to get frustrated if they perceive that people who are at the same level as themselves are making more progress. From a coaching perspective, you should encourage internal referencing, especially if you deal with competitors. A person with a healthy internal referencing attitude will tend to accept the inevitable ups and downs of competition with ease, provided that they can see that they are improving their performance regardless of the outcome of any given match. A person who uses external referencing will not weather these challenges so easily. All other factors being equal, internally referencing students with a healthy attitude who face a losing slump will tend to look within themselves for a solution, whereas the external referencing students will tend to look for outside causes for the problem.

Reinforcement: Reinforcement is an integral part of learning, precisely because it has such a big effect upon behavioral response. The use of B.F. Skinner's Operant Conditioning is one of the most effective ways of obtaining the best results from your students. According to Ormond (1999), Skinner's approach requires that drill practice should be supported by performance goals, clear guidance, and **immediate**, **constructive** feedback provided by the instructor. A direct result of the reinforcement is that the likelihood of a desirable behavior being repeated is enhanced.

Reinforcement can either be positive, which adds something desirable to the situation and which results in an increase in the frequency of a desired outcome; or negative, which removes something aversive from the environment and which also results in an increase in the frequency of a desired outcome (Klein, 2002; Ormond, 1999). Reinforcement, therefore, **always** results in an increase in a desirable behavior. When working to improve a player's performance use positive reinforcement to increase the likelihood of repeating the actions that are desirable (for instance: *"Great use of the chamber and re-chamber on that kick, you kept your weapon pointed straight at the target and were able to generate maximum power through your hips"*). Use negative reinforcement to increase the likelihood of developing desirable behavior by removing something aversive from the training situation (As an example, recall from Chapter 2, a child does not like to take falls because every time he lands he hurts his arm. By providing a softer falling surface and correcting the falling action (Figure 2.9), the coach is able to remove the aversive element of pain. If the child shows an improved performance, a negative reinforcement can be assumed to have occurred).

Another aspect of reinforcement relates to shaping. Shaping employs selective reinforcement of successive approximations that lead to a desired behavior (Klein, 2002; Le Unes and Nation, 2002). For instance, a player may be given a reward (for instance: specific praise) for the successful completion of an approximation of a desired performance goal (keeping weight on the opponent during grappling drills). As the player's ability to perform the skill increases, s/he may only be given the reward for more precise executions (does not put knees on the ground at all during a free-practice session). If we examine the same situation as a time-line, there was a time earlier in his or her training when the advanced student was rewarded for approximating a desired behavior but later, at higher levels of performance the student is only rewarded for excellent executions of the same behavior.

At this point it is worth mentioning that what represents reinforcement to one student and leads to improved performance may have no effect upon another student and exactly the opposite effect upon a third student. One student may feel that praise is a highly affirming event, which leads to improved levels of performance whereas another student may see praise as a form of condescension and responds negatively to praise. The point to stress here is that an instructor must not assume that reinforcement can be applied in the same way with all students all the time. It is also true that what represents reinforcement in one setting (the training session) may not work under a different set of conditions (a tournament setting). In order to find out what represents reinforcement to each student, instructors must study their students' behavioral responses to the coaching methodology used in each situation. **The key point is that what each player perceives as reinforcement is specific to both the <u>individual</u> and the <u>situation</u>** (Klein, 2002; Le Unes and Nation, 2002).

While we are discussing reinforcement, let's discuss what things constitute desired behaviors. Some of these will apply more readily to younger students, but many of them apply across the board (Le Unes and Nation, 2002). During class there are several behaviors that enhance both individual and group performance:

i) Regular attendance.

ii) Paying attention to, and obeying, instructions.

iii) Being considerate of, and taking care of, training partners.

iv) Proper use of training equipment.

v) Practicing the proper drill after instructions have been given.

vi) Continuing to practice without frequent stops.

vii) Seeking clarification and advice on skill improvement and acting upon information received.

viii) Use of appropriate levels of force, speed control and cooperation during activity sessions.

ix) Appropriate use of self-control, focus and concentration, determination, initiative, persistence, leadership and taking personal responsibility for acquiring the material being offered in the lesson.

Rewards: Reinforcement and reward are closely allied concepts. Reinforcement can be a reward of sorts, and vice versa, but not they are not synonymous terms. There are several places and times to reward your students, for instance:

i) Reward performance and effort, not outcome. Students cannot control all outcomes, but they can control their performance and effort.

ii) In the early stages reward little progress steps that lead toward the accomplishment of larger goals.

iii) Reward frequently in the early stages of training, less so in the later stages of development. This applies especially in children's classes, because children will tend to seek clarification for the parameters of appropriate behavior in all areas of their lives.

For advanced martial artists success is its own reward. But remember this: The successes that the advanced student enjoys are built upon the confidence that stems from positive self-expectancy, which was generated by building competence in the little things during the early stage of their training. I mention this because it implies that a very large collateral (trust) account has been built in the student by the instructor over time. All those early rewards still have value and although you may not reward as often because the student does not need so much outside affirmation, there is now a strong bond between student and instructor. Even having said this, however, you cannot make the assumption that the students know you think well of their efforts and performances, you still need to give praise, just not as often.

Reward immediately, when it is earned, because rewards should have meaning and value for your students. When you delay giving a reward, it loses meaning because the reward has lost contact with its reason for being given.

Motivation: Reinforcement and rewards will help you retain a student, but ultimately, you must motivate your students to take consistent action towards their goals. Motivating students is possibly one of the hardest of the psychological training skills to master. We tend to expect our adult students to be self-motivating, but as a general rule it is the instructor's task to keep students motivated, enthusiastic and coming back to learn more. So, what motivates a person? Most people are motivated to fulfill their needs. If you understand the needs of your students you can motivate them. So what are the needs of your students? In general terms there are three needs that most students have:

i) To have fun.

ii) To feel good about themselves.

iii) To have a sense of community, to belong.

It is perhaps an oversimplification to say, but, almost all other needs (such as tournament honors, belt promotions etc.) can be placed within one of these needs. Students will have fun in class if they reach optimal arousal, which will differ for each student. In states of optimal arousal "flow experiences" can occur, during which time just seems to "fly by" (Csikszentmihalyi, 1991; Goleman, 1995; Hawkins, 2002).

There are few moments for a player that have greater emotional impact than the achievement of a "flow" experience. During flow experiences, students immerse themselves so fully in what they are doing that they lose track of time and are unaware that concentration has become an automatic response. In some ways, there is no separation between action and performer, or between student and the art they are learning. In effect, your players will become so immersed in what they are doing, they forget "self" (Csikszentmihalyi, 1991; Doidge, 2007; Goleman, 1995; Hawkins, 2002).

In the Japanese martial arts, we talk about mushin (mind of no mind). When this sort of moment occurs in a tournament, or a class, the effects are deeply motivating, long-lasting and frequently result in a paradigm shift for the student. As an example of a paradigm shift, consider the impact of Roger Bannister's achievement of running a mile in under four minutes. Prior to breaking that barrier, the prevailing mentality was that a four-minute mile was beyond the limits of human performance (Hawkins, 2002; Maltz and Sommer, 2000). Once broken, the mile was run in under four minutes by several athletes and is now considered an attainable performance goal for most elite long-distance runners.

The flow experience is a very emotive phenomenon for both instructor and student. When we experience flow, we feel a great sense of calm and well being. Moments of flow, or mushin, are deeply etched into the memory and become events that the student wants to savor again. During flow we feel "at one" with what we are doing, our techniques become effortless and graceful, exquisitely controlled and appropriate for the moment. After a flow experience, a student will feel immense satisfaction and joy. As a student improves in skill development, moments of flow tend to become more common and are seen as the high points of competition and training to which we aspire (Csikszentmihalyi, 1991). An excellent description of flow is found in the following passage, which is quoted verbatim:

> *"High states of consciousness are also frequently experienced by athletes. It's widely documented that long distance runners frequently attain sublime states of peace and joy. This very elevation of consciousness, in fact, often inspires the prolonged transcendence of pain and exhaustion necessary to achieve higher levels of performance. This phenomenon is commonly described in terms of pushing oneself to the point where one suddenly breaks through a performance barrier and the activity becomes effortless; the body then seems to move with grace and ease of its own accord, as though animated by some invisible force. The accompanying state of joy is quite distinct from the thrill of success; it's a joy of peace and oneness with all that lives"* (Hawkins, 2002, p.172).

Flow events are, therefore, markers along the way that hint of what we could be both as instructors and as students. Flow experiences inspire players to exceed the normal limits of what was previously thought to be attainable. As is alluded to by Hawkins (2002), players in moments of flow will break through mental and physical barriers and open new vistas of possibility that go beyond previously established concepts of endurance, pain tolerance and quality of performance. Consequently, flow experiences are extremely powerful motivators that leave a very strong memory imprint of the potential that the student has to excel. The net result of flow experiences is, therefore, to destroy previously established mental paradigms of performance and build new ones that raise the bar for the athlete in terms of both endurance and performance, while at the same time raising the question of what else might be possible with higher levels of personal commitment. Flow experiences lead us towards our Zone of Genius (Hendricks, 2009).

Flow experiences also enhance the trust bond between student and instructor, because it happened in **your** class. Bringing an entire class to a state of flow is truly exhilarating, and bespeaks the intimate levels to which non-verbal communication can affect the entire class population.

There are several ways in which an instructor can enhance the possibility of reaching a flow experience:

i) Set challenging but attainable goals.

ii) Maintain variety; look for new ways of teaching the same skill.

iii) Maintain student arousal by teaching class-appropriate skills in an emotionally positive environment.

iv) Keep activity high, with very short precise periods of instructor talk.

v) Provide evaluations of progress; let the students know whether they are attaining the goals that you set.

Many people come to the martial arts to improve their self-confidence in some way. Self-confidence is an aspect of self-worth, and self-worth is tied to our ability to succeed at those things we choose to do. It is for these reasons that it is so important to demonstrate that **success lies in the performance, not the outcome**. Praise performance, demonstrate that the student is increasing in ability (intrinsic rewards) and, therefore, achieving success and the result will be that "winning" or "losing" in a competition will become much less of an ego roller coaster. Students equate success with competency, and seek some way in which to measure their success. Unfortunately, and all too often coaches and competitors equate success with winning matches and place undue emphasis on winning trophies (extrinsic rewards), which is an outcome dependent upon things over which neither the coach nor competitor has complete control. Good competition coaches emphasize performance regardless of outcome and encourage their athletes to do likewise.

As a tool for maintaining motivation, the instructor's goal should be to create success-oriented students. Under these circumstances, failure at a particular task is merely an opportunity for improvement, an indication that the student has not yet learned all s/he needs to, or that the student needs further work to refine some set of actions. The essential point in this: Every failure in the life of a success-oriented student is a motivator to renewed effort, every failure is a challenge to improve, not a threat to the student's sense of self-worth, every failure is an opportunity for growth. Failure in the learning curve is inevitable; it is a natural part of success. But also remember that success is a choice. We either choose to learn from our mistakes and improve or we choose to let failure undermine our sense of self-worth and cause us to feel that we are powerless to change our circumstances.

Success-oriented students are proactive and take personal responsibility for their actions, those who choose not to succeed will be reactive and seek to find excuses for their non-performance, they will blame all sorts of things from the weather, to the meal they ate last night, to the referee, to the stress in their lives - the list is as long as they want it to be. Success is a personal choice (Covey, 1989; Hendricks, 2009; Pitino, 1997). The fundamental issue is whether the student has the internal fortitude and courage to maintain a sense of self-worth in the face of the inevitable failures that appear along the road to great success. Only those who dare, will achieve. If a student wishes to succeed it is impossible to avoid the risk of failure. The successful instructor is the person who can bring his or her students to this realization and cause them to dare greatly and provide them with the tools to maximize their abilities and thereby increase their self worth. Herein lies the instructor's great reward.

If you set reasonable goals and challenges and expect success, your students will be generally happy to oblige. Children are a wonderful lesson in this regard. Quite frequently, if you ask a child to perform a difficult technique without hinting at the level of difficulty, they will not think twice, they will simply do it because you asked them to and expected them to be able to succeed. The only caveat here is that obviously the children must have been stair-stepped from the simple toward the difficult task, so that they have the necessary foundation upon which to perform with success.

There is an interesting side issue here, which relates to the willingness of children to step outside their comfort zones on a regular basis and the timidity with which adults sometimes greet the same opportunities. To children, life is a great experiment. For some adults life experience has taught them some lessons about failure, which leads to fear of making the attempt for fear of the bruising that ego will receive. How many times have you had adults watch a children's class and say things like:

    i)   I wish I could still do that.

    ii)   I'm too old to do that.

    iii)   I can't do that.

    iv)   I'll never do that.

    v)   How come they can do _____ and I can't?

If we engage in negative self speak, or make excuses for ourselves, it is a sure thing that we will not succeed. Jim Bregman, America's first Olympic Judo medalist and one of my mentors was very fond of using the line "*Whether you believe you can or you believe you can't, you're right.*" He was so right. As instructors, it is imperative that we replace negative self speak with positive self-expectancy in our students. First and foremost we must create a positive learning environment, but then we must also be able to encourage self-motivation in our students.

When students do something and fail in a positive environment, they will not feel threatened by the risk of failure. They will simply lower their sights to a slightly less challenging goal and succeed at that one. Once that goal is no longer a challenge, students in a positive training environment will tend to raise the ante so that they keep working at the upper limits of their current abilities. The essential truth here is that each student has a different "set point" for a given task and success for one student cannot be compared with the successes of another player of apparently greater ability who gives an effortless performance at the same level of activity. If an activity is a challenge for one student, but not for the other, it is unreasonable to have similar expectations of them both. It is also unreasonable to demand similar performances of them both and to praise only the successful player. Be sure that the goals you set are realistic for each student.

My final comment concerning motivation is that the instructor's responsibility is to help each student to see that his or her successes are found in exceeding personal goals rather than surpassing the performances of other students. The instructor's goal is to help students to find their own personal limits and push the envelope of performance beyond what they thought was previously possible (Hendricks, 2009). In the process of doing this, the instructor will build a very large trust account with the students that is built upon mutual respect.

Mentoring: One of aspects of long-term planning that we need to discuss in the section on psychology is the concept of mentoring because it can profoundly impact the nature of the teaching relationship. In his book "*The Courage to Teach*", Parker J. Palmer (1998) talks about what he calls "The Great Thing." The "great thing" in our case is our particular martial art style and if we place it at the center of our learning environments, then we create subject-based learning opportunities rather than a rigid hierarchic learning environment in which the instructor is the fount of all knowledge. To repeat what was said earlier, when a student comes to you the relationship may begin as a Teacher-Student relationship, but as you both learn and grow, the relationship should naturally evolve into more of a mentorship.

Mentoring is the art of being stunningly successful and completely anonymous. When we mentor people in life, we often do so in a specific area of performance or for a specific period in their lives. Mentors help their protégés to develop and acquire the skills that will ensure success. It is the protégé, however, who draws the adulation of praise for success…and this is exactly as it should be. Mentors are quiet, unobtrusive advocates for, and facilitators of, their protégés.

I see mentors as map-readers, mine sweepers and lighthouses. Mentors are map-readers because we are further ahead on our own journey. We have been there, done that. We know the lay of the land, the obstacles, pitfalls and challenges that lie ahead for our students. We are mine sweepers precisely because we **do** know the challenges ahead, and we can offer suggestions that might help our students avoid obstructions and achieve success sooner. Typically, protégés choose mentors whom they admire and respect and who can act as a guide, all of which makes the mentor a lighthouse, a beacon to a safe harbor on an uncertain ocean.

Frequently, protégés want to emulate some aspect of the mentor's character or success. The mentor in turn needs wisdom, understanding, tolerance, patience and above all compassion, because it is inevitable that protégés will make mistakes. Falling over is a necessary step in the process of learning…I truly believe we fail our way to success. I can think of hundreds of instances where I have fallen flat on my face or made the wrong choice in my own journey. But each perceived failure is an opportunity and a valuable lesson on our individual paths of discovery. I am still on my journey, learning and making new mistakes. In true Edison style, failure allows us to successfully discover the ways that won't work and draw us closer to the ways that will work. It also means that our students have to make their own mistakes to learn the necessary lessons that will ensure eventual success. Often the mentor can see pitfalls ahead and might even give warnings of their impending arrival, but ultimately it is up to the protégé to successfully negotiate the obstacle. When protégés make mistakes, mentors are patient and tolerant.

If mentors do their job well, protégés achieve success through synergy. Synergy occurs when a group of individuals combine their skills, knowledge, experience and talents to achieve more, sooner, than would have been possible had they acted alone. By drawing on the experiences of mentors, protégés can achieve higher levels of success, sooner. In an ideal world, martial arts instructors should want their students to be better and achieve more than they did.

Once the success has been achieved, it should be the protégé who draws the praise and the mentor should be in the background. It is not about my ego as a mentor, it is about the success of my protégé.

Winning the mental game: Another key aspect of coaching psychology is helping your students to develop mental toughness. Building a physical fortress for your players, but neglecting their mental ability to defend it will be costly for your students when the rubber meets the road and your players' skills are required in the environment of use (Janssen, 1996; Siddle, 1995). There are many important mental traits that your students will need to be successful, some are interpersonal and others are intrapersonal.

Interpersonal traits can be related to how your players deal with others and might involve such traits as good sportsmanship, honesty, integrity and a code of ethical behavior. Bear in mind, however, that your players will tend to model how you behave as a coach. Other interpersonal skills will be related to the ability of your players to truly listen both in the training environment and in the actual environment in which the skills will be used. The ability to truly listen and to maintain awareness even under stress will give your players an edge when they enter the Adrenaline Stress Response during stressful situations and respond with "hypervigilance" that causes a narrowing of the vision field and reduction of the auditory response (Siddle, 1995). One last interpersonal skill that will be is the ability to communicate well. If you, as the instructor do not understand your students or your students have difficulty communicating what they are feeling or need during their training, it will be easy to misunderstand each other. Building a long-term training plan will rest upon the foundations of quality communication.

Other mental traits are more of an intrapersonal set, which include the athlete's ability to focus and concentrate, dedication to process, degree of competitiveness, internal drive, determination, courage and ability to overcome obstacles and failure, desire to persist in the face of tough training, willingness to face personal fears and self-limiting beliefs, and lastly his or her strength of spirit, all of which relate to self-esteem and the self-concept. Recall that the main reason people begin doing something is to improve self-worth. When we fortify the physical side of training with mental skills, we are helping our players to increase their self-esteem and as they see the fruits of their labors, levels of self-confidence will likewise increase. Although the martial arts training will help our students to build the mental skills concurrently with their physical skills, there are additional forms of mental training that will help your students to face "reality-based" situations with a calm and focused mind, capable of clarity, discipline and resolve.

i) **Biofeedback Exercises**: Biofeedback exercises are designed to reduce performance anxiety and employ the Operant Conditioning procedures described by B.F. Skinner (Le Unes and Nation, 2002, Doidge 2007). Biofeedback exercises frequently involve attaching monitors to the athletes so that they can see their own body responses. In this way athletes can learn to control their own heart rate, and level of muscular relaxation.

ii) **Meditation**: Meditation can be performed in a variety of ways, but again, the purpose is to concentrate and focus, relax, clear the mind and permit the athlete to focus fully on his or her goals during times of stress in a non-attached way. Meditation teaches us to be mindful and be fully present in the moment (Huang and Lynch, 1992; Leggett, 1978). Being fully present in the moment creates higher levels of awareness, a skill that can be of great value in the competitive arena or the real world of self-defense. The ability to be fully present and not be distracted by external events is critical in both the training and the "real" environment. When martial arts are practiced with real intent and become an intense physical activity there is a remarkable ability to focus the mind. In such moments, martial arts can become a 'moving meditation'.

iii) **Visualization**: Visualization drills can be done to teach a player to see a perfect performance, to play out a scenario in his or her mind and see the strategy at work. Visualization drills can focus upon examining a specific aspect of performance or an entire match that is about to be played. Visualization can also be used to improve self-confidence, discover the fear of success and/or embrace success (Huang and Lynch, 1992; Siddle, 1995; Maltz and Sommer, 2000). Playing mental movies can improve attention to detail and also improve the physical performance. Visualization works well when "mirroring" is involved. Mirroring occurs when a student studies the actions of a more highly trained martial artist and then mentally practices the moves as though s/he were doing them personally.

Challenges, Progress and Retention: As a student moves from novice White Belt to Black Belt or as they move through the tournament tiers they will inevitably face a number of challenges, any one of which can be an obstacle to retention (Corcoran and Graden, 1998; Graden, 1997; Martens, 1990; NCCP, 1979). As an instructor, your retention performance goal is to maintain a high positive retention percentage. In a situation where retention stands at 70-80% or better, you are probably losing only those students over which you have no control such as: Those who move to a new town, or who graduate from university or high school and move away, or who get a new job, or through illness or accident can no longer train. It is easy to measure your percentage rate of positive retention if you keep monthly figures and statistics to compare newly enrolled students to the total numbers of students.

If you lose a student for any other reason, then it is because in some way, you failed to fulfill their needs or expectations, and you failed to provide them with value for time and/or money invested (Le Boeuf, 1987). If you recall the section on Conditions of Learning, we talked about "Value, Meaning and Benefit". Almost all challenges to continued training can be thus be seen as a balance equation between perceived value on one side of the equation and desire to continue the investment of time and materials on the other:

i) Does the student have any desire to continue through this challenge? (Thought process: *Do I want to do this anymore, or would I prefer to spend my time...*).

ii) Does the student perceive any value in continuing beyond the present challenge? (Thought process: *What's in it for me?*).

iii) Does the student see any meaning to what s/he is being asked to do in class? (Thought process: *Why am I doing this?*).

iv) Does the student perceive any practical gain or benefit for time and money spent in training? (Thought process: *How am I getting better at this?*).

If the answer to any of these questions is "*No*", then there is a high probability that you will lose the student. If you are honest with yourself as an instructor, when a student leaves your dojo and uses time or money as an excuse, you must accept that more often than not, it is because you have failed to provide a meaningful reason for them to **want** to continue to train. It's rarely about time; all of us will always find time to do the things we want to do. It is just as true that we will find reasons for not doing something that we do not want to do. Students will justify any activity they want to do, even in the face of demands to do something apparently more important. For instance: Ask any child who doesn't want to do their homework, or any adult who avoids doing a chore. Equally, it's rarely about money, students have a fixed amount of money and they will spend it on those things that seem to them to be of value. Students will find the money to do the things that they **want** to do. Very rarely is money a real issue, except where the family has faced true financial hardship, and even in those circumstances I like to think that there are possibilities.

Consequently, if the student is to stay the course and continue training, it is the instructor's responsibility to show the student the value inherent in the activity. Moreover, in so far as is practical, the instructor needs to be proactively aware of what challenges the student will be facing and be prepared to deal with them when the time arrives. The instructor who blindly teaches classes with no regard for the challenges in a student's training is going to be working in a reactive environment and will be putting out forest fires, rather than preventing them.

It therefore becomes important to know what challenges the students will face in their training and when they are likely to occur. As our students move up the ranks, step up to higher levels of competition, or faces a real self-defense challenge they will inevitably face **moments of truth** that will become thresholds of training. All students go through thresholds at some point in their training. Retention, therefore, is merely a matter of knowing the pre-incident indicators for any given threshold and providing the tools, which enable the student to successfully negotiate his or her way across the threshold to the next higher level of development. By providing tools to successfully negotiate a challenge to continued training, the instructor de-fuses the possibility of the student beginning to question the merit of continued training. At the same time, the instructor demonstrates a clear awareness of the student's needs, which in turn reinforces the mutual respect between both student and teacher and, therefore, increases the perceived value in continuing training.

Some challenges that the students will face are going to be physical and some will be mental; knowing how to meet these challenges is the difference between retaining and losing a student. Instructors with children's programs however, face two extra challenges: Dealing with the children (who are NOT miniature adults) and dealing with their parents!

Working with Children: When we look at the differences between children and adults from a developmental perspective the reasons for creating different teaching experiences become extremely pronounced. From the psychological perspective children in our classes are busy developing their thought processes and learning how to function in the world in which they live. In essence they are learning how to calibrate their brains, as well as receive and process information. When we teach martial arts to children, we are helping them to learn how to use their brains and their bodies at the same time (Figure 5.2). The implication is very clear: By teaching martial arts from the perspectives of creative, analytical and practical ability development, we **can indeed** work at multiple levels simultaneously.

Figure 5.2: When working with children, give them plenty of training time, but also encourage them to think and talk about what they are learning. In this way you can work the physical and mental aspects of training in mutually self-reinforcing ways.

The critical point to emerge from the foregoing, however, is that children at different ages will have very different needs because they are at different levels in the calibration process.

From birth until the age of three children are busy developing synaptic connections in their brains, until they have a staggering 15,000 for *every* brain cell. From the age of three through adulthood, children prune back those connections and create "fast tracks" in their brains that will ultimately become the ways in which they process information. Obviously, the way in which this process occurs profoundly affects whether or not a child develops certain types of talents or not. Synaptic pruning is what leaves one child "gifted" in a particular area and another child "gifted" in completely different ways (Buckingham and Coffman, 1999).

Since children tend to begin martial arts training at about six, (or, perhaps three or four if they are in Little Ninja or Little Dragons programs), the synaptic pruning process has already begun. It is critical, therefore, that our children's programs equally balance aspects of physical and mental training as well as touch on as many aspects of learning style as possible.

We can subdivide children's classes into three distinct educational groups according to their developmental stage (Corcoran and Graden, 1998; Kim, 1997; Ormond, 1999):

i) Ages 4 through 6 are the pre-school children.

ii) Ages 7 through 12 are the pre-adolescents.

iii) Ages 13 through 16+ are the adolescents.

According to Ormond (1999) one of the most influential thinkers concerning the manner in which children process information was the Swiss scientist Jean Piaget who studied patterns of cognitive awareness and development in children. According to the work of Piaget mental development amongst children results from how they interact in their physical and social environments. Moreover, Piaget recognized that cognitive development occurred in four distinct stages (Ormond, 1999), of which we are mostly interested in the last two:

i) Birth to two years old is the **Sensorimotor stage**. In this stage the "out of sight out of mind" thought process characterizes the dominant mental patterns. The end of the Sensorimotor stage is marked by the onset of symbolic thinking, which is the ability to see external events and objects using internal mental images.

ii) From about two until six or seven years old is the **Preoperational stage**. At this stage language exponentially develops and these children are very talkative. They need and want to use their new skills and build upon their language skills. Dominant thought patterns might appear illogical by adult standards. Such thought patterns tend to confuse psychological events with physical realities. Preschoolers are curious and want to experiment and want to find out what they are "good at." They want to impress adults with what they can do, but rarely do preschoolers have a good concept of team behaviors. Preschoolers are looking for boundaries and limits and appreciate being encouraged in their activities. Activities that are appropriate for this age group include simple physical skills that build co-ordination and balance and which work major muscle groups.

Figure 5.3: Children in the pre-operational stage will readily learn how to grapple, even if they don't remember the names of the skills that they can use.

Children under six may have a difficult time figuring out the differences between one kick and another or one throw and another, but will quite readily learn how to kick, punch, trip, fall and grapple (Figure 5.3). With this group of children it is much better to work on correct body action, rather than memorizing a series of moves.

iii) From about seven until eleven or twelve is the **Concrete operational stage**. In this stage children begin to develop logic-based thought patterns. School-aged children will tend to make sense of information by transforming it as they are presented new data. They begin to develop a sense of classification and start to build sets. As these children begin to develop sets of data, they become capable of learning a sequence of moves. Prior to this stage, children have difficulty putting three events in series. Between the ages of seven and nine children begin to develop a strong sense of independence and a need to be self-sufficient. At this point in their development, children want to be shown something and then be left to figure things out on their own. Enquiry-based learning and discovery-based learning methodologies can work really well with this group of students. Frequently children at this level of development have great confidence but tend to overestimate their true abilities. Equally, children at this stage are very strongly influenced by the opinions of other people in their world; this applies both to adults in their world as well as the children's own peer group. By the time they are ten to twelve years old, concrete operational children will start to develop cliques and be very comparison conscious. Feelings of inferiority within the clique or the risk of public embarrassment of getting something wrong can be devastating to children at this stage of development. Their physical actions are much more refined and accurate than those of the younger group. By the time children in this group are about nine years old, they are capable of very refined hand-eye co-ordination. At the later end of this stage gender differences begin to emerge, with boys developing more strength than girls of the same age. Children will also start to learn a sense of proportion at about eleven or twelve, which affects concepts such as using half-power on a punch or a kick. Prior to developing a sense of proportion, power is either on or off, there is little "in-between". Children at this stage of development like to be active in highly energetic games. In this stage of development training drills should emphasize control, timing, reflex and co-ordination.

iv) From about twelve through to the onset of adulthood behavior is the **Formal operational stage**. At this stage of development, children prefer to be treated like adults. Adolescents can think in abstract terms and build hypotheses, theories and conclusions. With this new ability adolescents can be taught to think strategically and solve problems. It has been suggested that not all children reach this level of development because they are not exposed to advanced educational challenges. The quality of educational experiences can, therefore, profoundly impact the transition from the concrete operational stage and development with the formal operational stage (Ormond, 1999). Gender differences become marked and hormone-driven growth spurts affect both bones and muscles. Adolescents may tend to feel awkward or clumsy because they are not "used to" their new bodies or have not "grown into" their new shape or size. These factors combined with the onset of sexual characteristics can leave adolescents feeling very self-conscious, regardless of gender. Adolescents need appropriate role models, mentors and behavioral reinforcement to develop a positive sense of self. Additionally, students in this age group relish the opportunity of being given responsibility and being asked to fill leadership roles like an adult. Duncan (2002) discusses the merits of transferring children at this stage of development into the adult classes. The children appreciate being included in the adult group and will tend to rise to the challenge. Adults on the other hand will tend to "mentor" the younger adolescents when they enter the adult environment and "take care" of them. Having said that, peer pressure is a big factor in determining what is "cool" and what is "nerdy."

Although Piaget's view of mental development is considered by many to be the "standard", it is clear that children do not fit neatly into these groups, for instance some children can show much more sophisticated thinking patterns at earlier ages than might be expected (Ormond, 1999). It is important however, to recognize that thought processes are distinctly different at each stage of development and will require distinctly different training drills both for physical and mental growth. Another factor that bears consideration is the fact that children can demonstrate an "actual developmental level" when left to themselves and yet the same children can accomplish much more complex tasks when coached by someone at a higher level of development thereby demonstrating a "potential developmental level" (Ormond, 1999).

In conclusion it is critical to their development that children be placed in learning environments, which suit their level of development and allow them to reach the full potential of their abilities. Since most of the children enter martial arts at in the four-to-six range, the majority of children can be taught in a learning environment that favors the **concrete operational** stage. By the time children are about twelve or thirteen, most of them can be moved up into the adult class, which makes teaching children just a little bit easier. The difficult part of all of this is developing the correct communication patterns that reinforce the positive aspects of student growth.

Dealing with "difficult" children: One of the great pleasures of being a martial arts school owner is working with young people and watching them grow and mature. As the young people grow up, they will go through some "difficult" stages and there will be some children who seem to be "difficult" from day one. Knowing how to deal with challenging children and difficult moments can make the difference between what is a great class and a class that is a struggle from first to last! If you are going to instruct children, then it a good idea to know ahead of time how you will deal with the difficult times. An excellent resource that will give you a lot of great ideas about how to improve your communication with children is the book "*How to talk so kids will listen and listen so kids will talk*" by Faber and Mazlish (2002). In their book, Faber and Mazlish (2002), go through a series of specific exercises that can have a powerful impact on the quality of the learning experience for your children's classes. Aspects of the text that bear particular scrutiny are the sections on "cooperation", "alternatives to punishment" "giving praise" and "encouraging autonomy." In each section the authors give a series of exercises that you can complete on your own or role-play with your assistant instructors if you have them, as part of your instructor training classes. Each section allows us to explore possible communication pathways from the perspective of both the parent and the child and also from the positive and the negative consequences of each pathway.

Remember that you are only seeing a child for a couple of hours a week and without support from home and school, you may have limited success in obtaining behavioral modification. One of the things that parents often ask is "Will martial arts teach my child self control and/or discipline?" The answer to this question will depend largely upon the ability and willingness all parties involved, including the parents, and the school teachers act as a team, and reinforce expected standards of behavior all the time, everywhere. In her book "*Don't Be Afraid To Discipline*", Peters (1997) emphasizes that setting and maintaining boundaries for acceptable behavior is a critical element in the development of a child's character. Moreover Peters (1997), demonstrates that children who learn to live within appropriate boundaries and who also develop self-control and self-discipline are much more likely to become successful in their coping strategies as adults. Consequently, when dealing with children who "lack self-control", who are "discipline problems" or who are "difficult" it is important to be consistent, set clear and unambiguous boundaries and be prepared.

The first part of dealing with "difficult" children is to know ahead of time how you plan to deal with situations that will inevitably arise in class. Next, you need to define and enforce very clear behavioral boundaries for your children. Make sure that your children and their parents all know what is considered acceptable behavior and what behaviors are unacceptable. You will also need to repeat the expected behaviors and reinforce the boundaries on a consistent and regular basis. Reward positive behavior patterns and draw attention to students who are exhibiting the expected behaviors (for instance, you could praise a student who is paying particularly close attention when you are giving a demonstration). Children who know what is expected and where the lines are drawn are much more apt to behave well than those who do not.

It is also important to understand the motivation for errant behavior patterns. If misbehaving is an unusual phenomenon in a particular child, then when s/he misbehaves in class, you can almost guarantee that there is a specific reason, which may or may not have anything to do with your class. Under these circumstances, you might need talk to the child directly, and find out what is at the root of the behavior. When a child habitually misbehaves, you may be dealing with much deeper challenges such as problems in the home or at school, or lack of confidence and lack of self-esteem, or maybe even medical or allergy issues.

Also, when dealing with a child, provide options. Find out what motivates the children you teach. Pleasure seekers will do a thing because they stand to gain some reward or personal satisfaction from the activity. It is helpful when dealing with pleasure seekers who are being difficult, to point out the benefits of good behavior. Conversely, pain avoiders do things because if they do not, they stand to lose something of value to them. When dealing with these sorts of children, behavior modification may be achieved by taking away a privilege. Understand though, that each child will be a pain avoider in some circumstances and a pleasure seeker in others, so you cannot assume a one-size-fits-all approach, you must carefully study your students.

Another way of dealing with difficult children is to give them responsibility, and hold them accountable. In this mode, you are attempting to draw on their leadership capabilities and using their behavioral strengths in a positive way. In a lot of ways, you are simply channeling their disruptive activities into a more constructive path.

It is important to be firm, fair and consistent when disciplining children. Discipline and punishment are acceptable forms of behavior modification when set in a framework of caring. When faced with a situation in which you would normally resort to punishment, something that you can use before you resort to punishment is induction discipline. Induction discipline is concerned with allowing the child to see the effect of his/her behavior on someone else. In effect you are teaching the child how to empathize. Let's say a child kicks another child in class out of frustration and anger or maybe simple spite. You were teaching the child how to kick, but the child chose to use the kick out of context. You can punish the child by removing them from class or you can use induction discipline by asking the child what s/he would have felt if the action had been done to them. What happens during induction discipline is a series of steps that naturally flow from each other: Event > Intervention > Questioning > Reflection > Guilt > Atonement > Empathic Resolution. We have used this behavior-shaping tool for a long time, but it is only recently that it is being recognized as a powerful mechanism for teaching empathy-based morality (Rifkin, 2009). The point here is that if a child knows that s/he is genuinely cared for and that it is a behavior that is being disciplined then the student is much more likely to respond positively than if s/he feels that you do not care about them. Peters (1997) and Rosenblum in Corcoran and Graden (1998) emphasize several key elements disciplining children:

i) Set very clear boundaries of behaviors. Once you have set a rule, stand by it and follow it.

ii) Discipline should occur immediately upon the performance of unacceptable behavior.

iii) Discipline should be placed in the context of what was unacceptable.

iv) Discipline should be consistent and be the consequence of every instance of a particular form of misbehavior. It must be applied in the same way, every time.

v) Discipline should be significant **in the mind of the child**. If the punishment has no effect, it is probably not significant to the child.

vi) Allow the student to return to class and/or status after the punishment has been fulfilled.

vii) Use induction discipline rather than punishment.

viii) Use punishment as a last resort. Whenever possible use reinforcement and teach desirable behavior patterns. When a child uses appropriate behavior, give specific praise and draw attention to the good things that the student does.

ix) Always maintain respect and caring for your student. Emphasize that you are punishing an unacceptable behavior. Punish without using anger and do not make personal attacks on the child. Do not shame a child.

x) Remember to focus on the fact that we are engaged in a long-term project and not a short-term solution.

Lastly, when there are behavior problems with a child, make sure that you communicate with the parents face-to-face whenever possible. Parents may have insights that could help you, and just as possibly, you may be seeing some behavior pattern that the parents do not see at home. Remember that you are part of a character-building team. When you work with the parents and schoolteachers, you are much more likely to obtain a positive outcome to any challenging behavior patterns.

Dealing with "difficult" parents: If working with children can be one of the great rewards of running a martial arts school, then one of the great challenges of being an instructor, can be dealing with the parents of your children (Corcoran and Graden, 1998). There can be many reasons for this. "Problem parents" begin to surface when there is poor communication between the coach and the parent. One of the first things to do is listen to, and talk to, the parents when they enroll a child in your program. Find out why the child is being placed in your care:

i) Are there discipline problems at home? At school?

ii) Is the child being bullied?

iii) Is the child inactive?

iv) Is the child hyperactive?

v) Is the child shy and/or lacking in self-esteem?

vi) Does the child suffer from ADD or ADHD?

vii) Does the child have any medical or allergic conditions?

viii) Has the child been referred by a teacher, counselor or health professional?

ix) Has the child been pestering mum and dad to do "Karate"?

x) Is it an activity to fill the off-season between soccer and baseball?

xi) Is it an activity to fill the hours between school and the time one of the parents gets off work?

xii) Does the child have a friend in you program?

xiii) Do the parents just want to find out if their child will like this?

From the foregoing, it is clear that your job in the enrollment process is to find out several very different, but interrelated things:

i) What are the needs of the child?

ii) What are the needs of the parents?

iii) Do they match your programmatic goals?

iv) Will the parents be supportive of your training policies?

v) Do they understand and support your ranking policies?

vi) Will they support your tournament participation policies?

vii) Will the parents encourage the behaviors at home (such as respect and courtesy) that you enforce in the martial arts school?

The answers that you get to these questions, will go a long way towards telling you what kind of parent you will be dealing with, and whether the client is a compatible match for your student population. Unfortunately, you will also have to deal with some less than ideal parents. Henkel (2002) discusses several different types of "difficult" parents:

i) The drop-off parent. These parents drop off their children and you never see them.

ii) The instructor parent. These parents like to coach from the sidelines.

iii) The distracted/forgetful/negligent parent. These parents send their children to class with dirty uniforms or missing belts etc., but what is more significant they may deliver children late and forget to pick them up. Yes, it does happen.

iv) The distracting parent. These parents talk or generally make enough noise to interrupt your class while they sit at the edge, and yes, parents who have cell phones with loud ringtones count here too!

v) The excuse-maker parent. These are the parents who always seem to have some sort of family crisis or problem, or there is always some reason for any perceived lack of performance.

vi) The "Glory Days" parent. These parents are attempting to live out their wishes through their children.

In almost all these cases three very simple proactive approaches can make your life as a children's instructor much more enjoyable.

Firstly, set clear behavior codes for both the children and the parents. Be polite, but firm with the parents. Set clear boundaries and don't be afraid to enforce them. But if you do have to enforce a boundary, do it politely and privately with the parent. For instance: If you have a parent that keeps talking loudly during class, explain that too much noise at the edge of the mat can be distracting to the children. Ask for *active* parental support of your behavior policies and ask **the parent to help you** set the example for the children (Appendix 4).

Secondly, make time to meet with the parents (Figure 5.4), especially those you don't see very often. Make it a policy to chat at least briefly with the parents at least once a week, and know them **by name.** For parents who drop off their kids and who never see the inside of the school, call them and ask if they are happy with their child's progress and invite them to come to class. Ask specific questions that allow you to gather information that can help you keep the child in your program and motivate the parents to become more involved.

Figure 5.4: Make it a point to chat with the parents. In this example, the assistant instructor is showing excellent listening skills, great eye contact, facial mimicking, and an open, facing posture as she listens to the parent discuss his expectations and hopes for his son's performance in class.

Thirdly, keep the parents informed. Give the parents a manual of skills their child will be learning, along with your rules of behavior, some explanation about how your specific martial art works and invite them to take a class or two. Often when a parent tries Judo or Karate for the first time, they gain a new appreciation of what their child is attempting to accomplish in class and can become a lot more supportive.

Remember that you have been doing your art for a while and it makes sense to you, to the parents its some strange thing they don't understand. Your job is to help them to understand, and to gain their assistance in keeping the child motivated and progressing.

Emphasize to the parents that you are part of a team to help the child mature. A lot of the time, parents just need information and reassurance. Once they have these two things and you understand their needs, running your children's program can be very rewarding. As with many things, once you start getting parents on the sidelines to support your program and enforce your behavior guidelines, a snowball effect occurs and you find that more of the parents start supporting your efforts and asking questions about how they can help your program.

In simple terms there are two groups of problem parents: those that don't **appear** to care about the program and those that **appear** to interfere too much. In both cases engaging the parents directly and helping them to understand what you are doing, will reap major rewards in the long-term. The parents that don't seem to care may want to be involved, but may be simply so busy or have such poor time management skills that they never find the time to stop off at the dojo and watch their child perform. They may be very appreciative if you could meet them at the curbside with their child once in a while at the end of class, or call them at home to discuss their child's progress. Some parents simply don't care. It's unfortunate but a reality you may have to face. When dealing with "don't seem to care" parents, your main goal is to emphasize the benefits of your program, not as you see them, but as the parents want them. We all know what positive benefits we gain from training, so talk to the parents and find out what they want to get from your program.

Once you have found the "hot buttons" for the parents, talk to them about your class in terms that meet the parents on ground that is important to them. When dealing with "seem to care too much" parents, education is important. The parents need to know what is acceptable and what is not acceptable in your program. More specifically, if you can get this type of parent on your side, you will develop a very strong advocate for your program. In both cases however, it always comes back to the child and the benefits that the child will gain in the long-term from staying in your program. Parents want to know that they didn't make a mistake and need to be reassured that you are the right person to be training their child, so the more you can stress the benefits, talk to them about the progress of the child, inquire if there is anything happening at home or at school that you could help with through your classes, the better will be your relationship with the parents.

Remember, in the final analysis, that teaching children is about teaching life skills. If you remember this, and talk to the parents regularly, you will find that the majority of them want to be helpful in some way. Most of them may not even realize that their actions are a distraction or undermining your efforts. The majority want to help, they just don't know how to, because no-one has taken the time to chat with them about what they can do to help. It all comes back to communicating your program goals.

Chapter 6

PHYSIOLOGY OF TRAINING

What is "fitness"? How is fitness measured and how can we monitor changes in fitness level? How does "fitness" change with age? These are the sorts of questions that we will answer as we go through this section together. We will include information about the principles of fitness and explain how the body manufactures energy for use in physical activity and stores energy for future use. We will discuss training methods and monitoring, and specifically address warm-up, cool-down and stretching protocols. Since energy production is a matter of diet, we will also look at nutrition, and lastly, we will investigate injury and recovery. So, to set a foundation let's begin with a discussion of the principles of fitness.

Fitness Principles: It is possible to look at fitness in terms of a) body composition, energy fitness, and muscular fitness, and b) strength, flexibility and endurance (ACSM, 1995; Cooper Institute, 1999; Mitchell, 1988; Martens, 1990; NCCP, 1979; Powers and Howley, 1990).

Body composition is concerned with the ratio of fat to lean body tissue. Energy fitness is concerned with the ability of the body to generate the energy necessary to perform work and involves all the cardiovascular support units. Muscular fitness, in comparison, is concerned with muscular endurance, strength, flexibility, power and speed (ACSM, 1995; Cochran, 2001). Muscular fitness is, therefore, not simply linked to the ability to use the energy provided by the cardiovascular support systems, but is also linked intimately with the nervous system and all neuromuscular support systems. Since the human body is a machine fueled by food to supply energy for work, we will start our investigation by looking at how the energy systems work and build up from there.

Energy Systems: Muscles derive the energy they need to perform work from a biochemical energy donor called Adenosine Triphosphate (ATP). When ATP is broken down to ADP (Adenosine Diphosphate), energy is released in the muscle cell, which can be used to perform work. The body generates ATP using three energy systems (Figure 6.1) that are employed according to the availability of oxygen and the duration and intensity of the activity (Powers and Howley, 1990; Fox 1993). The three systems are the:

Energy System	Fuel Source	Duration	Type of Activity
PHOSPHAGEN	Cellular stores of ATP	Few seconds	Short burst
ANAEROBIC GLYCOLYSIS	Non-oxidative breakdown of muscle glycogen	Less than two minutes	High intensity
AEROBIC	Oxidation of carbohydrates and fats	Long duration	Low intensity

Figure 6.1: The three energy systems of the human body.

Energy fitness is, therefore, concerned with all three of these energy systems and will require specific training mechanisms to develop them. The aerobic pathway is the most efficient of the energy production pathways and creates fewer waste products and less heat than anaerobic activity (Powers and Howley, 1990).

When muscles are recruited for physical activity, each of the energy systems is used in accordance with the type of work being required of the muscles. The muscle cells only store limited amounts of ATP and, therefore, the energy demands of the work to be performed must be balanced by the supply of ATP if the work is to be completed. Remember that the ATP is broken down to ADP, and it is during the breakdown process that energy is generated for work.

The most rapid way of supplying ATP to a working muscle cell is to simply reconstitute the ATP as quickly as it gets used up, and this is the job of the Phosphagen system. The problem is that there is a very small supply of the molecule (CP) required to reconstitute ATP in the muscle cell. The reaction looks like this:

$$CP + ADP > ATP + C.$$

Once the CP in the cell has been used up, the cells must get the ATP from a different source. The Phosphagen system is, therefore, useful only at the onset of muscular activity and can be used to provide energy for very short-term, intense bursts of activity that can be completed in a few seconds. An example of an activity in which only the Phosphagen system is recruited for work would be when a student breaks a board with a single kick. I chose this example because it is important to recognize that for the CP system to be initiated there must be a physical demand placed on the body. For instance, scratching an itch is a short-term action, but does not trigger the CP system because scratching an itch does not create an excess demand upon the normal energy expenditures of the system.

The second energy pathway is the anaerobic pathway, which breaks down stores of muscular glycogen or glucose into lactic acid. During this process, called anaerobic glycolysis, ATP can be reconstituted from ADP, and can, therefore, be used to provide energy needed for work. The anaerobic system is capable of sustaining short, intense periods of work for less than two minutes, after which the muscles cells must change to the third energy pathway. The changeover point in a tournament is often obvious when a student works well for about two minutes in a match and then starts to "suck wind."

The third energy pathway is the aerobic pathway and can be used to sustain long-term muscular activity beyond the two-minute range. In the aerobic pathway, carbohydrates and fats are broken down in the cell using oxygen in order to allow for the reconstitution of ATP. The aerobic pathway takes place (and produces ATP) in special organelles inside the cell called mitochondria.

An examination of energy yield emphasizes the difference between the anaerobic and aerobic pathways: For every molecule of glucose used in the anaerobic process 2 molecules of ATP are produced. Conversely in the aerobic pathway, for every molecule of glucose used 38 molecules of ATP are produced, which means that the aerobic system is much better at producing ATP for use in a working muscle. Even having said that however, the aerobic pathway only has a 40% efficiency rating, with 60% of energy being lost as heat.

Without getting bogged down in biochemistry, it becomes clear that each energy system is dependent upon two things: The presence of a source of fuel in the working muscle cells **and** a mechanism for burning the fuel so that ATP can be generated. From this perspective it is equally clear that the longer the period for which the activity must be sustained, the greater will be the need to replenish the muscle cells with an adequate supply of fuel and remove the waste products generated in the muscle cells by their activity.

Knowledge of these facts is of great value in the development of solid lesson plans that will help your students achieve sustainable, demonstrable and incremental improvements in personal physical fitness over time. The energy pathway information is, therefore, critical to understanding what happens during a typical class, training cycle or a typical tournament and how our training process should be modified or developed to improve the fitness levels of our students over time. By understanding how the energy systems are recruited and used, we can begin to understand both the short-term and long-term training goals that will be needed for each student.

For instance: Beginning students may need to build an aerobic base first and then start working on the ability to produce anaerobic bursts of energy. In this instance classes that are filled with sustained low intensity activity will be most beneficial. Conversely, a highly-trained student may need specific drills that improve performance when anaerobic energy pathways are recruited. In this case, an example might be a Judo lesson plan that includes intense, explosive throwing drills separated by periods of lower intensity recovery time. If you recall what we discussed in the section on pedagogy, when we take a longer-term view, training for the energy demands of a competition season will be different from the training demands of the off-season and these factors will need to be considered in the development of meaningful and useful lesson plans.

In throwing and striking arts, many individual actions involve short, high intensity bursts of energy, although continued performance requires long-term endurance. For martial artists it is, therefore, critical to have a well-developed aerobic foundation **in addition** to being capable of producing sudden, short-lived, very high-intensity actions. Although martial arts training includes both anaerobic and aerobic activities, when a new student begins training it is still a good idea to build an aerobic base before emphasizing the anaerobic system.

The key here is the intensity level of the training. Low intensity activities will tend to lead to improvements in aerobic capacity (Figure 6.2). As new students progress through their first few weeks of classes, they will often see dramatic improvements in a number of key areas of aerobic fitness (Powers and Howley, 1990; Fox, 1993):

i) The ability of the lungs to collect oxygen and discharge carbon dioxide.

ii) The ability of the heart to pump oxygenated blood to the muscles.

iii) The ability of the heart to pump deoxygenated blood to the lungs.

iv) The ability to supply enough oxygenated blood to the active muscle groups.

v) The ability to get fuel and oxygen from the blood into the working muscle cells.

vi) The ability of the muscle cells to efficiently use the supplies received.

vii) The ability to remove waste products from the working muscle cells.

We can, therefore, define aerobic fitness as being directly related to the ability to take in, transport and use oxygen efficiently in the production of energy. Training for improvements in aerobic fitness is based upon low intensity, long duration activities that improve all aspects of cardiovascular endurance. As endurance improves, it is possible to overload the aerobic pathways with greater intensity or longer duration exercises.

During the early stages of training, the instructor must emphasize that students need to stay within their limits and not overdo things. The instructor must continually emphasize that the fitness performance goal of these activities is to build an aerobic foundation. Related to improvements in aerobic fitness will be improvements in how the student feels about him or herself. There will be greater levels of confidence associated with a desire to take on more demanding tasks. It is exactly this desire that can sometimes cause a student to overdo things.

An instructor must be aware of this possible outcome and act quickly to keep the students focused on the purpose of this level of training. Obviously, as your students improve in aerobic fitness, it will be necessary to train the anaerobic system, because, as we just said both energy systems are important. One of the main things to consider here is that students are individuals with specific training needs. Some students may be ready for more intense activities before other students and one of our jobs as coaches is to develop appropriate training plans for each of our athletes as opposed to using a one-size-fits-all approach.

Once an aerobic foundation has been established, the next stage in training is to raise the anaerobic threshold. The anaerobic threshold is the point at which the intensity of the workload causes the muscles to change from aerobic respiration to anaerobic respiration. As a guide, the anaerobic threshold is at about 85-90% maximum heart rate. Maximum heart rate is normally calculated by subtracting the student's age from 220. In order to raise the anaerobic threshold the student needs to be engaged in class activities, which will keep the student working at close to 85% of maximum heart rate. Continuing to work at this level during practice sessions over several weeks will help to raise the anaerobic threshold.

Anaerobic energy pathways are trained through short, intense periods of activity that overload the aerobic energy system (Figure 6.2). In order to train the anaerobic pathways, the student needs to increase intensity of effort and decrease duration of activity. A good method of training the anaerobic system is interval training, which involves short bursts of intense activity followed by a period of low intensity activity as a resting phase for the anaerobic system. The "active rest" period allows the muscles to cool down and wash out the waste products such as lactic acid. Too much anaerobic training, however, will lead to chronic fatigue, susceptibility to injury and a loss of self-motivation.

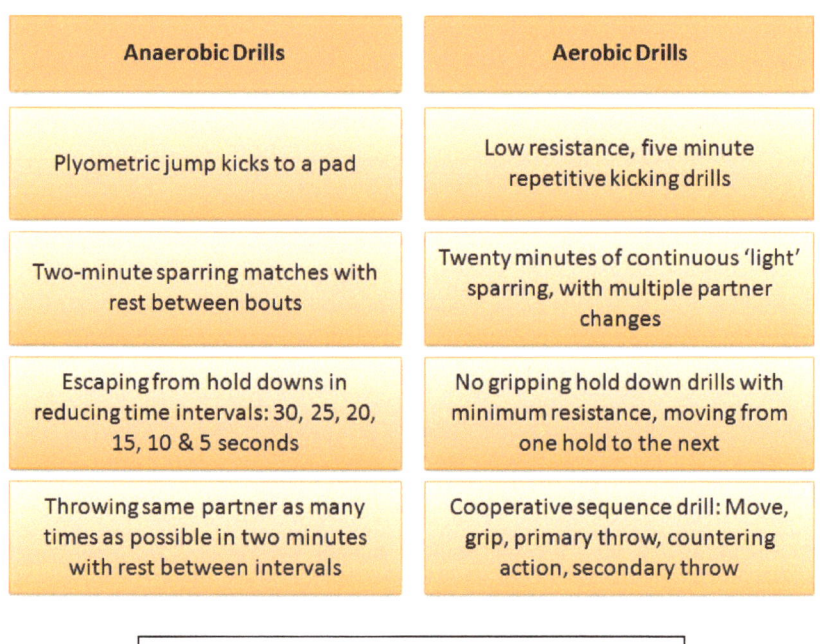

Figure 6.2: Anaerobic versus aerobic drills.

Muscular Fitness: Muscular fitness includes parameters such as muscle flexibility, strength and endurance. Before we get into these areas, however, we need to understand that there are different types of muscle fibers in the human body. Essentially there are three types of muscle fibers (Powers and Howley, 1990; Fox, 1993):

i) Fast-twitch.

ii) Intermediate.

iii) Slow-twitch.

Fast-twitch muscles fibers (Figure 6.3), are rich in glycogen stores, but have a low resistance to fatigue and have small numbers of mitochondria. Fast-twitch fibers contract very rapidly and are capable of producing more force than slow-twitch fibers. Fast-twitch fibers derive their energy from anaerobic glycolysis. Conversely, slow-twitch muscle fibers have a high resistance to fatigue; have large numbers of mitochondria and low stores of glycogen. Slow-twitch muscles are also fed by more blood capillaries than fast-twitch muscle fibers, which is important for keeping the fibers supplied with oxygen for the aerobic energy pathways to be sustained. Slow-twitch muscle fibers (Figure 6.3) produce less power than fast-twitch muscle fibers and contract more slowly. Intermediate muscle fiber types possess characteristics between those of the fast and slow-twitch muscle fiber types. Each person is genetically coded with fixed percentages of fast-twitch and slow-twitch muscle fibers; it is impossible to change a slow-twitch muscle fiber into a fast-twitch muscle fiber, or vice versa. It is important to realize though, that often the differentiation of muscle fibers does not begin until the onset of puberty.

Fiber Type	Energy System	Fatigue Resistance	Power Output
FAST TWITCH	Anaerobic	Low	High
SLOW TWITCH	Aerobic	High	Low

Figure 6.3: A comparison of fast and slow-twitch muscle types.

Intermediate muscle fibers can be altered to become more like "fast" or "slow" twitch according to the type of training they receive, but the essence of the matter is that "sprinters are born, not made." The implication of muscle typing is that training can improve the performance of the different muscle types, but cannot change the overall nature of a fast or a slow-twitch fiber. For sustained work, slow-twitch muscle fibers are needed. For short, powerful bursts of energy, fast-twitch fibers are recruited.

If we consider standing posture versus dynamic action for a moment, most of the muscle fibers that are recruited to maintain a standing position are of the slow-twitch type. Conversely, creating an explosive technique like a powerful kick or throw will require the recruitment of fast-twitch muscle fibers. Emphasis is placed upon the recruitment of slow or fast-twitch muscle **fibers** because each muscle is composed of a mixture of slow, fast and intermediate fiber types and the work that the muscle is called upon to do will affect the types of fibers that are recruited to do the work.

Going back to our example, in a standing posture the gastrocnemius (calf) and quadriceps (thigh) leg muscles rely mostly upon slow-twitch fibers to help sustain body posture, but when used to push explosively, the same muscles recruit fast-twitch muscle fibers to generate the power necessary to do the work (Figure 6.4).

Figure 6.4: In a Judo tournament, throws are often sudden events that use a lot of explosive power and recruit fast-twitch muscles.

The discussion of muscle type was necessary to lay a foundation for understanding muscle endurance. Muscular endurance can be either short-term (anaerobic) or long-term (aerobic) endurance. We can think of muscle endurance as the ability to withstand fatigue, which results when the muscle is no longer capable of performing work. Endurance training will:

i)   Improve Oxygen uptake.

ii) Increase numbers of capillaries feeding the muscle.

iii) Increase numbers of mitochondria in the muscle cells.

iv) Lower the rate of glycogen depletion during activity.

v)   Decrease the amount of lactic acid produced during activity.

Endurance training, therefore, improves **performance** of muscles but will not however, increase the size of muscles (Powers and Howley, 1990). Activities that build endurance will tend to be low intensity activities that keep the students active for a prolonged period at the target heart rate. Target heart rate is found using the Karvonen Formula as follows:

i) Measure the **Resting Heart Rate** at either the carotid (side of the neck) or radial (thumb side of the wrist) pulse site by counting the number of beats per minute. (Use first two fingers to feel and count the pulse).

ii) Calculate the **Maximum Heart Rate** = 220 minus student's age.

iii) Calculate the **Heart Rate Reserve** by subtracting the resting heart rate from the Maximum Heart Rate.

iv) Calculate both 60% and 80% of the HRR.

v) Add the Resting Heart Rate back to the results of the last step. The two figures will be the lower (60%) and upper (80%) limits of the **Target Heart Rate**.

vi) Example: An active 40 year-old male with a resting heart rate of 60 beats per minute.

   a. Step 1: 220 - 40 = 180bpm. This is the Maximum Heart Rate.

   b. Step 2: 180 – 60 = 120bpm. This is the Heart Rate Reserve.

   c. Step 3: 60% of 120 = 72 and 80% of 120 = 96bpm.

   d. Step 4: 72 + 60 =132bpm and 96 + 60 = 156bpm. This is the Target Heart Rate range.

By way of contrast, if muscular strength is required, then it is necessary to increase the **size** of the muscles through a process known as "hypertrophy" as well as increase the numbers of muscle fibers recruited during a contraction. Muscular strength is built by using resistance training, because the resistance overloads the muscle fibers. Improvement in muscle strength also results in:

i) An increased ability of nervous stimulation to recruit more muscle fibers for a given activity.

ii) An increase in the strength of connective tissues.

iii) An increase in the amount of muscle protein mass.

To build strength, students should perform activities that involve low numbers of repetitions but offer a high resistance. To be effective, strength-training needs to be done three times a week, with a rest day between each training day. If the student can do more than ten repetitions of any training exercise, then the resistance needs to be increased for strength benefits to be produced. The overload principle requires that the resistance level needs to be set such that the student can do about 7-9 repetitions and then increased when the student can consistently perform ten repetitions.

Resistance-training programs need to be carefully designed and properly supervised. Delavier (2001) is an excellent source for building a strength training program for your students, which lists more than one hundred exercises dealing with almost every muscle group in the body and shows you which muscles are receiving a training effect from each exercise.

Another aspect of muscular strength that is important in martial arts, is plyometric power. Plyometric power is concerned with generating a very fast, very forceful burst of action (Chu, 1992). Plyometric training, therefore, aims to improve the velocity of a performance and affects activities like exploding into a throw or escaping from a hold down. Training plyometric fitness involves learning about elastic recoil limits of the muscles (Luttgens and Wells, 1989). Plyometric actions involve a rapid relaxed stretch phase prior to a forceful contraction phase in the same muscle. It takes two muscles on opposite sides of a joint to produce a plyometric action (Figure 6.5). When the agonist muscle (on one side of the joint) is maximally contracted, the antagonist muscle (on the other side) is maximally stretched and when the agonist contraction is released the elastic properties of the stretched muscle will cause it to begin contracting (myotactic stretch reflex).

Figure 6.5: A plyometric throw in the moment of execution. The quadriceps muscles of the thigh are used to generate the power needed for this Seoi Nage (shoulder throw).

Training methods, which involve body actions that work against a resistance provided by items such as a medicine ball or a rubber strap can train plyometric response. Chu (1992) provides an excellent review of plyometric drills and training regimens many of which can be modified or used in your classes. As a warning, however, plyometric training exercises can be very damaging if it not done carefully, especially if done without an adequate warm-up or attention to the accuracy of biomechanical actions.

The last aspect of muscular fitness to examine is that of muscular flexibility. Muscular flexibility is related to joint range of movement (ROM) and is limited by changes in the elasticity of the tendons, muscles and ligaments. In any joint, the muscles work the joint, tendons join the muscles to the bone and ligaments are bone-to-bone connectors that hold the joint together. When students are improving flexibility of a joint, they can stretch the muscles and tendons because they are both elastic fibers. Ligaments, however, are non-elastic, which means that they can be stretched, but once stretched, they will not return to their **original** size. The goal of flexibility training is to increase the range of motion for a joint by lengthening the tendons and the muscles, but without compromising the integrity of the ligaments.

In summary, whatever fitness drills you employ, remember that you must consider the starting fitness level, body type and age of your players.

Age-Specific Physiology:

Before I go on to a discussion of training principles, I'd like to spend a few moments chatting about the physical differences between adults and children. When dealing with children it is good to be aware that there are three types of age: chronological age, mental age and biological age. What we may infer from this is that it is quite possible for a ten-year-old male to have the physical development of someone two years older but the mental maturity of someone a year or two younger. Moreover you should be aware that the adolescent growth spurt may begin as early as 11 or as late as 16 in boys and as early 8 or as late as 15 in girls. Consequently, it is a good idea to recognize that children grow and mature at different rates and that blanket statements about training are unwise. Having said that, let's look as some of main physical differences between adults and children.

The most obvious physical difference between adults and children is that children are still growing, therefore, their bones are softer and there are "growth plates" (epiphyseal plates) made of cartilage in the long bones that have not yet calcified fully (Powers and Howley, 1990). Less obvious, but just as important, is that prior to the onset of puberty children do not have the same circulating hormones as adults.

Children respond well to organized physical activity that promotes cardiovascular development and aerobic endurance (Powers and Howley, 1990; Micheli, 1995), but there are some things that as coaches we would do well to remember. In terms of performance, children tend to have a lower cardiac output, and a lower sweat rate than adults, which means that they can become overheated more quickly and are susceptible to heat intolerance. Also, if you recall earlier when we discussed fast versus slow-twitch muscles, we noted that the differentiation does not occur until puberty. As a result, children tend to have lower percentages of fast-twitch muscles (Mitchell, 1992), and thus, have a lower anaerobic capacity, which limits power output and may cause children to tire more readily.

Given the differences that we have just discussed, the two areas where the physical differences between children and adults become a really big factor are strength training and flexibility training. There are two sources of concern: Firstly, Micheli, (1995) discusses the absence of circulating androgens (hormones that are associated with puberty), which limits the development of muscle mass in children. Secondly, Powers and Howley, (1990), Mitchell, (1992), and Micheli, (1995) all comment that as a direct result of the growth plate in the long bones of a child's body, the **inappropriate** use of strength and/or flexibility training can result in arrested growth, tendon separation from the bone, and growth plate damage and the development of scar tissue in ligament tears.

In conclusion, I would like to mention an article that I read several years ago that made a big impact upon me (U.S. News and World Report, April 8th, 2002) because it drew attention to the increasing numbers of **preventable** injuries that occur in children who are engaged in sporting activities. The article clearly demonstrated two things:

i) That many injuries suffered by children can be prevented with well-designed and properly supervised sports fitness programs.

ii) That children engaged in sports are sometimes practicing **too much**.

What we should keep in mind when coaching children is that we want to create life-long habits of personal fitness, not create chronic injuries due to overtraining. It is a wise coach who is governed by the

Goldilocks Principle, which, when applied to training athletes simply implies that mild stimuli have little effect, moderate stimuli are useful and excessive stimuli are harmful (Figure 4.11).

Training Principles: Regardless of age, there are several training principles worth considering that will enhance the process of student development (Abernethy et al, 1997; Bompa, 1999; Graden, 1997; Judo Canada, 1983; Martens, 1990, NCCP, 1979; Wiley, 1995). The most important thing to remember, however, is to take a long-term perspective. By setting a reasonable pace with reasonable goals, our students will improve in their fitness and skill levels with lower risk of injury, frustration, burnout or boredom. Let's take another look at the Goldilocks Principle. We want to moderate stimuli so that our players receive a training effect and are not subject to burnout, frustration or overuse injuries. Training effects are, however, cumulative, so in our training plans we want to create moderate stimuli even while the intensity of what we do increases and our students improve. The trick is to recognize when a stimulus that was "moderate" has become "mild" and no longer has any training effect, and to increase the stimulus, but not overdo it and load too much, too soon. Accordingly, let's look at some training principles that might act as a guide to the development of appropriate training strategies:

i) **Adaptation over time**: It requires months of training for improvements in overall fitness to accumulate as a result of regular training. The daily improvements are very small, but when measured over a period of months, clear improvements can be seen in cardiovascular endurance, blood circulation, heart function, muscular strength and endurance, as well as bone, ligament and tendon strength. In the early stages of development provide reinforcement often, even for seemingly small improvements. It is easy for beginning students to watch advanced students and feel as though they will never reach those levels of performance, so it is important to remind your students that they **will** acquire of skill, strength, stamina and flexibility through commitment to training over time. Encouraging your students to keep a training journal will help them to see the progress being made, and also act as a catalyst for setting new, loftier goals.

The most visible changes in fitness also occur in the early stages of training when our students drop excess weight, burn away excess fat, build muscle and reshape their bodies with improved muscle tone. Student will also notice the cardiovascular gains that they make because they have more energy and more endurance. At the advanced levels of training when are dealing with well-conditioned athletes, the improvements are smaller, more subtle and incrementally not so noticeable.

ii) **Frequency**: For students to benefit in all areas of fitness it is important that training involves at least two classes per week of about one hour each. Attending class is absolutely essential for continued development. Sporadic or short bursts of training will not only be ineffective, they also increase the risk of injury. It is the instructor's responsibility to instill a "work ethic" and aid in developing time-management skills early in the student's training. In order for the long-term benefits to occur, our students must develop the discipline to stick with their training, and not get side-tracked by other distractions. Unless you have a mitigation plan in place, seasonality can adversely affect student retention in your school. Many students will train during the spring and then take off the entire summer and lose a lot of ground when (and if) they come back in the fall.

iii) **Inactivity and Injury**: It takes longer to recover lost levels of fitness than it does to lose them. Any reduction in the training regime over a protracted period will result in a loss of training adaptations. According to Martens (1990) and Powers and Howley (1990) bed rest can result in a loss of aerobic fitness at the rate of 10% per week or 25% after 20 days of bed rest. Students returning after injury or a period of inactivity should be made aware of the fact that they will not be as fit as they were prior to the lay off. We should also encourage our returning students to bring themselves back up to their pre-lay off conditioning slowly and not to demand too much from themselves, too quickly.

Additionally, it is important to remember that there is always a psychological injury that goes along with any physical injury and that the psychological trauma may take longer to heal than the body. Sometimes, a student may be physically prepared to return to training but may be reluctant to engage in certain activities due to a lingering fear that s/he has yet to resolve. The fear can be particularly evident when a student returns to training after an injury that involved a surgical intervention, regardless of whether or not the injury occurred as a result of martial arts practice. If a student does sustain an injury in class, the activity that directly relates to cause of the injury will often be the last activity to which the student will return (Estwanik, 1996).

iv) **Individual Response**: Different students will respond differently to the same stimuli. Moreover, the same student may also respond differently at different times to the same stimulus. The differences that a coach notices between performances of different students and performances by the same students at different times can be attributed to a variety of factors. Some factors that create interpersonal differences in response are genetic and include inherited characteristics of physiology such as muscle fiber composition and the genetic aspects of cardiovascular function (Powers and Howley, 1990). Other factors, which may impact responses by different individuals and also by the same individual at different times may include both genetically and non-genetically influenced responses to changing environmental influences such as heat, cold, altitude and humidity (Haymes and Wells, 1986). Lastly, a student's performance may vary as a function of factors that include personal stress, fatigue, rest and sleep cycles, illness or injury, motivation, nutrition, emotional maturity and level of fitness. It is this last group of factors over which the individual player will be able to exert the greatest control.

v) **Intensity**: When a new technique is presented or when a student first starts a drill (especially at the novice level), it is important to go slowly during the first few repetitions of the drill and build up to increased speed and power. There are several reasons why this makes good sense. First and foremost, safety considerations dictate that if students practice slowly at first, they will be less likely to injure themselves or their training partners, as a result of poor control or poor biomechanics. Secondly, working through a drill slowly will allow students to get a feel for the body placement and biomechanical actions necessary for successful execution of the skill. Advanced players will be able to start out with faster paced repetitions because they already have an experiential base upon which to build. It is important to practice the drill and do the repetitions at the intensity level that will be required in the actual field of application as soon as possible. The merits to this approach for improving skill, deriving greater fitness benefits and obtaining the greatest degree of transference from the training experience should be obvious.

A second aspect of intensity is related to the nature of each class and also the duration of the training season. Aim to do the most intense work in the middle of a class once the class has been prepared physiologically and motivated psychologically for more intense work. It is also sensible to come back down again from a high level of intensity before the end of the class to allow the students to return to pre-class levels of physiological and psychological arousal. Finishing a class at its intensity peak without a cool-down period can lead to muscle cramping and possible injury. Finishing at the peak of intensity will also lead to a sense of disappointment rather than euphoria.

vi) **Monitoring**: Improvements in both fitness and ability must be monitored, so that your students can see for themselves the improvements that they are making. Regular evaluation of performance ability can be a very powerful motivator, especially when students compare where they started to their present level of fitness or their present level of skill development. While the progression of the colored ranks towards Black Belt is a form of self-monitoring, it is the instructor's responsibility to provide more detailed monitoring mechanisms for the students. The concept of monitoring is an integral part of long-range planning and is, therefore, related to your ability as a coach to understand the student's needs and personal goals within your program. Consequently, monitoring depends upon excellent communication skills and is an indispensable part of reinforcement and encouragement for your students. Since monitoring deals with results-based feedback concerning skill development, technical ability and fitness level, it is possible to initiate the process of coach-mediated self-monitoring very early in the training process by providing clear measurements of improvements in each of these areas.

By monitoring fitness gains combined with individualized fitness prescriptions, the instructor is indicating a commitment to the long-term development of the student in a personal, practical and verifiable fashion. The result of this sort of interaction enhances the instructor's trust account with the student and will further motivate and inspire the students to continue their training. By ensuring that the early training goals lead to successful and measurable outcomes, and by using a monitoring process that can demonstrate the success to your students; you will help to build the self-confidence of your students and increase their awareness of what is possible. In this manner it is possible to create a positive feedback loop (Figure 6.6). Taken together, these sorts of monitoring tools will cause the student to build a high level of confidence in the instructor's ability to help the student achieve his or her personal goals.

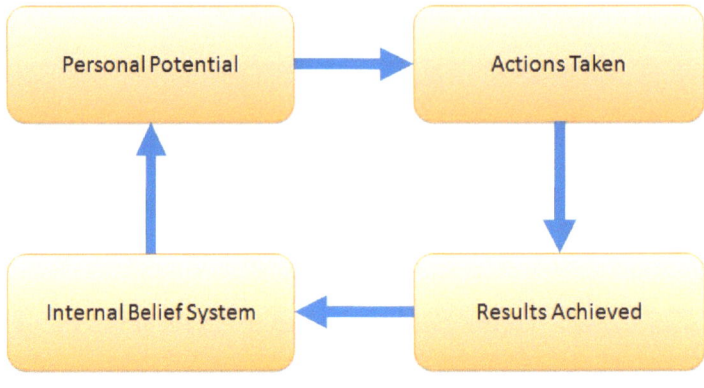

Figure 6.6: Personal success cycle.

vii) **Overloading**: There are two distinct aspects to overloading. Firstly, there is the principle of physical overloading, which is responsible for improving our level of fitness. Secondly, there is mental overloading, which is related to providing more technical information than the students can handle. As stated earlier, in order to improve their fitness level, our students must exceed the typical demands of their bodies. As students adapt to the increased physical requirements, greater demands can be introduced according to the Goldilocks Principle. The early training, therefore, prepares our students for the greater physical demands and more complex techniques of the later training. Physical overloading of students too early will lead to rapid burn out and increased likelihood of injury due to a lack of readiness. Moreover, mental overloading of beginning students with detailed technical information is almost guaranteed to lead to confusion, frustration and a high dropout rate. The time to begin physically overloading your students is when they are mentally willing to commit themselves to the training. The time to mentally overload your students is when they have a very strong foundation of skills and are able to abstract data from a history of personal training experiences.

viii) **Overtraining**: It is possible to have too much of a good thing. Overtraining is the result of excessive training demands over a protracted period of time with little or no chance for rest and recovery. Overtraining can result from increasing the intensity, frequency or volume of training too quickly and without building sufficient recovery time into the training process. We can look at training as a form of stress, because we are exceeding the normal demands of the student's body. Following the dictates of the Goldilocks Principle (Figure 4.11), the externally applied stress of training will either be so slight as to create no discernable result, so severe that the player is being over-trained or balanced in such a way as to ensure that player receives maximum benefit from the training. The student's response to his or her training is, therefore, an internal strain to the system. Consequently, training can be viewed as an externally applied stress, which creates an internal strain response (Figure 6.7). The diagram can be applied to physical materials, psychological settings and for physiological responses to training. The curve indicates that there is a yield point before which the external stimulus is too slight to cause a permanent response and a fail point at which the system fails. Although we will use physical training as our example in the strain responses itemized below, don't lose sight of the fact that the curve applies to mental aspects of training as well. The strain response can, therefore, be of three types:

i. Elastic: Under elastic strain conditions, the student's body returns to its original state with no discernable training effect, once the training stress is removed. In short, the training stress was too slight.

ii. Ductile: A ductile strain is one in which the student's body responds by making physiological adaptations to the demands of training stress. It is the ductile area of response that is most beneficial for the player and the area that leads to improvements in conditioning.

iii. Collapse: If too much training stress is applied, the student is overtraining and the result will be a physiological failure of some sort.

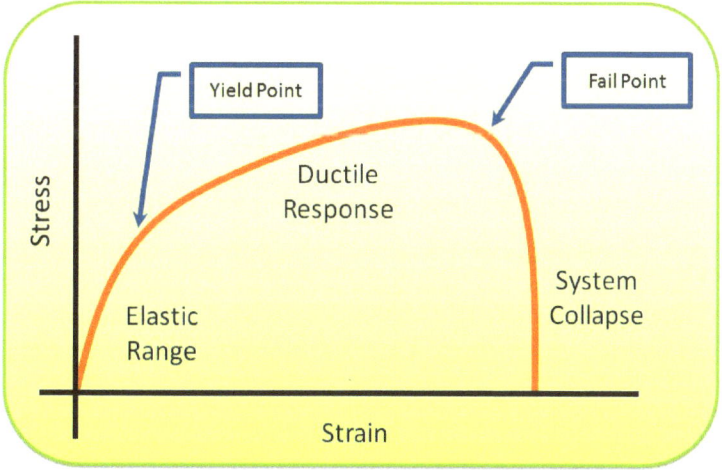

Figure 6.7: Stress and strain diagram.

ix) **Periodization**: We have already discussed this principle at some length in the section on pedagogy (Chapter 4), so we're not going to repeat it here.

x) **Progression**: Improvements in fitness and skill will be the result of setting appropriate goals of duration, frequency, intensity and overloading of training. By helping our students to see their own adaptation to the training over time, we will be in a position to assist them in creating new training goals and aspire to higher levels of performance. Consequently, our students will require training that keeps them pushing the edge of their performance envelope in order to maintain optimal arousal and excitement. The clear implication is that our students will need to train more often, harder and/or for longer. Obviously though, you cannot keep training longer and harder. There are limits imposed by the age, goals and external commitments of your players.

Training programs, therefore, need to be appropriate for the level of development and performance goals of the student and be individualized on daily, weekly, monthly and yearly cycles. Once a student shows an adaptation to training, it will be necessary to increase the training demands and raise the performance bar **in a way that is meaningful to the student**. Progression must, however, also allow time for recovery, so in a period of several months, the student should work up to a peak, slack off a little and then build up to the next peak, and so on.

xi) **Readiness**: Be sure that your students are ready for the training that they are being given. Students must be both physiologically **and** psychologically ready for their classes. By setting and achieving reasonable goals and by overcoming obstacles in an environment of appropriate reinforcement our athletes will develop the commitment and discipline to follow through as the physiological demands of the training increase. There is little point setting high physical demands for your students if you have not prepared them psychologically to commit to intense levels of physical training. Although it is axiomatic that we will be working on several aspects of physical and mental development concurrently and that each student will have individual and specific needs and abilities, the principle of readiness suggests that during the early stages of training, emphasis should be placed upon building mental commitment, developing simple skills and preparing the athlete for the greater physical and mental demands that will come later. In intermediate levels of training more emphasis can be placed on developing a more complex integrated skill set, supported by greater demands in strength, endurance and flexibility. The later development will tend to bring it all together in the creation of a self-disciplined, confident, motivated, highly skilled, physically fit and psychologically tough martial artist.

xii) **Recovery**: It is essential that our students have adequate time to recover from their training both physically and mentally. The time required for recovery is a very important element in the adaptations that our students make to training. In simple terms we want our students to be overloaded during their training so that they exceed the normal requirements of their bodies and then be given time to recover, so that they are ready for the next stage in the development process. We do not want to work our students to a state of chronic fatigue by continuing to apply the overload requirement without adequate rest. Consequently, recovery is something that should be an integral part of each class **and** be incorporated as a component of all longer-term training cycles.

xiii) **Reversibility**: The anatomical adaptations that occur due to training will only last for as long as the demands are present. As we just mentioned in the section on inactivity and injury, training effects are lost very quickly. The process of loss begins within days of the cessation of training. As a rule, however, fitness levels take less effort to maintain than the original investment of effort needed to obtain them. Consequently, training volumes can be decreased during a maintenance stage of training, without loss of the training effect.

xiv) **Specificity**: The main significance of specificity is that whatever you do in training will create specific physiological and psychological responses and adaptations. It is therefore important to understand that training for an increase in strength will require different training programs than training for improvements in endurance. Likewise increased flexibility will require specific training tools.

A second aspect of specificity is that training in a particular way, prepares you for what you have trained. It should be fairly evident that if you train for recreation, then you are not training for competition. What is sometimes less evident is that merely repeating a set of self-defense moves does not prepare you for the highly charged moment of actual combat (Siddle, 1995). Likewise, skill in a tournament environment does not necessarily translate to an ability to defend yourself on the street, if the need arises. The point is simply this: Specificity dictates that if you want to prepare your students for a particular performance environment, then it behooves you to train them in conditions that as nearly approximate the actual environment in which the skills will be used, as soon as possible.

xv) **Variety**: It is impossible to keep training at the same level all the time in the same ways and expect to maintain progress and motivation. Training must include variety in order to provide continued physical benefits and avoid boredom. From a physiological perspective, our bodies get used to doing the same things over and over, so variety keeps the body from getting too comfortable. Instructors then, need to be masters of innovation and disguise. It is important to find diverse ways of teaching the same skills in such a way that the students do not realize that they are repeating a drill. The issue of disguising repetition is particularly acute in children's classes where the attention spans are shorter, and impulse control is not as great as in the adult classes. Regardless of the age group you are teaching, simply remember that variety is all about hiding repetition while maintaining a training effect for both the body and the mind.

Training Protocols: Aside from the skill-training component of each lesson plan, there are three additional training protocols that must be addressed in each class. Each of the next three protocols will have a profound effect upon your ability to adequately prepare your students, help them to gain fitness benefits and enhance your student retention.

The Warm-up: The warm-up is an indispensable part of reducing the likelihood of injury in class (Byl, 2004; Corcoran and Graden, 1998; Martens, 1990; Mitchell, 1988, NCCP, 1979; Nishiyama and Brown, 1960; Powers and Howley; 1990, Scott, 2005). A thorough warm-up allows the student to become both psychologically and physiologically prepared for the more intense activities to follow. As such, the warm-up bridges the gap between coming to class and doing the work expected in the lesson plan to be presented. One of the most important aspects of doing a warm-up is that it increases the state of psychological arousal by inducing the secretion of endorphins that stimulate the body to perform at a higher level. A warm-up should be a whole-body experience, using all the muscles that will be used during the class (Byl, 2004). Warm-ups should include range of motion exercises as well as cardiovascular and mild stretching components but should be tailored to the fitness level and age of the students. Warm-ups should be rhythmic and be accompanied by activities that emphasize the full range of movement (ROM) for all joints that will be used in the practice. Excellent warm-up drills include lower intensity versions of movements that you will use later in class.

It is very important to develop a wide range of warm-up exercises, so that you can vary the warm-up procedure over time. All too often we fall into the trap of using the same warm-up exercises repeatedly. By varying the warm-up, instructors are able to minimize the level to which the warm-up loses its efficacy because the student's minds and bodies have adapted to the drills used in the warm-up. By varying the warm-ups, students will remain motivated, their bodies will not fall into a "warm-up comfort zone" and the students will continue to derive both psychological and physiological benefits from the warm-up itself.

Warm-ups also act as a good time for the students to indulge in relaxation (stress release), focusing, meditation and/or visualization.

If your players have received an adequate warm-up the physical and mental preparation for class will inevitably lead to a reduction in the risk of injury which will, in turn, promote better technical accomplishments and a more relaxed and enjoyable training environment.

In summary then a warm-up should:

i) Build fundamental psychomotor skills.

ii) Involve large body actions using full range of motion exercises.

iii) Use body movements that simulate actions that will be required in the lesson plan.

iv) Elevate core and muscle temperature.

v) Increase heart rate.

vi) Increase breathing rate.

vii) Increase circulation of blood to the muscles.

viii) Stimulate joint lubrication.

ix) Include a mild stretching component, once the body is warm.

x) Stimulate endorphin release for optimal physiological and psychological arousal.

xi) Stimulate psychological arousal ensuring the players are mentally motivated, prepared and focused on the class ahead.

Stretching: In any joint there are two sets of muscles needed to work the joint. The two-muscle sets work as a pair and are known as the agonist and antagonist muscles (Luttgens and Wells, 1989). When the agonist muscle is contracting and shortening it changes the joint angle, and the antagonist muscle on the other side of the joint must relax and lengthen or else the two sets of muscles will be working against each other.

The purpose of stretching is, therefore, to increase the range of motion for a particular joint; which presupposes that the joint we wish to stretch is well-lubricated and relaxed, i.e. warm and ready to do work. Since the joint structure is a limiting factor, the only things that we can change are the elasticity of the muscles, tendons and ligaments surrounding the joints. Muscles work the joint, tendons attach the muscles to the bones and ligaments join bone to bone across the joint. Muscles and tendons are elastic, which means that if they are stretched they can return to their original size when the stretching force is removed. Ligaments are non-elastic, but can be stretched, which means that they do not return to their original length once the stretching force has been removed. As a consequence, once a ligament has been stretched the joint will have a greater range of motion and a lower level of stability than before. It is, therefore, inadvisable to stretch ligaments.

One of the very best forms of stretching exercise is called proprioceptive neuromuscular facilitation (P.N.F.). Stretching using P.N.F. involves holding a muscular contraction followed by relaxing the muscle and allowing it to stretch, then repeating the cycle (Anderson, and Anderson, 2000; Estwanik, 1996; Luttgens and Wells, 1989). As a teaching drill, emphasize to your students that P.N.F. stretching involves four stages:

i) Bending (flexion) of the joint to develop relaxed muscular stretch.

ii) Resisted muscular contraction for a slow count of ten.

iii) Increase in relaxed bending (flexion).

iv) Repetition of the cycle three times.

P.N.F. stretches can be done on your own, but also work very well when you have a partner who cooperates with you during the exercise. Since both people are working together, P.N.F. stretching is an excellent way of cooling down a class both physiologically and psychologically (Figure 6.8).

Figure 6.8: P.N.F. stretch of the hamstring.

Static Stretching involves holding a slow, smooth stretching action. During a static stretch one set of muscles (agonist) is used to stretch the opposite muscles (antagonist) on the same joint (Anderson and Anderson, 2000; Luttgens and Wells, 1989). For instance, an example of a static stretch involves using a contraction of the quadriceps muscles of the thigh to stretch a relaxed hamstring muscle on the opposite side of the leg (Figure 6.9).

Figure 6.9: Static stretching of the hamstring muscles and lower back.

In older training protocols a form of bouncing, called ballistic stretching was frequently used, but is now contra-indicated. Ballistic stretching is damaging to muscles because it results in an automatic reflex muscle contraction, and can lead to high incidences of injury (Estwanik, 1996).

A warm-up combined with **mild** stretching before a vigorous work out reduces the risk of injury and increases the range of movement for the joints (Corcoran and Graden, 1998; Judo Canada, 1983; Mitchell, 1988, NCCP, 1979, Scott, 2005). It is important to recognize that stretching is not a warm-up in itself, but that once the body temperature, heart rate and blood circulation rate have been elevated, stretching can be used as part of a warm-up (Anderson and Anderson, 2000; Herbert and Gabriel, 2002). The point here is that it is the warm-up that reduces the risk of injury, not the stretch.

Stretching should be taken to the point of discomfort, but should not feel painful. Each stretch should be held for about ten seconds at the maximum stretch, followed by a ten-second relaxation and a repeated stretch (Anderson and Anderson, 2000; Corcoran and Graden, 1998). Estwanik (1996) recommends that for actual lengthening of muscle and tendon fibers, three to five repetitions of a thirty-second stretch in a relaxed maximally lengthened position are required. Stretching should be smooth and steady and can involve resistance or non-resistance.

When doing mild stretching in preparation for a martial arts class, it is important to emphasize range of motion exercises for the ankles, calf muscles, the quadriceps, hamstrings, hip adductors, lower and upper back, sides, shoulders, fingers and wrists. Stretching is also good after a class as a cooling down activity. In either warm-up or cool-down, move from large muscle groups to small muscle groups and work methodically through the whole body.

Cool-down: The cool-down is a mechanism by which our students reduce their state of arousal and also bring physiological parameters such as breathing and heart rate back down to normal levels. Although it should be obvious that to suddenly stop working can lead to increased risk of injury, we also need to consider the benefits of a cool-down:

i) **Physiological**: The obvious physiological benefits of a cool-down are in returning heart rate, blood pressure, breathing and core temperature to normal levels as well as the removal of metabolic waste products from their sites of production. Cooling the system down and allowing the body to gradually return to more normal levels of activity, places less strain on the heart and lungs and related (circulatory) systems. During physical training, about 80% of the available cardiac output is being pumped to the big muscles groups, which means that less than 20% is going to the visceral organs and the brain. In actual fact, although the brain only receives 3-4% of the available cardiac output during physical activity, the absolute amount of blood going to the brain goes up slightly because the heart rate has increased. When you stop activity, blood can pool in the muscles and needs to be redirected to normal flow patterns. If blood is allowed to pool in the muscles then the percentage of the available cardiac output going to the brain may go back to about 15%, but the absolute volume of blood drops because heart rate has declined and because of blood pooling less blood is being pumped through the heart. Failure to redirect blood flow to normal patterns can, therefore, cause fainting (Corcoran and Graden, 1998; Powers and Howley, 1990).

Additionally, intense physical activity burns metabolic materials in the muscles and produces metabolic waste. When the activity stops, waste products can pool in the muscles which can result in cramping or muscle soreness. Using a cool-down drill as a less intense form of activity at the end of class helps to flush out waste products produced by working muscles.

The cool-down is a good time to do a stretching component because the muscles are already warm and the joints are well-lubricated. A stretching cool-down is a good way to enhance venous return, promote waste removal and release muscular tension. Additionally, a stretching component to the cool-down can enhance the overall psychological state of relaxation after intense effort and promote physiological well-being.

ii) **Psychological**: If a cool-down is not employed as an integral part of the lesson plan, the intended effect of an intense and rewarding physical activity can marred by a sense of disappointment rather than a sense of euphoria and enthusiasm. When we are physically active the release of endorphins raises our level of arousal. If we have to stop what we are doing without a cool-down, those same endorphins are still cruising through the body and we are eager to keep going. So without a cool down, instead of feeling good when we leave class, we actually leave class feeling a sense of disappointment.

Nutrition: We are all familiar with the analogy of the human body to a car engine, and an athlete to a high performance racing car. No one expects a car to run with clogged fuel lines, poor quality gas and without regular oil changes or maintenance. The human body works in much the same way; the quality of the fuel that we take in has a lot to do with our efficiency and our ability to do work. Extreme media-related and societal pressures affect our dietary habits and frequently it takes a great deal of effort and even a force of will to replace soda with a glass of water, or cut out salt, sugar, refined flour, high fructose corn syrup, artificial flavors, artificial colorings and preservatives from our diets. As martial arts instructors, however, we cannot expect our students to perform at their best unless we also give guidance when it comes to the foods that they are eating (Nurchis, 2002).

Purpose and Components of Good Nutrition: The purpose of nutrition is four-fold:

i) Build body tissues.

ii) Repair body tissues.

iii) Provide the body with energy.

iv) Maintain body functions.

When a body does not receive sufficient, or appropriate fuel for the required work, it starts to cannibalize its own proteins (Glazier, 2002a), which means that by studying levels activity and comparing them to caloric intake it is possible to establish dietary norms for a particular student. Depending upon age, size and level of activity a human needs between 2,000 to 3,000 calories of energy every day to function efficiently. The figures are generalizations and only serve as a guide for comparison. Highly conditioned athletes may require a higher caloric input because they are so much more active than "average" people. As an example, according to Nurchis (2002), Judo players may need from 750 to 900 calories **per hour of training** in order to maintain their performance level. Having said that, some (not always accurate) assumptions are often made with regard to the suggested caloric intake values:

i) Women will plot at the lower end of the caloric range than men.

ii) Children will require a higher caloric intake for body and mind development.

iii) Larger people will require a higher caloric intake just to move the larger mass.

iv) Older people will require less caloric intake because they are less active.

v) Athletes and people engaged in occupations involving high levels of physical labor or exertion will require a higher caloric intake because they are more active.

A typical diet is composed of six main components. Fats, carbohydrates and proteins can be referred to as "macronutrients", whereas vitamins and minerals are often referred to as "micronutrients":

i) **Fats**: Another word for fats is "lipid". In, fact a "fat" is a solid lipid at room temperature and a liquid lipid is an "oil" at room temperature. Lipids are a necessary part of any diet. Lipids play a vital role in building our cellular membranes, and our brain and nervous tissues. Fats also aid in the absorption of certain vitamins that are essential for proper body functioning. Fat cells are also stored as an energy reserve. Dietary "fats" are of great interest to the health community because of the differences between unsaturated fats and saturated fats, which are considered to be "good" and "bad" respectively.

ii) **Carbohydrates**: Carbohydrates include all the sugars and starches. Also included within the carbohydrate group are all the indigestible fibers (such as cellulose, which is insoluble and pectin, which is soluble) that we eat. The body generates energy by consuming carbohydrate molecules. Carbohydrates are broken down during digestion and transported by the blood (primarily as glucose) to the liver and the muscles. Glucose is stored in both of these sites as glycogen, and it is the muscular glycogen stores that are used to fuel muscular activity. Glycogen is released from the liver stores to maintain sufficiently high levels of blood glucose for delivery to the brain and the muscles so that neither brain function nor muscular function is impaired. You may recall from the beginning of this chapter, that anaerobic pathways consume glycogen without the aid of oxygen; whereas aerobic pathways obtain the energy from glycogen with the aid oxygen.

iii) **Proteins**: Proteins are important in the construction of many body components, including muscles, bones (collagen), ligaments, tendons, skin, hair, nails and blood. Proteins are built from building blocks called amino acids, of which there are about twenty that are significant for human protein construction. Eight of these amino acids are considered essential. Body proteins are in a constant state of flux because new proteins are being made to replace old proteins. Under stressful conditions, the body can use its own proteins as a fuel from which to derive energy.

iv) **Vitamins**: Humans need about a dozen vitamins, to function normally. Some of the vitamins dissolve in fats, some in water. The B complex of vitamins and Vitamin C are water-soluble. Vitamins A, D, E & K are fat-soluble. Each vitamin permits very specific reactions to occur within the body. If the vitamin is not present, the reaction is impaired. Vitamin overdoses can present just as much of a health risk as vitamin deficiencies. Vitamins act mostly as catalysts to chemical reactions, because they can affect the rate of reaction but are not consumed by the reaction. Normally, we only need small quantities of each vitamin in our daily diet and there are "recommended **dietary** allowances" (USDA RDA) for each vitamin. When you read an RDA label on a food item you will, however, be reading the "recommended **daily** allowances." Vitamins, like proteins, need to be replaced on a regular basis.

v) **Minerals**: The body needs at least twenty minerals to function effectively. Some of these are needed in "trace" amounts (for instance Selenium and Cobalt); others are needed in larger amounts (for instance Phosphorous and Calcium). Minerals are normally what are called "inorganic" elements other than the four main elements used in the construction of "organic" molecules (Carbon, Hydrogen, Oxygen and Nitrogen). Like Vitamins, the minerals have very specific functions. Some are used in the construction of body tissues; others are required for the correct operation of specific biochemical pathways within the cells. Also, in the same way as vitamin deficiencies, mineral deficiencies can result in functional or developmental impairment and overabundance can be toxic.

vi) **Water**: Water is essential to life. As much as half to three quarters of the body is composed of water so dehydration can be a life-threatening condition. Although difficult to measure for the instructor, clinical studies show that as little as a 5% reduction in the amount of body water can seriously affect athletic performance. The reason water is so important is because many of the chemical reactions that occur in the body do so in water. The body loses water through breathing, urine and sweat. It is, therefore, critical that water reserves be continually replenished and the harder a person works, the more important it is to replace lost water and keep the body hydrated.

Now, if we examine the foods we eat we can break them down into six major groups:

i) Milk and milk products contain proteins, minerals, vitamins and fats.

ii) Breads and cereal grains are composed of carbohydrates, vitamins and fats.

iii) Meats and meat substitutes are a primary source of proteins, fats, minerals and vitamins.

iv) Fruits and vegetables contain mostly carbohydrates and some vitamins.

v) Nuts and beans are a significant source of protein, fats and some vitamins.

vi) Fats, oils and sweets contain mostly fats and refined carbohydrates.

The goal of a healthy diet is to maintain water, protein, vitamin and mineral intake while at the same time minimizing saturated fats and placing more emphasis on whole grain, intact, unprocessed carbohydrates (Nurchis, 2002; Willett, 2001). For instance, a typical diet in western society may contain as much as 40% (saturated and unsaturated) fat and only 45% carbohydrate with 15% protein (Martens, 1990; Powers and Howley, 1990). These percentage, however, obscure some of the truth. Lumping fats together as a single percentage is not a good idea because unsaturated fats have proven health benefits whereas diets that are rich in the saturated fats found in meats and dairy products lead to health problems (Nurchis, 2002; Willett, 2001). Unsaturated fats including "HDL" (high density lipoprotein) cholesterol are found in nuts, olives and avocadoes, and have been shown to assist in preventing blood clotting within the arteries, reducing the development of erratic heartbeats, helping the blood vessel linings to handle stress and supporting brain function. Consequently, simply replacing fat with carbohydrate is not necessarily a good thing because the reduction of total fats in the diet brings with it the loss of unsaturated (good) fats (Willett, 2001). Another problem with carbohydrates in today's world is that we eat so-called "refined" sugars that are quickly absorbed into the blood and can raise glucose and insulin levels in the blood, leading to greater risk of non-genetic diabetes and other cardiovascular problems (Willett, 2001). In reality, what we mean by "refined" is that much of what we really need from whole grains and cereals has been "refined" out. The key here is to eat as close to nature as possible. Aim to eat whole grains, fruits and vegetables, intact and unprocessed. Remember also that the primary role of carbohydrates in the body is primarily energy production. The direct outcome for people who are inactive is that they will be putting the fuel in, but driving nowhere (to return to our car analogy). It is therefore easy to see why high carbohydrate/low fat diets do not necessarily help a person to control weight.

Consequently, the essential components of a healthy diet might include (Willett, 2001):

i) Replacing saturated fats with unsaturated fats.

ii) Replacing refined carbohydrates with whole grain carbohydrates.

iii) Eating a wider choice of proteins, trading red meat for nuts, chicken, fish and beans.

iv) Eating plenty of fruit and vegetables.

v) Drinking a lot of water.

If you are going to supplement your diet with minerals and vitamins it is better to take them in the form that your body can absorb (Cochran, 2001). The goal of taking mineral and vitamin supplements is to make up for any deficiencies in the diet and to get them into the blood stream so that they can be distributed to the places where they will be required. It is essential, therefore, that any vitamin and mineral supplements be balanced to the needs of the athlete and taken in appropriate amounts (Nurchis, 2002). Many solid capsule and pill supplements do not get digested in the alimentary canal and are consequently voided before they do any good. It is better to take dietary supplements that are readily digestible such as gelcaps or powder-filled caplets. Minerals are best taken in colloidal suspension and not as solid pills, because many of the minerals are used by the body in their ionic form and are more effectively taken in solution. Bare-Grounds (2001) and Willett (2001) both recommend a multi-vitamin supplement "to be on the safe side." Very detailed advice concerning a large number of supplements used by athletes is given by Headley and Massad (1999). It is an unfortunate reality that intense agricultural practices (Brown, 2009) have depleted the quality of the soils in which we grow our food; therefore, the crops contain fewer of the essential minerals, making mineral supplements a necessary part of the dietary support system.

Beyond the basics of diet, however, our students will have specific needs according to the types of training in which they are involved. Certainly, the diet of a high-performance athlete will require both increased water intake and higher carbohydrate intake to offset fluid loss and energy output. It is also possible that activities, which lead to building or repairing muscle tissue, will require protein-enriched diets. It is clear then, that an athlete's diet will need to change according to the:

i) Seasonality of training.

ii) Energy requirements of training.

iii) Intensity and frequency of training.

Pre- and Post-Tournament Nutrition: Diet on its own will not allow a player to turn in a stellar performance in competition. Conversely, eating a poor diet or not considering the energy needs of the performance before a tournament can easily affect match performance (Nurchis, 2002). If you coach competitors it is important to recognize that during performance the blood is diverted from digestion to muscular activity (Powers and Howley, 1990). It is therefore better encourage your athletes to eat several hours before a work out or tournament, so that the body has time to digest the meal (Glover, 1996; Martens, 1990).

One of the pre-tournament dietary myths that has been common for many years is that "carbohydrate loading" can lead to better performance (Cochran, 2001; Martens, 1990; NCCP, 1979; Powers and Howley, 1990). Classical carbohydrate loading involves having a very long work out (to deplete the muscular glycogen stores) about a week before a tournament, followed by three days of low carbohydrate meals (and continued workouts) and then three days of high carbohydrate meals (to "supercharge" the glycogen stores). Modified carbohydrate loading does not emphasize the three days of depletion while continuing to work out, which can be extremely difficult for the athlete and lead to fatigue and irritability, dizziness and nausea as well as loss of appetite, blood chemistry imbalances and other metabolic changes in order to find fuel sources for both brain and muscle activity (Boeckner, 1998; Burke, 1998). If your players are already eating enough carbohydrates to meet the energy needs of their performance, it is unlikely that carbohydrate loading will be of any benefit. According to NISMAT (2002) carbohydrate loading is only of use when athletic performance is going to last more than 90 minutes and exhaustion is possible. Moreover, some authors (Cochran, 2001; Coyne, 2003) indicate that recent research emphasizes that if blood glucose levels can be maintained, then carbohydrate loading is unnecessary for most athletes, and may in fact only be beneficial for untrained players. The pre-tournament meal should, therefore, be about 500-1,000 calories (Glover, 1996; Nurchis, 2002; Powers and Howley, 1990) balanced, rich in whole grain and complex carbohydrates but low in fiber, low in proteins and low in fats (emphasizing unsaturated fats over saturated fats).

During the tournament there will be two major dietary needs: Maintaining hydration and keeping the glycogen stores topped up. These needs can be met by drinking 8-16oz of water in the hour before a match and eating small quantities (a few ounces) of complex carbohydrates per hour during the tournament day (Bare-Grounds, 2001). Maintaining high levels of blood glucose and preventing dehydration will promote higher levels of performance during the competition day. Dehydration resulting in the loss of water equal to 2% of an athlete's body weight can negatively impact performance due to increased demands that the loss places on the circulatory system. When dehydration occurs, the blood is more viscous and there is less of it, both of which mean that the heart has to work harder to maintain adequate flow to the brain and working muscles. Dehydration also leads to elevated core temperatures and an increasing difficulty in regulating body temperature (Haymes and Wells, 1986).

During the tournament, sports drinks, energy bars and whole fruit are favorites among competitors, but simple, refined sugars (especially candy and sodas) should be avoided. Some sports drinks contain a large amount of sucrose-based corn syrup and high fructose corn syrup, so it is often better to read the labels first or drink water and eat natural, carbohydrates and fruits. Complex hormonal and circulatory changes occur with the onset of physical activity, which cause the blood to be re-routed to the areas of highest need. Eating little during the tournament is, therefore, better than eating a meal between bouts because there is a finite amount of blood in the body and when it is required to do muscular work, it is diverted from digestion. Powers and Howley (1990), indicate that during exercise, cardiac output (amount of blood pumped by the heart per unit time) may increase five-fold to 25 liters per minute over the resting cardiac output of only 5 liters per minute. Also, at rest while 25% goes to the gastrointestinal tract and 15% goes to the brain, only 15-20% goes to the muscles. During activity only 3-5% goes to the digestive system, 3-5% goes to the brain and a whopping 80% goes to the muscles.

Typical coaching wisdom tells us that after tournament the body has two major needs and a secondary need:

i) Replace lost fluids and the electrolytes lost in sweat.

ii) Replace depleted glycogen stores with carbohydrates.

iii) Repair damaged tissues with proteins.

Accordingly, the most immediate post-tournament needs are to drink fluids, replace the glycogen stores by ingesting high quality carbohydrates and make sure that the electrolytes lost during the tournament are present in the fluids and foods that the athlete consumes. The main electrolytes lost in sweat include sodium and chlorine although magnesium, potassium and zinc are also lost in lesser amounts (Glover, 1996; Haymes and Wells, 1986). The main point here is that as body water volume is decreased during sweating, the **actual concentrations of electrolytes will increase**, because they are being lost at a lower rate than the water. It is far more important to replace the fluids than the electrolytes (Haymes and Wells, 1986). For the purposes of replenishing the glycogen stores and rehydrating the body, return to the advice of Willett (2001), and recommend to your competitors that they eat a balanced meal including unprocessed, intact, complex carbohydrate-rich foods and drink plenty of water.

Body Composition and Maintaining Weight: It is clear that not all human bodies are the same. According to a classical study by Sheldon involving a study of 4,000 male college students in 1940, there are three distinct physique types:

i) Endomorphs: Soft, round, people with a large digestive tract.

ii) Mesomorphs: People with a relative preponderance of muscular tissues.

iii) Ectomorphs: Thin, lanky people, with a high surface area to volume ratio.

The study in itself is not necessarily indicative of what is "good" and what is "bad" (Powers and Howley, 1990) because it is possible to change body type by making behavioral changes in diet and exercise. Although there may be a genetic component to body typing, each person's body type can be as much to do with lifestyle as genetics. What is most important is to gain some idea of how much fat each of your players is carrying and establishing whether or not the fat percentage is healthy. Given that *excess* weight is stored as fat tissue, a high fat percentage relative to **age** (for an adult) indicates that the athlete is overweight. Children go through growth spurts at different ages, and it is, therefore, unwise to use fat percentages as indicative of obesity in children. In the cases of children, lifestyle and developmental history will be much more helpful in determining whether or not a child with a high percentage of fat is obese.

In finding the ideal weight for your athletes, there is a simple test, which can be administered (Abernethy et al., 1997; ACSM, 1995), called the Body Mass Index (BMI). The Body Mass Index is calculated by dividing weight in kilograms by the athlete's height in meters squared (wt/ht^2). The desirable range of BMI for both adult men and women is 19-24.9 kg/m^2. ACSM (1998) produces a chart, which provides the BMI in a matrix of weight plotted against height. Be aware though that protein (lean muscle mass) is denser (heavier per unit volume) than fatty tissues, elite athletes will tend to be heavier per unit height and, therefore, generate a higher BMI than is shown as being healthy on the ACSM chart.

If we are going to build a long-term plan for the development of our students, then it is important for us to know what is healthy for them in terms of their performance weight. The next step, therefore, is to either get to, or maintain, the desired weight. A prescription of activities, attention to diet and even lifestyle changes may be necessary to change a student's weight. If you are not an expert in nutrition, then consult with one so that you can ensure that any weight gain or loss is done in an appropriate fashion. There are however some simple, common sense rules that you can apply:

i) **Do not change weight, just for competition**. Our athletes should change weight because it is a healthy choice. For some coaches, working with elite athletes, weight changes for competitive purposes may be necessary, but do not lose sight of the fact that the competitor should return to his or her normal weight after the tournament season.

ii) Make weight changes gradually. Plan ahead if one of your competitors needs to change weight divisions. An athlete should "make weight" with plenty of time before the tournament, so that your player will feel comfortable moving at the new weight. We're talking weeks here, not days.

iii) Do not cut weight at the expense of endurance. If a competitor has to lose weight, then monitor endurance performance as the weight drops. If your player starts to lose stamina, re-evaluate the **rate** of weight loss and adjust the diet accordingly. Check with a nutrition expert to find out what is an appropriate rate of weight loss.

iv) Burning about 3,500 calories is equivalent to a one-pound weight loss and the difference between calories in and calories burned should not be greater than 1,000 per day for optimum weight loss, without loss of endurance (Martens, 1990).

v) If weight gains are required, monitor the diet components carefully and combine increases in food consumption with an increase in the prescription requirement for anaerobic activities such as a strength training program, so that new body mass is added as lean muscle, not fat.

vi) If you want to increase muscle mass, it will be necessary to increase the percentage of proteins in the diet.

vii) If weight gain is the objective, it is better to graze with several small, well-balanced meals each day. Conversely, if weight loss is needed, eat only at meal times. Eliminate snacks.

viii) To increase weight, it might be necessary to use a lighter prescription of aerobic endurance training. Be careful here, because you do not want to compromise performance.

ix) Keep a daily log so that you as the coach, and the athlete both know how many calories are being taken in as part of the daily diet and know how many calories are being burned in exercise. The difference will either be translated into weight loss or weight gain.

x) Know the calorific value of the foods your players are eating. Know the calorific demands of the workouts in which your players are engaged. Keep records.

xi) Don't use hormone or steroid therapies to either gain or lose weight.

xii) Do not eat to satisfaction. Digestion is promoted by not being completely full at the end of the meal.

xiii) Get professional assistance from a certified nutritionist and work with your students so that they understand what is needed.

Injury and Recovery: Even if your athletes are fit and well-fed, there may still be times when training or performance situations lead to injury. The first thing to mention in this section, therefore, is that unless you hold a specific qualification in the medical field (such as an EMT, MD or RN), you are not a qualified expert in the area of diagnosis and treatment either legally or medically. As a martial arts instructor however, you will probably find yourself in the position of being required to administer first aid and recognize when an injury needs medical attention. Often you will be the first responder in an emergency situation and the choices that you make in those critical moments can have far reaching effects. It is for these reasons that coaches are urged take First Aid and CPR courses on a regular basis.

You should expect to treat minor cuts, scrapes, bruises and abrasions that are a natural part of martial arts training. Unless you are a qualified medical professional however, you should **not** treat any suspected joint, muscle, bone or head injury. Gary Berliner MD, an international-level Judo competitor, referee and coach gave me this statement several years ago, and it bears careful study:

"Treatment, as such, implies that the provider is the primary care-giver and adequately suited and trained for complete management of [the] injury, to include recognition of complications which may ensue, that services may be remunerative, that judgment must be exercised for the necessity of further testing, referral to specialists, or tertiary care" (Gary Berliner M.D., Pers. Comm., 2001).

When we talk about being a provider of emergency assistance, however, we are referring to your ability to do four things (American Red Cross, 1993; Handal, 1992):

i) Follow an Emergency Action Plan.

ii) Check the injured person's ABC's (airway, breathing, circulation). Ensure that the player is breathing freely, has a pulse and check for bleeding.

iii) Ensure that an injured person is as stable and comfortable as possible.

iv) Sustain the well-being of the injured player to the best of your ability until Emergency Medical Service providers arrive.

When the injury is beyond the realm of simple first aid, obtain medical assistance as soon as possible, or advise the student to do so if the need is not immediate. In essence it is your responsibility to do no more and no less than you are **qualified** to do for the injured student. Let us suppose that a student breaks a bone in your class and the bone is protruding through the skin. Although you are not qualified to reset the bone; as a first aid provider, you should immobilize the injured limb to prevent further trauma, do what you can to control the bleeding, calm the patient, keep him or her as comfortable as possible and activate the EMS (Emergency Medical Services). As soon as possible complete an accident report as part of the student's permanent file.

Glossary of terms: Before we get too involved our discussion, it might be a good idea to create a frame of reference to which you can refer, and which covers many of the terms that you will encounter when dealing with athlete injury.

Abrasion: Abrasions are most commonly frictional scrapes to the outer layers of the skin. Abrasions can involve the exposure of, and oozing of blood from the capillary bed.

Acute Injury: Generally sudden injuries to skin, muscles, tendons, ligaments, bones, blood vessels, nerve fibers and /or internal organs.

Artery: Blood vessel, which carries blood away from the heart.

Avulsion: An avulsion occurs when soft tissue is completely torn away from its connection to another body part.

Blister: A fluid filled sac between skin layers.

Bruise: Injury resulting from bleeding within the skin layers and/or the muscular tissues.

Break: See fracture.

Bursa: Bursae are fluid filled sacs found between bones, muscles and tendons and are intended to reduce the friction generated as the different types of tissue move against one another during movement.

Bursitis: An inflammation of a bursa. Bursitis occurs when a bursa is irritated and swells.

Capillary: Small blood vessel that feeds the body tissues and is the primary sites of gas, nutrient and waste exchange between the blood and the tissues.

Cartilage: Gristly tissue that occurs at the ends of bones. It protects the surface of the bone, absorbs the force of impact and protects the bones when they rub against each other during joint activity.

Chronic Injury: Generally long-term injuries resulting from extended wear and tear. Chronic injuries are often also called "overuse" injuries in many textbooks, but overuse is only one aspect of chronic injury. An untreated acute injury such as a sprain or a strain may also become a chronic problem if not treated properly when it first occurs.

Concussion: A concussion results in a temporary impairment to the brain function. Frequently, concussions are an acute brain injury resulting from a blunt force trauma to the brain when it makes contact with the inside of the skull and cause actual brain damage.

Contusion: A medical term for a bruise.

Convulsion: see Seizures.

Dislocation: The result of the forceful separation of bones where they meet at a joint. Hitting or twisting the joint may apply a dislocating force, causing the bones to move out of their natural position and remain out of position after the force has been removed. Dislocations will also generally involve the straining of muscles and tendons and spraining of ligaments associated with the joint.

Fracture: A fracture is a crack, break, splintering or shattering of a bone. Open fractures break through the surface of the skin, closed fractures do not.

    i)   Simple Fractures: A simple fracture is a break in which the bone is almost always broken into two pieces.

    ii)   Compound Fractures: In a compound fracture, the bone is broken and at least one end of the break is protruding through the skin.

    iii)   Comminuted Fracture: Fractures that result in bones being broken in several places along their length.

    iv)   Complicated Fractures: Complicated fractures involve not only the breaking of a bone, but also involve collateral nerve or blood vessel damage.

    v)   Greenstick Fracture: A greenstick fracture is one in which the bone splinters or splits along one side only, but does not break all the way through.

    vi)   Stress Fracture: Stress fractures are the result of repeated minor traumas that lead to the formation of small cracks in the outer layers of the bone. Continued trauma leads to the development of more cracks and can possibly result in sufficient weakening of the bone that a relatively minor incident can cause the total fracture of the bone.

Hemorrhage: Extensive bleeding, internal or external.

Incision: An open cut, with straight edges that exposes tissues below the skin. Incisions tend to bleed freely.

Joint: Places where bones meet. Joints frequently (but not always) permit a range of movement between the bones. For the purposes of this course we can think of joints as being complex musculo-skeletal articulations often involving muscles, tendons, ligaments, bursae, cartilage and bones.

Laceration: A jagged cut or skin tear. Lacerations, like incisions, will bleed freely.

Ligament: Flexible, non-elastic soft tissues that join bone-to-bone.

Nausea: A feeling of sickness, which may or may not be accompanied with active vomiting.

Puncture: A puncture is a stab wound. The entry point is normally small, but this is no indicator of the severity of the puncture. Shallow punctures penetrate the skin, whereas deep punctures may penetrate muscles and internal organs.

Rupture: A rupture is a complete tear involving soft tissues. Ruptures can affect muscles, tendons, ligaments, cartilage and/or internal organs. See also: Sprains and strains. Third degree sprains and strains are the most severe injuries to ligaments and tendons respectively and result in complete tearing of these tissues.

Seizure: A seizure involves abnormally high levels of electrical impulses from the brain to the muscles. Seizures often involve sudden involuntary muscle contractions and diminished awareness.

Shock: Shock occurs when, due to trauma, the body restricts blood flow (and therefore oxygen) to the extremities of the body. The intent of this automatic response is to protect the brain and internal organs. The result can be irreversible tissue damage and under extreme circumstances can lead to death.

Spasm: Involuntary muscle contraction.

Sprain: A sprain is caused by stretching, tearing or rupturing of ligaments that hold bones together. First degree sprains are minor sprains involving stretching and possibly micro-fiber tears; severe sprains involving the tearing of ligaments are third degree sprains.

Strain: A strain is caused by stretching, tearing or rupturing of muscles and/or tendons. First degree strains are minor strains involving stretching and possibly micro-fiber tears; severe strains involving the tearing of muscles or tendons are third degree strains.

Subluxation: Normally an acute injury in which a bone is forced out of joint and then immediately returns to its original position. A Subluxation may occur when a joint is hit or twisted, causing the joint to distort and the bones to move out of position. Although the bones return to their original positions, subluxation will often involve spraining of the ligaments that hold the joint together. Since ligaments are non-elastic, severe sprains can increase the likelihood of repeated subluxation and the development of a chronic condition.

Tendon: Tendons are the tough, narrow, elastic ends of a muscle, which attach the muscle to a bone.

Tendonitis: An inflammation of the tendons. Frequently, tendonitis is the result of overuse or may also result from excessive expectations in the use of weak muscles.

Vein: Blood vessel that carries blood towards the heart.

Type of injuries: In a discussion of injury and rehabilitation, we can separate three distinct types:

i) **Acute injuries**. The most common acute injuries that affect martial artists will tend to fall into three groups:

   a. Abrasions, cuts, scratches and burns, which affect the body surface.

   b. Strains, sprains and breaks, which affect the muscles, bones and joints.

   c. Concussions, which affect the brain.

ii) **Chronic Injuries**. Chronic injuries tend to occur because of inattention to a minor, acute injury or inadequate rehabilitation time.

iii) **Other medical situations**. These would include other disorders that the coach may have to face, such as problems related to heat and or cold, dehydration and other environmentally mediated conditions. The coach may also have to deal with genetic and non-genetic conditions such as diabetes and asthma.

I am not a medical professional, so I will only touch on some of these situations.

i) **Acute and Chronic Injuries**: Acute injuries that our students suffer during their activities tend to occur suddenly, but that does not mean that they were not preceded by a slow degeneration or weakness that built up over time. Think about what happens when a student suffers what s/he thinks is a minor injury during practice and shakes it off, and never gets medical attention. The original injury seems to heal (no more bruising, pain or swelling), but there is a deeper more chronic problem that should have been dealt with. An example might be when a student twists poorly during a throw or lands poorly from an aerial kick and "hurts" his knee. The knee swells, and the student sits out a couple of classes until the swelling goes down, but "feels" fine and comes back to class without seeking medical attention because there is a tournament at the end of the month and he doesn't want to miss it. Months later in class the knee "gives out" completely and the student collapses to the ground with the

"Terrible Triad": Anterior cruciate ligament (ACL) rupture, medial ligament rupture and medial meniscus tears. The first injury may have been a minor ACL tear, which weakened the knee, creating a chronic condition, but the last two injuries are acute injuries caused by the lack of proper care and rehabilitation of the original acute injury. **Do not attempt to be your own physician or orthopedist, get professional help.** It is much better to take what seems to be a minor acute injury to the doctor and get professional guidance than to assume that it is healed and risk a much greater injury, later.

ii) **Surface injuries**: The majority of abrasions, cuts, scratches and burns, which affect the surface of the body, can be considered minor, treatable events. For most of us, simply washing the wound with an antiseptic soap, applying an antibiotic cream and a covering with a sterile dressing will be sufficient (Flegel, 1992). The majority of cuts and scratches in the martial arts are caused by finger and toe nails or by uncontrolled or accidental strikes. Martial artists also suffer from various types of abrasions and burns that can often be related to the uniform being repeatedly pulled across the skin or friction burns from the mat surface (especially to the back of the foot in grappling classes). Friction burns should be covered with a sterile dressing and kept clean and dry. They will tend to weep and the dressing will have to be of a kind that will not stick to wound. Occasionally, longer or deeper cuts might require medical attention and need a suture or stitches. One other soft tissue injury that we should consider is trauma to the eye. Occasionally a student will get hit in the eye during sparring, throwing or groundwork and get a black eye. The immediate action after the impact, if no serious injury is suspected, should be to apply an ice pack over a towel to the eye to reduce swelling and have the student seek medical attention to ensure that no serious damage has been done. More serious trauma to the eye should be cause to activate the Emergency Medical System.

iii) **Musculoskeletal injuries**: Strains, sprains and breaks, which affect the muscles, tendons, ligaments, and bones, can be studied by examining the major joints in the body from head to foot. Again, remember that this manual is not intended to be a medical treatise; this is simply an overview of the more common injuries that your students may face when they are engaged in martial arts. There are several books to which you should refer concerning these types of injury (Canney, 1991; Estwanik, 1996; Grisogono, 1984; Micheli, 1995).

a. **Neck**: Injuries to the neck can have dramatic and potentially life-threatening or life-altering consequences. Obviously, the neck is the site of major structures such as the cervical vertebra (Figure 6.10), the spinal cord and other nerves, the esophagus, the trachea, and major blood vessels to and from the brain.

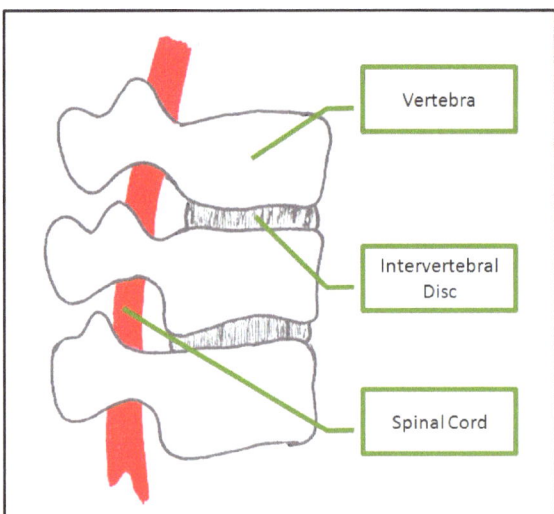

Figure 6.10: Simplified vertebral column.

Damage to the spine can lead to permanent paralysis and even death. When the cervical vertebrae are damaged, a dislocation between the vertebrae may sever the spinal cord and paralyze the body from the dislocation downward (Figure 6.11). A fractured vertebra, however, can cut through the spinal cord and also cause paralysis. Moving the injured person's head will initiate movement of the vertebra and can have dire consequences. **<u>Never</u> move a suspected neck injury, activate the EMS immediately.**

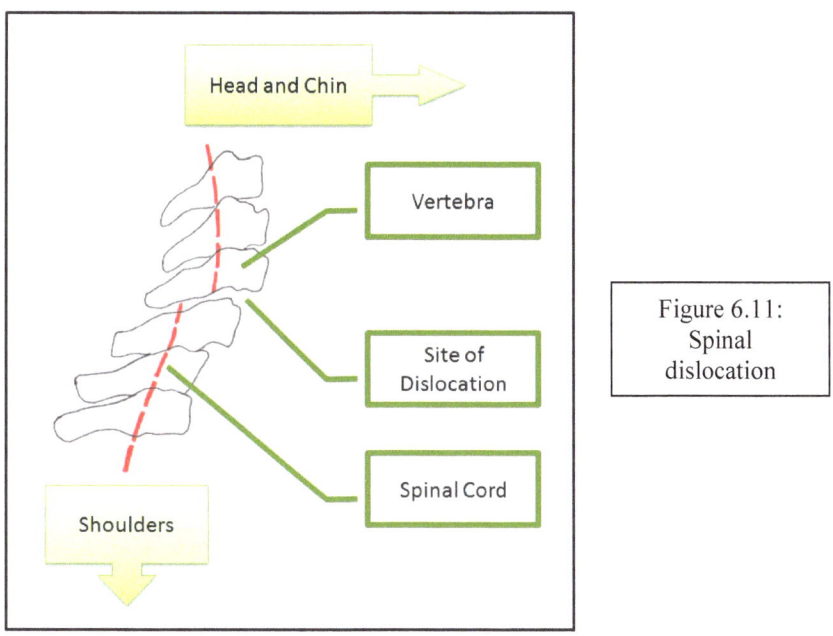

Figure 6.11: Spinal dislocation

b. **Shoulder**: A-C (acromio-clavicular) joint separations, collarbone fractures and rotator cuff injuries are the most common types of Judo injuries that affect the shoulder (Kujala 1995). The A-C joint is held together by muscles, tendons and ligaments. The relationship between the humerus, clavicle and scapula are very complex and do not easily fit the image of a hinge joint like the elbow or a ball and socket joint like the hip. The collarbone simply sits above the head of the humerus and the in front of the scapula (Figure 6.12).

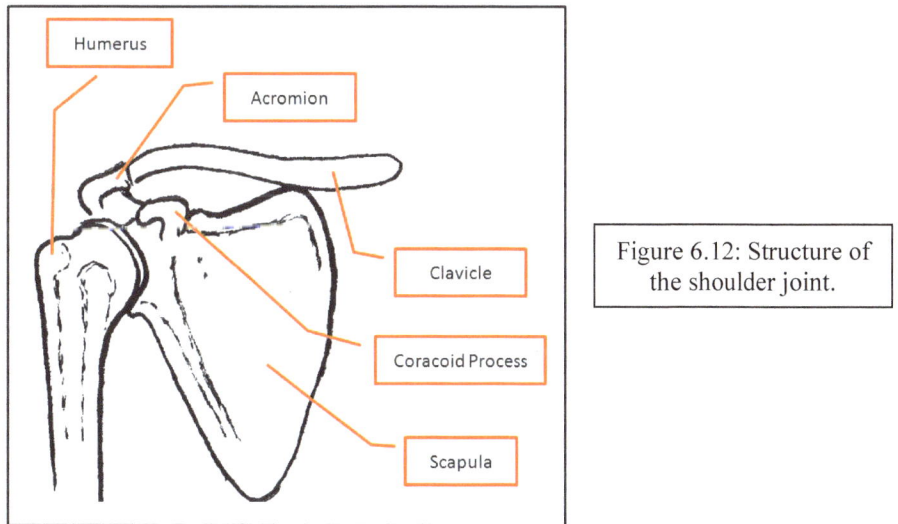

Figure 6.12: Structure of the shoulder joint.

Muscles, tendons and ligaments hold the whole structure together. Typically an A-C separation means that the ligaments that hold the clavicle in place have been torn. Under such conditions the clavicle is no longer attached by ligaments to the scapula (Figure 6.13). Clearly then, martial artists involved in throwing and grappling are susceptible to A-C joint injuries when they fall on the shoulder or take a particularly hard fall and the A-C joint takes the full force of the impact. A-C injuries need medical attention; certainly an X-ray should be taken to gain an appreciation of the degree of sprain or separation. It would be good at this point to mention two great principles of injury management: The first principle is **Immobilize and Transport**. When you suspect a sprain or separation of any joint, immobilize the joint and/or the patient and transport to a medical facility by activating the EMS (Flegel, 1992; Handal, 1992). The second principle is **PRICE**, which is an acronym for **P**rotect, **R**est, **I**ce **C**ompression and **E**levation (Flegel, 1992).

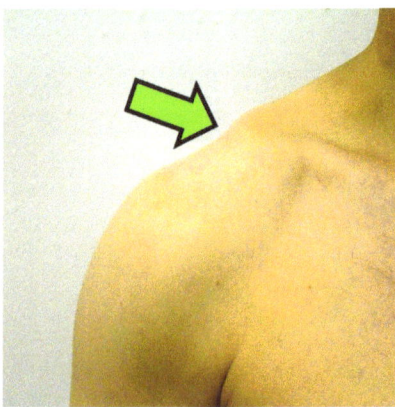

Figure 6.13: A-C separation

Collarbone fractures need immediate medical attention and are typically caused by falling or rolling incorrectly and transferring the force of the impact along the collarbone in such a manner that it breaks. The rotator cuff is a group of four muscles that hold the head of the humerus in place during punching, throwing, pinning and rolling drills. They are damaged when the bursa, which overlies the muscles, gets swollen and pinches the muscle compartment. Continued activity can then lead to tendon damage and eventually a rotator cuff tear.

The last shoulder injury is the dislocation of the joint. You probably know someone whose shoulder is "double-jointed" and seems able to move the joint in and out of position freely with no discomfort. Subluxations of the shoulder occur when the head of the humerus pulls out of the socket and then reseats itself. They are no less important than a full dislocation in which the humerus does not go back to its original position. Subluxations and dislocations need medical attention and may involve ligament damage. **Do not attempt to pop the joint back into place because injury to the surrounding nerves and blood vessels could result. Follow the first principle: Immobilize and transport.**

c. **Elbow**: The elbow is a hinge joint that allows the radius and ulna bones of the lower arm to articulate with the humerus bone of the upper arm. The ROM for the joint is normally from $0°$ with the arm straight (extended) to about $140°$ with the arm bent (fully flexed). Problems occur when we exceed the ROM of the joint. Typically this occurs when the elbow is hyperextended as can happen during the application of arm-locks or overextending a punch. Since arm-locks are common in a lot of martial arts styles, damage can occur when the lock is applied too quickly (Figure 6.14), with too much force or when a student refuses to tap out once the lock has been applied. Hyperextensions can also be caused when a student reaches for the mat to take a fall and the impact of both students is absorbed through a locked elbow. If the fall is fast enough and has enough force, the elbow can be dislocated and the radius and ulna bone can be fractured. Hyperextensions of the elbow can cause ligament sprains and tendon strains. If enough force is applied tearing of ligaments and tendons can occur. Initial treatment of minor strains and sprains is going to be PRICE, but it is wise to see an orthopedist to check the injury. An acute tendon injury from a hyperextension can easily become chronic tendonitis without adequate rehabilitation. What is often referred to, as "Tennis Elbow" is a chronic injury caused by repeated poor biomechanical actions or overuse. TE affects the outside (lateral) tendons of the elbow and is most frequently caused where the student repeatedly overextends, and locks out the elbow at the end of the punch.

Figure 6.14: A combination throw to arm bar. Drills that involve joint locking actions should always be performed with due care and consideration to prevent injury.

d. **Wrist and Hand**: Wrist and hand injuries include broken and dislocated fingers, and sprained wrists. Sprained wrists can occur from punching a pad or a board with poor weapon alignment, from reaching for the mat during a fall and taking the force of the impact with the hand bent backwards. As with any joint action that moves beyond normal the ROM for the joint, ligament and tendon damage can result. PRICE is again, the answer for minor sprains and strains, but an X-Ray should be taken to ensure that the small bones of the wrist (the carpal bones) are not damaged or broken. Although finger dislocations and fractures may be painful, they tend not be life-threatening, so first aid can be applied by using an ice pack to reduce swelling, a bandage to support the hand and then making sure that the player seeks medical attention. Fingers get dislocated and broken in martial arts when players misalign a fist during punching drills against a hard target, when students jam fingers into the mat or get them caught in the jacket, sleeve or pants leg during throwing and grappling drills.

e. **Hip and thigh**: The hip joint is an immensely strong, ball and socket structure that involves the pelvic girdle and the femur. The head of the femur fits into a socket called the acetabulum. Due to its function as a weight-bearing and locomotory structure, the hip is fairly resistant to injury. Thigh injuries, however, tend to be associated with inadequate or insufficient warm-up followed by powerful throwing or kicking actions that can result in a hamstring tear for the student's supporting leg or a hip adductor. Hamstring tears frequently give pain at the insertion point of the muscle at the hip when the knee is extended and the hip is flexed. Hamstring tears also lead to bruising in the muscle depending upon the severity of the tear. The answer to such injuries is prevention through adequate warm-up exercises and rehabilitation using PRICE and muscle strengthening to prevent repeated injury. Chronic hip problems can result from repeated misalignment of the joint during kick actions, so pay particular attention to correct biomechanical action when teaching kicks. Remember that skills are learned and we can become very good at doing the wrong thing, if we do not get adequate correction during the early stages of learning.

f. **Knee**: The knee is perhaps the most vulnerable joint for martial arts of all types. The speed with which pivoting and rotational actions can occur during active training places tremendous stress on the knee. Stresses can be hyperextensions that lock the knee from front to back, lateral stresses that push the knee joint from one side, and rotational stresses that cause the upper leg to rotate over the lower leg. Typical knee injuries include cartilage and ligament tears and much more rarely knee dislocations. The "Terrible Triad" is an acute knee injury that tears the Anterior Cruciate Ligament, the Medial Collateral Ligament and the Medial Meniscus (Figure 6.15). Although a student can continue to be active even with an ACL separation, the knee is significantly destabilized and requires surgery to fix.

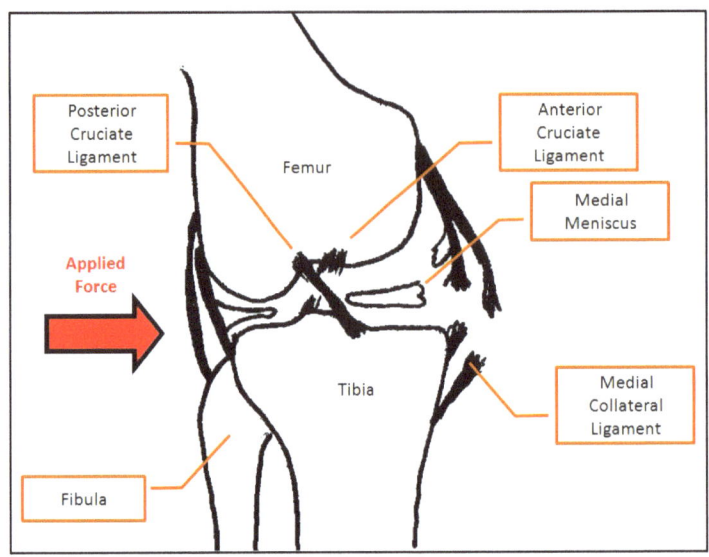

Figure 6.15: The "Terrible Triad."

Once cartilage is torn within the knee, it is vulnerable to folding over in the joint and may "lock" the joint, causing significant pain if the student attempts to change the angle at the joint. Moreover, a grinding sensation in the joint called "crepitus" is caused by the ends of the bones rubbing on each other and, therefore, indicative of cartilage damage. In recent years two supplements have been shown in clinical studies to promote the protection and repair of cartilaginous tissues. These supplements are Glucosamine sulfate and Chondroitin (Glazier, 2002b). Glucosamine stimulates the production of the molecules necessary for construction of cartilage and Chondroitin helps to form a gel-like substance that helps to give elasticity to the cartilage and increase the cushioning effect when the joint is active.

g. **Ankle and foot**: Typical ankle and foot injuries are sprained ankles and broken toes. Toes get broken when they get caught or twisted when students are turning or pivoting. Occasionally a student can break a toe from incorrect weapon formation when kicking a hard target (Figure 6.16). As with any broken joint, it is not a good idea to attempt to reset a broken toe, more damage can be done to blood vessels and nerves. Also, in much the same way as a broken finger is not a life-threatening condition, the best response is to apply the principle of PRICE, wrap the foot and immobilize the toes as best as possible and seek medical attention.

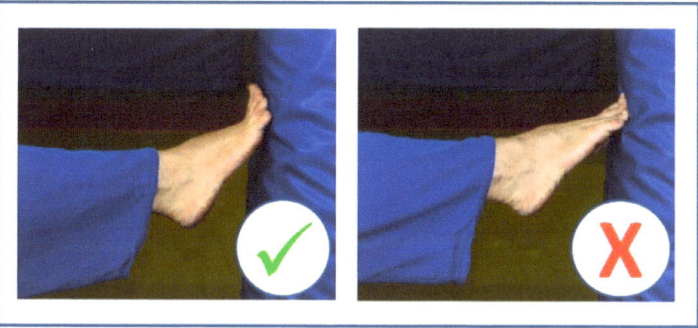

Figure 6.16: Good and poor weapon formation when kicking. Broken toes can result from poor weapon formation when kicking a hard target.

Ankle injuries are also normally caused during pivoting and frequently result in sprains. Severe sprains can lead to separations and ligament tears. There are three types of turning actions for ankles: Inversion (Figure 6.17), Eversion (Figure 6.18), and Plantar flexion (Figure 6.19). Inversion is when the medial border (big toe side) of the foot is raised and eversion of the foot occurs when the lateral border (little toe side) is raised. Eversion injuries, therefore, are caused when the body weight comes to rest on the inner edge of the foot and ankle, whereas inversion injuries tend to occur when the weight is pushed over the outside edge of the ankle and the blade edge of the foot. Plantar flexion injuries can occur when a player gets a foot caught under the body as s/he is moving forward, or in a ground position when the body is being pulled back over the foot while the toes are flat to the mat. Treatment of breaks and sprains would follow the twin principles of Immobilize and transport and PRICE. In the case of a sprain, the student should be advised to keep from weight-bearing until advised to do so by a qualified physician.

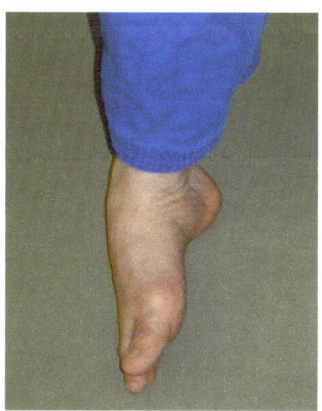

Figure 6.17: Inversion of the foot.

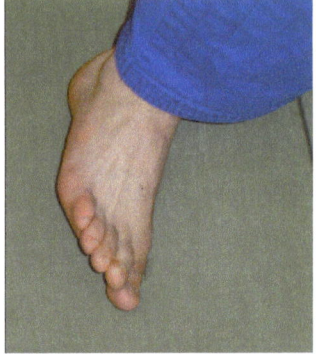

Figure 6.18: Eversion of the foot.

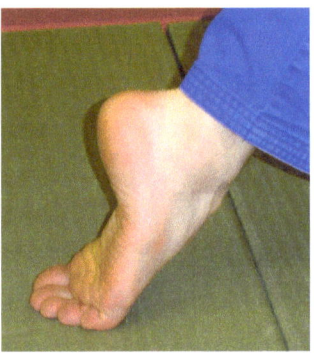

Figure 6.19: Plantar flexion.

iii) **Other medical and emergency conditions**:

a. **Heat Problems**: The body strives to maintain a condition called "homeostasis", which can be interpreted to be an optimal internal environment, despite external conditions (Haymes and Wells, 1986). When the internal temperature conditions get too high or low the body has problems and must re-establish the homeostatic conditions before metabolic problems develop. There are three heat-related conditions: heat cramps, heat exhaustion and heatstroke. Prevention of heat-related conditions involves giving your students time to acclimatize to high heat and humidity conditions as well as ensuring that they replace lost fluids. Remember that one of the ways in which the body cools itself is through evaporative heat loss via sweat. Failure to replace lost water will result in dehydration and other problems associated with more viscous blood. When the body is dehydrated, there is less actual blood volume, which means that the body has to work harder and the heart has to pump more often to maintain circulation to the working muscles.

The first stage of heat-related illness (Dominguez, 1979; Flegel, 1992) is the onset of heat cramps, which are severe muscle spasms resulting from dehydration. Rehydrate and you fix the heat cramps. The second stage is heat exhaustion, which is a shock-like condition resulting from an inability to cool the body associated with higher levels of dehydration. Symptoms of heat exhaustion include headaches, nausea, dizziness, chills, fatigue and excessive thirst. Students suffering from heat exhaustion have cold, clammy skin, dilated pupils, are sweating profusely and may experience a loss of coordination. It is important to cool the student's body and apply ice packs over a towel to the neck, armpits, back and stomach. If the student is conscious give water to drink. If the student does not improve or the conditions worsen, activate the EMS. In the third stage, which is heat stroke, the condition is severe enough to be life-threatening. In essence the core temperature has risen so far that the natural cooling mechanisms are unable to cope. The student is so dehydrated that s/he is no longer sweating. The dehydrated state has reached a level where the temperature control center in the brain has lost the ability to regulate body temperature. The student's skin will be hot, dry and red, the pupils will be small, the core temperature will be over $103°$ and there will be rapid breathing and a rapid pulse. The student may experience dizziness, confusion, diarrhea and vomiting, as well as seizures and loss of consciousness. Under extreme conditions the student can suffer from cardiac arrest. Heatstroke is a condition to be treated by the EMS, but until they arrive do everything that you can to lower the student's temperature. Apply ice packs and have the student drink cool water if s/he is still conscious. Monitor the ABC's and if necessary administer CPR. Make no mistake; heatstroke is a life-threatening condition (Flegel, 1992). It is your responsibility as a coach to monitor your student for signs of heat-related injury and deal with them early on, rather than allow heatstroke conditions to develop. Heatstroke is the result of a progressively worsening set of conditions for the student and each stage in the process has a series of clearly recognizable signs and symptoms.

b. **Concussion**: A concussion can be induced by any impact to the head and involves the temporary malfunction of the brain (Canney, 1991; Estwanik, 1996). In simple terms, the brain floats inside the skull, immersed in cerebrospinal fluid. When the head takes an impact, the brain does not move until it is pushed by the skull, and accelerates across the brain cavity. Likewise the brain will not stop moving until it reaches the opposite side of the skull and is decelerated by the second impact. Brain damage can, therefore, occur on **both** sides of the brain, not just the side of the initial traumatizing impact (Estwanik, 1996). Concussion involves the impairment of brain functioning, which means that a person does not have to be rendered unconscious to suffer a concussion. Concussions can result in a variety of symptoms including: Loss of short-term or long-term memory, short-term confusion and disorientation, dizziness, nausea, headaches, dazed and unfocussed eyes, double vision, ringing in the ears, inability to concentrate, inability to perform mental calculations, loss of eye muscle co-ordination, slurred speech and seizures.

If a concussion is suspected, do not ignore it. Get medical attention and do not allow the player to return to active participation until s/he has been released by a doctor. A significant point here is that if a second concussion occurs before the first one has healed, the damage can be ten times greater than the initial injury (Canney, 1991).

c. **Choking**: Choking does one of two things: it either compresses the airway or it shuts off the blood supply to the brain (Estwanik, 1996). The blood supply includes the carotid artery, which brings oxygenated blood to the brain and the jugular vein, which takes de-oxygenated blood away from the brain. Choking techniques used in Judo, Jujutsu and Hapkido normally attack the blood supply to the brain, thereby robbing it of essential oxygen (Figure 6.20). Properly applied, chokes can become effective in less than ten seconds. When a blood choke is applied a player will experience a narrowing of vision, ringing in the ears and then a loss of consciousness as a result of the restriction of oxygen to the brain. At this point the person being choked goes limp, although some people exhibit involuntary body spasms as they lose consciousness. In most martial arts styles that employ chokes, students have the option of tapping out.

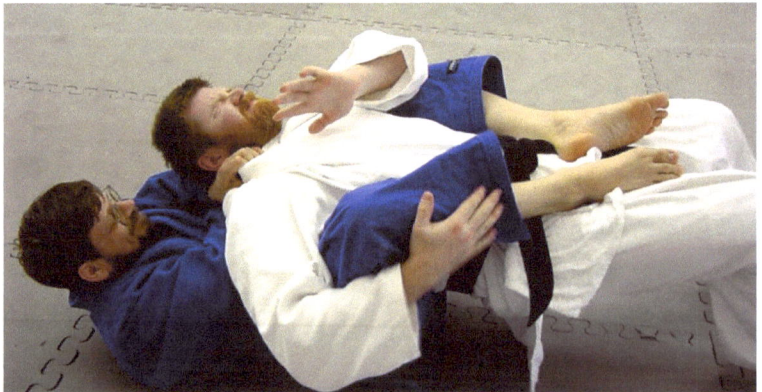

Figure 6.20: Demonstration of a blood choke from the rear, using the uniform to cut off the blood supply. Note the use of the feet to immobilize the hip block.

If a student does lose consciousness, then regaining consciousness is related to the ability to restore the blood flow (and therefore the oxygen supply) to the brain. The simplest way to accomplish this is to lay the student on his or her back, check the ABC's (Airway, Breathing and Circulation) and raise the feet. As a final comment about health risks involving choking techniques, there has been much interest in recent years concerning the incidence of strokes related to dislodging plaque from the carotid artery during blunt trauma (Moore, 2000). A "stroke" is a term used to describe any vascular injury to the brain and the compressional force applied during a choke is an example of a blunt trauma to the carotid artery.

d. **Diabetes**: Diabetes is associated with the inability of the body to correctly metabolize carbohydrates because there is not enough insulin. Insulin is produced by the pancreas and controls the uptake of glucose by body tissues. When insulin levels are compromised one of two conditions can occur: In hyperglycemia, there is too much glucose in the tissues and in hypoglycemia there is not enough. Normally, diabetes is controlled by careful attention to exercise and diet, although medication and in some cases insulin injections may also be needed (Bare-Grounds, 2001; Flegel 1992). Since insulin levels can be affected by exercises it is important to monitor your diabetic students for signs of diabetes-related problems. There are two possible scenarios to watch for. One is insulin shock the other is diabetic coma (Flegel, 1992). Insulin shock results from a sudden drop in glucose levels due to high insulin levels (hypoglycemia). Diabetic coma results from the opposite condition, when there is too much glucose in the blood (hyperglycemia). A side-effect of hyperglycemia is that the body attempts to flush the excess glucose by increasing urination, which can then lead to dehydration. Symptoms of insulin shock include dizziness, headache, hunger and weakness. The student's skin may be cold, even though s/he is perspiring freely, coordination may be compromised and there may be a sense of confusion or disorientation. Activate the EMS and give sugar in the form of a fruit juice to a conscious athlete. Students who are susceptible to insulin shock will already know this and you should advise them to keep fruit juices or an easily metabolized form of sugar handy. Early symptoms of an impending diabetic coma include headaches, nausea and abdominal pain together with things that we tend to associate with dehydration such as thirst and dry mouth. Someone suffering from hyperglycemia will have dry, warm skin, may be breathing heavily and urinating a lot. In this case, activate the EMS.

e. **Asthma**: Asthmas may affect as much as 5% of the total population and involves a restriction of the airways. A diminished inflow of air means that lesser amounts of oxygen getting to the alveoli-blood boundary. Students may experience shortness of breath, a tendency to hyperventilate and potentially lose consciousness. Asthma attacks may be induced by activity or allergy and is often medicated using an inhaler to keep the airways open. If you have an asthmatic student ensure that s/he has an inhaler at the edge of the mat and available in case it should be needed.

Chapter 7

PHYSICS OF COACHING

Many martial arts actions can be related to simple biomechanical principles and basic physical laws, which govern the movement of bodies through space. The references cited give some account of some of these principles, but are not intended to be either inclusive or comprehensive (Campbell, 1974; Judo Canada, 1983; Leggett, 1978; Luttgens and Wells, 1989; Watanabe and Avakian, 1960; Weers, 1995, 1996, 2003).

Adversarial Psychology: This is not exactly a biomechanical principle so much as a psychological tool. Adversarial psychology essentially dictates that in an attacker-defender situation, an attacker will want whatever the defender does not want. Adversarial psychology, therefore, has a lot to say about how to deal with an opponent who is attempting to grip you or is exerting some force against your body. If, for example, an opponent grabs your wrist, s/he expects that you will pull away. If you pull away, then the opponent will want the exact opposite, so s/he grips more tightly and tugs against your pull. The logical action is to respond when your opponent tugs at the wrist by adding your force to your opponent's in the direction of the pull. It is then easy to capitalize on your opponent's grip and turn it to your advantage. The physical principle, which emerges from this, is the principle of realignment and redirection of force.

In many free fighting settings in Judo and Jujutsu, the exchange often looks more like a tug of war between opposing forces, than a flow and counter flow of energy between two bodies. Resisting a push will only create an antagonistic tug of war, which the stronger player will win. By way of contrast, blending with the oncoming force and redirecting it will cause attackers to over-extend and off-balance themselves, because the expected reaction force never materialized. Judo forms (and perhaps most especially Ju No Kata) teach us this principle over and over, which is perhaps why Leggett (1978) was such a proponent of learning kata. Instead of meeting a push head on and creating a reaction force against it, skilled martial artists will realign themselves with the force and redirect it to their own advantage.

Sun Tzu (Ames, 1993) states that *"We are most vulnerable when we consider ourselves to be invincible"*. Whenever an attacker commits fully to a technique be it a throw, hold or strike, adversarial psychology dictates that there is an expectation of resistance. When the resistance (reaction force) does not materialize, the attacker is frequently left in a vulnerable position. By combining the mental concept of adversarial psychology with the biomechanical principle of realigning and redirecting force, a skilled martial artists can make the most efficient use both offensive and defensive actions.

Attack Space: The attack space is the distance between two players. According to Sun Tzu (Ames, 1993), "*Whoever enters the attack space first, loses.*" An example of this principle at work is found when a student back-steps into a forward throw without first causing his or her partner to fall into the attack space by virtue of a superior off-balance. If the partner is falling into the attack space because the thrower's **movement** created an off-balance and **then** the attacker back steps under the person being thrown, the technique will be successful (Figure 7.1).

Figure 7.1: Back-stepping into a throw after creating an off-balance. Notice that the player in blue has been induced to lean into the attack space and is rising up on his toes. The player in white is entering the throw and is still moving his right foot under the opponent to create a driving force for the completion of the throw.

If the thrower back steps without adequate preparation (person being thrown is still balanced), the attack is sure to be countered thus fulfilling another of Sun Tzu's statements: "*Invincibility lies in defense, the possibility of victory lies in the attack.*" Martial artists who understand the attack space and how to control it, also know:

i) What strategic actions will be effective for any given attack space.

ii) Which attacks need to be blocked and/or countered and which ones do not constitute a real threat.

iii) What attacks and counterattacks can be launched effectively.

iv) How to lure another player into the attack space in order to create vulnerability.

Balance and Posture: The irreducible essence of all martial arts activities concerns an understanding and appreciation of posture and position. Remember that without good posture and position it is difficult to execute an effective offense or defense, therefore, "Position is King". Although he is writing specifically about Judo, Weers (2003), makes a very valid point that we tend to forget to teach posture as a fundamental skill. Put another way, we tend to forget about the significance of posture to the development of skill until we see bad posture and then we act to correct it. The statements holds true regardless of whether we are talking about the execution of a strike or a throw. It would be better to emphasize the elements of good posture as an integral component of skill set acquisition from the onset of training.

Do not forget however, that posture is not just the spatial arrangement of the human structure. Posture is also an attitude of mind and condition of spirit (Herrigel, 1953; Leggett, 1978; Morgan, 1992; Nakamura, 1992), which is often revealed in the physical posture. Where the mind goes, the body is sure to follow. When correcting balance for a student executing a class drill, it is important to recognize that there are probably psychological as well as physical factors at work. As an example, think about the posture of someone who is confident about what they are doing, versus someone who lacks confidence in the expected performance.

For the sake of this discussion, however, we shall confine our thoughts to the physical aspects of balance. There are three aspects of balance:

i) Visual, based upon what our eyes tell us concerning our position in space.

ii) Vestibular, based upon the response of the inner ear to gravity and motion.

iii) Proprioceptive, based upon a muscular awareness of pressure changes in our joints.

We obtain a visual awareness of our position in space through the use of environmental cues that provide information concerning our orientation relative to the environment in which we are moving. Secondly, vestibular balance awareness is provided by the inner ear, which collects static and dynamic equilibrium information. Static equilibrium is obtained through an awareness of the body's position with respect to gravity, whereas dynamic equilibrium relates to maintaining posture in the face of changes in body velocity and or body rotations. Thirdly, small-scale muscular and joint adjustments provide proprioceptive information concerning balance as we move. Proprioceptive movements are neuromuscular reflex actions that finely tune the body as it moves. Proprioceptive awareness provides information concerning changes in muscle tension and changes in the position of a joint. It is the proprioceptive aspect of balance that is so critical to the martial artist. It is possible to train proprioceptive awareness using one-leg balance drills, or ball-balancing drills. It is also possible to take away our tendency to rely upon visual cues by working with eyes closed and "feeling" the position and balance of our opponents (Luttgens and Wells, 1989).

The maintenance of positional stability in a dynamic combat training environment is the result of developing and practicing good balance and good posture. Being aware of the position of your center of gravity and keeping it within the base of support through the use of good posture is essential to developing good balance. Good balance can be defined as (Gleeson, 1967; Leggett, 1978; Nakayama, 1978; Weers, 1995, 2003):

i) Keeping your weight evenly distributed.

ii) Weight over the balls of the feet.

iii) Head up and centered over the shoulders.

iv) Hips unlocked.

v) Center forward.

vi) Center of gravity directly at, or below, the center of balance and centered over the base of support.

vii) Keep your nose between your toes.

Balance Lines: A balance line is an imaginary line that joins the balls of the feet (Figure 7.2). The easiest off-balances are produced by creating force perpendicular to a balance line. Any static stance is a target for the application of force. Consequently, if a martial artist is frequently changing stances in a dynamic setting, s/he will be less vulnerable to attack, especially if the stances are accompanied by good posture.

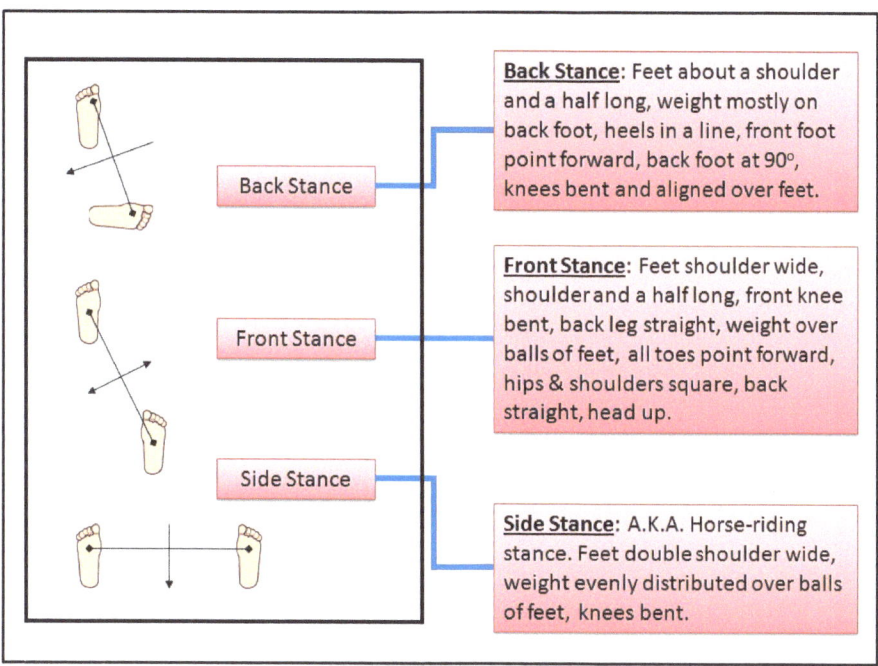

Figure 7.2: Balance lines for the basic Karate and/or Taekwondo stances.

In a normal, upright stance with the feet about shoulder wide and center faced forward (square mobile posture), it is possible to off-balance the body to the four corners, the front, the rear, and to the sides (Figure 7.3). The off-balance to the rear is easiest to create simply because our toes point forwards. Another excellent off balance is to draw a player out over the little toe side of the foot, where again, there is no base of support for the upper body. **The key to any off-balancing act is to separate the player's upper body from his or her support structure and in so doing, create an unstable body arrangement** by either: a) holding the upper body in place and removing the base of support or b) holding the support structure in place and extending the upper body beyond its support.

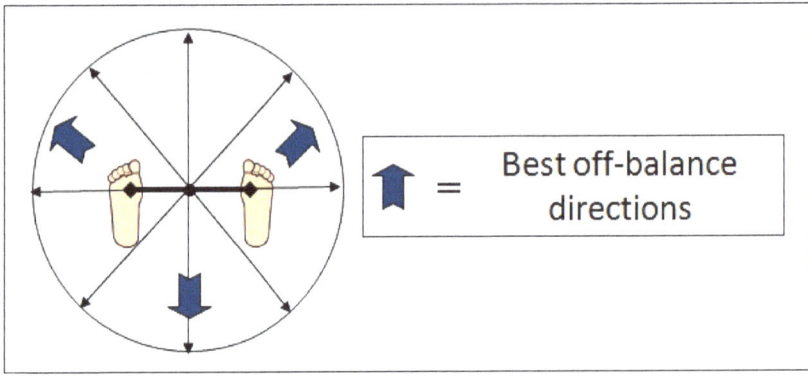

Figure 7.3: Off-balance directions and preferred off-balance directions for a square, mobile posture.

There are several principles of balance (modified from Kano, 1986; Luttgens and Wells, 1989; Nakayama, 1978) with which martial artists will become intimately acquainted as they journey through the learning process.

i) Stability is greatest when the center of gravity is directly over the mid-point of a line drawn between the balls of the feet.

ii) Stability decreases as the center of gravity moves towards the outside edge of the foot (little toe side).

iii) Stability decreases as the center of gravity moves towards the heels of the feet.

iv) The lower the center of gravity, the greater the stability of the body.

v) The wider the base of support, the lower the potential for mobility.

vi) The greater the mass, the greater the stability, or resting inertia.

Biomechanics and the Summation of Forces: The human body is a lot like an erector set. Humans are a collection of plates and rods and the connectors that enable the plates and rods to move relative to each other. From the perspective of movement, the human body consists of articulating joints composed of bones, which provide the structural framework; muscles and tendons, which work the joints; and ligaments that hold the joints together. In terms of biomechanics, the joints of the human body can be used to create only pushing, pulling and twisting actions.

In order to effect any actions, the joints must be used in a specific order. For instance: In order to push effectively with a hand and arm, you must unlock and rotate the shoulder girdle, and then unfold the arm at the elbow and then open the hand and rotate the wrist. As a direct consequence of their construction, each human joint is capable of only certain types and ranges of motion. For instance, the knee joint is primarily a hinge joint, which can open and close, whereas the hip joint is a ball and socket joint, which can complete a wider range of motions. It is therefore possible to define types of joint action as follows:

i) Flexion and Extension. Flexion decreases the angle at the joint, whereas extension increases the angle at the joint (e.g. bending the knee and straightening the leg in a front kick action, Figure 7.4).

Figure 7.4: Bending the knee in a front kick. Extending the leg to make the kick is an extensional action that increases the joint angle (E), whereas folding the knee to either chamber, or re-chamber, the kick is a flexional action that decreases the joint angle (F).

ii) Abduction and Adduction. Abduction moves a limb away from the body, whereas adduction brings the limb closer to the body (e.g. abduction at the shoulder during a ridge hand strike, Figure 7.5).

Figure 7.5: Abduction (Abd) of the shoulder joint and girdle moves the arm away from the side during the execution of a ridge hand strike. Adduction (Add) brings the arm back down to the side.

iii) Rotation. Rotation of a joint involves a turning or twisting motion of one surface of the joint relative to the other (e.g. turning the wrist over during a punch, Figure 7.6).

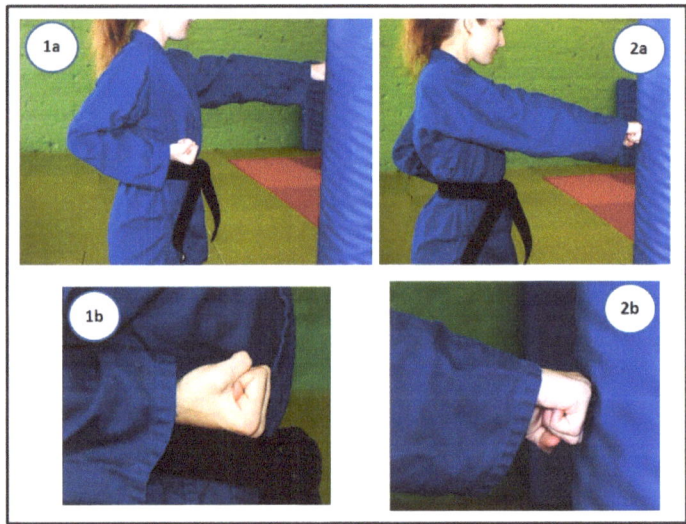

Figure 7.6: Rotating the wrist during a reverse punch. When chambered (1a, 1b), the wrist is rotated with the palm up. In the last instant as the punch is delivered, the wrist is rotated with the palm down (2a, 2b).

The point to all of this, is that in order to understand how a throw or a strike can be achieved most effectively, it is necessary to recognize that during the action, each joint required to complete the skill, will need to generate part of the necessary force at a specific moment in the process. Equally, other joints may be required to support the weapon platform at specific moments during the process. During any throwing and/or striking action, therefore, the student's joints may be required to support the student's weight, support the opponent's weight and/or provide part of the force that projects the opponent to the planet surface or the weapon into the opponent.

From the foregoing, it becomes clear that martial arts skills are necessarily very complex, full-body actions that involve many joints working together to create the forces required to complete the action. It is important, therefore, that each joint be used in the correct sequence and at the correct time to deliver the maximum power output at the moment of execution.

The summation of forces, therefore, requires that joints be used in order from large joints to small joints during the execution of any technique. By linking back to the psychology of coaching, if your players can create an approximation of a required skill using large body actions, it will then be possible to use reinforcement to refine the skill by paying attention to both the specific types of joint actions and the timing of the actions. It is for this reason that you are encouraged to teach gross biomechanical actions first and worry about the details later. After all, what does it matter if your player has his or her little finger in exactly the right place if the hip block is completely out of alignment?

Body Turning and Rotation: For the execution of powerful throws and strikes it is necessary to turn and rotate the body, often in more than one plane at a time. Vertical rotations involve actions such as bending at the knees, or bending forward at the waist, whereas horizontal rotations include actions such as hip and shoulder rotations. In order to make effective throws it is necessary to employ both vertical body rotations and horizontal body rotations. By way of example, when an effective hip throw is executed, it is necessary to bend the knees, twist the hips and turn the head in the direction of the throw as the thrower bends forward (Figure 7.7). When an effective strike or block is executed, it is necessary to rotate the hips and project the striking/blocking weapon in the direction of the target/offensive weapon. For most strikes, (depending upon the height of the target relative to the weapon being used), horizontal body rotations are used more often than vertical rotations (Nakayama, 1978).

Figure 7.7: Many forward throwing applications involve both vertical and horizontal body rotations.

When good balance is combined with good posture and appropriate body rotations, it becomes possible to "center" the weapons and apply them with considerable force (Nakayama, 1978). Being biomechanically centered involves keeping your hands in front of your shoulders and your shoulders in front of your hips (Figure 7.8). Also make sure that your elbows are kept down and in towards your sides. If the hands are not centered, then they are in a weak position relative to the application of the power needed for a throw or a strike. If the hands are in front of the shoulders and the shoulders in front of the hips, then the body rotations will produce maximum efficiency in the action (all other factors being equal).

Figure 7.8: In striking drills, it is important to keep the weapon centered; the elbows close in to the sides and to deliver maximum power to the weapon through the hips in the moment of the strike.

Driving Leg: All martial actions, whether they are strikes, hold-downs, throws, or joint locks or whether they are simply aspects of movement and gripping, derive their power from pushing against something stable. The most stable object, against which we can push, is the planet, so the driving leg pushes into the planet, which creates a reaction force. By pushing into the planet, we can then push into our opponent. The forces generated are in conformity with Newton's third law of motion, which states that to every action there is an equal, and opposite action. Consequently, if a technique is to be successful, it is necessary for the driving leg to be placed opposite the destination point of the technique (Campbell, 1974), that is to say be parallel to the direction of application of the force (push). The valuable insight that a student can gain from an understanding of the driving leg is that **all** kicking and punching actions and **all** throwing actions and **all** ground holds are necessarily **pushing actions**. In his work on Judo skill development Weers (1995, 2003), makes this point very clear, but the premise holds true in the striking arts as well. A punch or a kick is a very forceful pushing action that is dependent upon the availability of a driving leg for the generation of power in the first instance.

The Hole: If you think of a human being as not having enough legs, then the idea of a hole is easy to understand. Basically, if you are off-balance, you must move a foot or lean against something in order to re-establish positional stability. If you fail to do this, you fall over. It's that simple. In fact, if you think about it, the whole process of walking is about deliberately losing and regaining balance just before we fall over. It follows then, that since we do in fact only have two legs, any time that our center of gravity falls outside of the base of support we experience a positive response to gravity unless the base of support can be re-established below the center of gravity. We can call space into which we fall "the hole."

If throwing and striking actions are pushing actions, whenever an opponent is being thrown, there is only one location into which s/he can be effectively thrown with the minimum application of force. Likewise when you punch or kick, there is only one place in which your opponent will receive the full impact of a well-delivered strike, and this will be the hole into which the person striking would fall without something there to hit. It follows from everything else that we have said in this chapter concerning balance, balance line and the driving leg, that the hole will be located directly in front of the direction of the off-balance and that the attacker's driving leg must be placed directly opposite the hole, so that the push will be directly into the hole. Any other configuration of the two bodies will result in an ineffective throw or strike.

If we start with one partner in a square mobile posture (weight evenly distributed, feet about shoulder wide, center faced forward), and the other player **not** in a square mobile posture, there are only three fundamental positions for the opponent's **support** foot, Knowledge of these positions will indicate the location of the hole (Weers 1995, 2003):

i) If the two players are facing each other, and the opponent's support foot is to the rear, then the primary hole will be to the front corner in front of the rear foot (Figure 7.9).

Figure 7.9: Tai Otoshi, (body drop throw) from Judo as an illustration of the location of the forward hole.

ii) If the two players are facing each other, and the opponent's support foot is forward, then the main hole will be to rear corner behind the front foot, (Figure 7.10).

Figure 7.10: O Uchi Gari (major inner reaping throw) as an illustration of the location of the rearward hole.

iii) If the two players are at (or near) right angles each other, and the opponent has actively "trespassed" his/her support foot between the two players, then the main hole will be to the rear corner behind the opponent's weighted foot, (Figure 7.11).

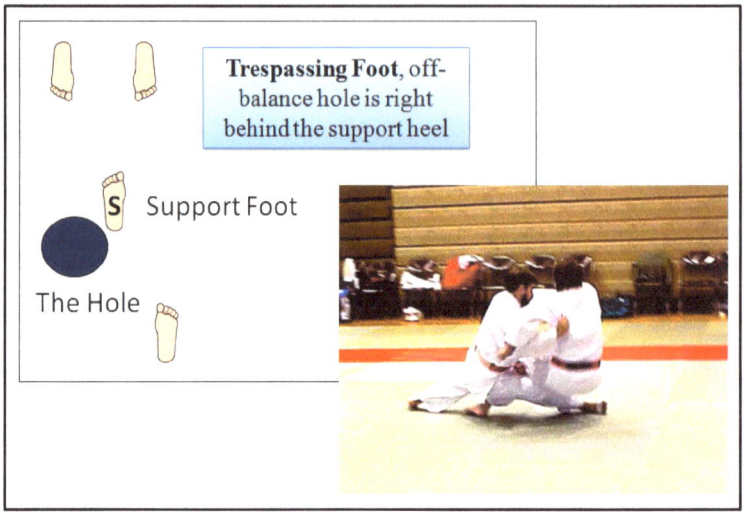

Figure 7.11: Tani Otoshi (valley drop) as an illustration of the location of the trespassing foot.

If we look at the situation where the two players are facing each other and the opponent's weight is evenly balanced, there is no immediate hole into which s/he will fall. In the square mobile a player can choose to move to either side for offense or defense. Until the balance has been compromised in some way, it is unwise to attack. Sun Tzu (Ames, 1993) puts it rather neatly "*Know where your opponent is strong and avoid him there.*" A student in the square mobile posture must, therefore, be induced to step before a hole can be established if a throwing opportunity is to be considered.

The Hop Reflex: In throwing actions, there are times when it is possible to create a reflex action in your partner's supporting foot that actually helps to create an opportunity to throw. In effect, your partners will throw themselves. If you draw someone forward to an off-balance position over his or her lead foot, there will come a point when your partner is standing on one leg and the heel of the support (lead) foot will come up. At this moment all the weight will be centered over the ball of the foot and the knee on the support leg will lock. If you extend the off-balance just a little further your partner will "hop" to regain balance. The hop is also called the "metatarsal stretch reflex." The direct application of the reflex is that if you apply a throwing technique to the support leg at the exact moment that your opponent hops, your opponent will be completely dependent upon your body for positional stability.

Levers: Knowledge of levers is critical to the student of the martial arts, since levers provide a mechanical advantage when applying force to a resistance. Most players use levers at an intuitive level and could not tell you that a specific skill requires a specific type of lever in order to be effective. Indeed an intimate knowledge of levers by your players will not necessarily improve their performance. Conversely, the ineffective execution of a skill can sometimes be related to the ineffective placement or use of a lever. Consequently, the coach who can see that it is the lever that needs to be adjusted will be able to coach his or her players more effectively. There are three classes of levers (Figure 7.12).

i) Class one levers have the fulcrum placed somewhere between the force being applied and the resistance to the force. The greater the distance between the applied force and the fulcrum, the more effective the lever. Many throws are class I levers (Figure 7.12 & 7.13, 7.14).

ii) Class two levers place the resistance between the fulcrum and the force being applied. Once again, the closer the resistance is to the fulcrum the more effective is the lever (Figure 7.12 & 7.15) Foot stopping throws are examples of class two levers (Watanabe and Avakian, 1960).

iii) Class three levers place the force being applied between the fulcrum and the resistance. In this case the force being applied needs to be closer to the resistance to maximize efficiency of the lever. A lot of armbars are class III levers (Figure 7.12 & 7.16).

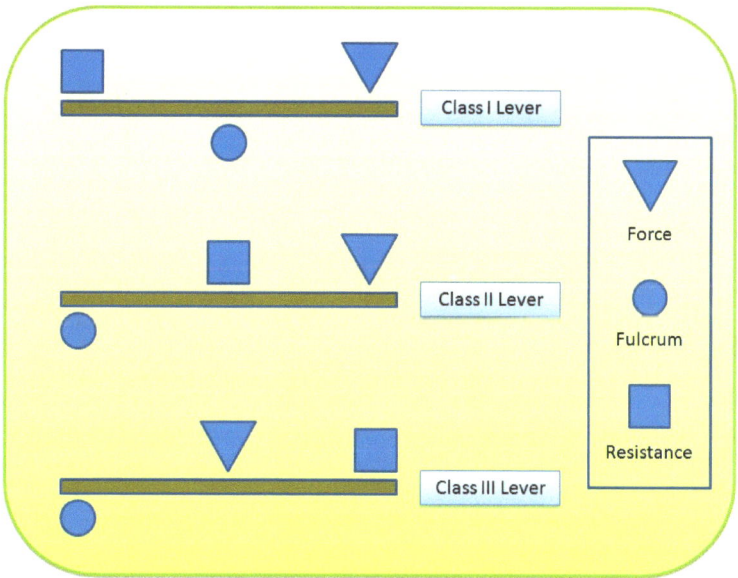

Figure 7.12: Classes of levers.

Figure 7.13: O Soto Gari (major outer sweeping throw) as a classic example of a Class I lever. Note that the fulcrum is at the hips, the force is at the shoulders and the resistance is at the feet.

Figure 7.14: Uchi Mata (Inner Thigh throw) as another classic example of a Class I lever. Note that the fulcrum is at the hips, the force is at the shoulders and the resistance is at the feet. The only real difference between O Soto Gari and Uchi Mata is that the person throwing is facing the other direction; the thrower's actions are essentially the same.

Figure 7.15: Kubi Guruma, head wheeling throw against a punching attack, used to demonstrate a class II lever. The fulcrum is at the attacker' foot, the force is applied at the attacker's punching hand and the resistance is close to the attacker's center of mass.

Figure 7.16: Ude Gatame, armlock against a grabbing attack, used to demonstrate a class III lever. The fulcrum is at the defender's shoulder, the force is applied at the attacker's elbow and the resistance is close to the attacker's shoulder.

Moving Off-line: It is axiomatic that the best way to avoid a trap is to not be there when it is sprung. The same principle is evident throughout martial arts training. In the movie "*Dune*", the Mentat Thufir Howat, tells young Prince Paul Atreides that the first step in avoiding a trap is knowing of its existence. The advice implies that you have an awareness of your opponent's actions.

A clear understanding of body movement will supply pre-incident indicators of an impending attack. There are only so many ways in which a human body can move and given one starting position, it is possible to predict with reasonable accuracy, what will happen next as a consequence of any movement emerging from the original position. Highly skilled martial artists, who have either seen combat in real-world settings or in competitive environments, where rules of engagement apply, seem to know this reflexively. Skilled martial artists with years of live combat or competitive experience can read what will happen next and be waiting for their opponents to move. For such players tactical combative responses are predictable.

Learning to avoid an attack by moving off-line and being able to redirect the opponent's energy is one of the key performance goals of the skilled martial artists. Moving off-line requires that we not resist our opponent's attacks, but rather flow with them and use them to our advantage. Weers (2003), provides an elegant discussion of the development of timing in the use of countering skills in Judo. Ultimately the best use of countering skills is when an attacker commits fully to his or her attack and there is "nobody home". When this happens, the defender sees the impending attack as it develops and is able to place his or her body in a position that maximizes any opportunity for exploiting the initial attacker's actions. Similar opportunities exist in the striking arts when one player evades, rather than blocks, an incoming strike. The player who makes the initial strike expects to encounter a resistance (satisfactory impact of the weapon or a blocking action), but when the resistance does not materialize s/he overextends the weapon and loses positional stability, creating an excellent opportunity for counter-strikes (Figure 7.17). The tricky part to all of this is to keep the opponent thinking that we are unaware of his or her strategy until s/he has fully committed to a course of action and cannot alter the plan of attack.

Figure 7.17: A tactical sparring drill in which a student is learning to move off-line and exploit an over-extended punch with the application of a counter-strike. Drills can be used that emphasize moving off-line to the outside and to the inside. Once the drill has been polished and internalized through repetition, students will automatically move off-line in the direction of a scoring opportunity.

Plyometric Action: A plyometric action uses the elastic properties of a muscle to assist in a forceful contraction. You may recall from the section on stretching that two sets of muscles are used for flexing and extending any joint (Figures 6.8, 6.9). These two-muscle sets work in such a way that the contracting muscle (known as the agonist) creates the joint movement while the antagonist muscle on the opposite side of the joint relaxes and stretches (Luttgens and Wells, 1989). During plyometric action the agonist muscle (on one side of the joint) is contracted so much that the antagonistic muscle (on the opposite side of the joint) is stretched to its elastic limit. When the agonist is relaxed, the elastic stretch reflex causes the antagonist muscles to start contracting, allowing for a more rapid and forceful generation of power. The elastic stretch reflex occurs because once a muscle is fully stretched it automatically contracts; this is also known as the "myotactic stretch reflex."

A good example of this principle at work involves the sudden, powerful burst of muscular effort used in a throw during which the thrower coils like a spring immediately prior to pushing into the throw. Two good examples in Judo are the drive out of a deep squat into a Seoi Nage type action (Figure 6.5) or the application of Ura Nage (Figure 7.18).

Figure 7.18: Ura Nage (rear throw), is arguably one of the most plyometric Judo actions and requires a tremendously explosive push from the thighs to generate the power for a successful outcome.

In the striking arts, powerful jumping and flying kicks (Figures 7.19, 7.20), so typical of Taekwondo and Hapkido (Chun, 1982; Tedeschi, 2000), derive their force from the plyometric action of the jump.

Figure 7.19: Jumping kicks generate power from the force of the plyometric launch.

Figure 7.20: Flying kicks often have more penetrating power because the plyometric jump is associated with a forward motion that carries over into the kick.

Power Curve: Every technique has a power curve, which is related to energy generated and distance traveled over time. In the simplest example, any strike or throw can only produce a finite amount of power during its execution and amount of force generated will obey the equation $F = M \times A$, where:

F = Force upon impact,

M = Mass of the body,

A = Acceleration (rate of increase in distance traveled per unit time).

There comes a point however, on the journey that any throw or a strike will reach its maximum velocity and since the projected mass has not changed, the force produced will peak. It would be expected then that once an action has reach its peak, the energy will be dissipated and the action will lose power. In the case of a throwing action, however, once the power has peaked, a well-executed throw will derive **additional** force from the acceleration due to gravity. It is for this reason that powerful throws continue to pick up momentum as the thrower's energy is replaced by the acceleration due to gravity. Conversely, any travel **parallel to, or away from** the planet surface after the attacker's power spike is reached, will cause the dissipation of energy and the loss of power.

A simple rule that can be applied to the power curve is that maximum power is achieved in the last few inches of a technique. By way of example, board-breaking techniques must reach their maximum potential power as the weapon penetrates the board, and not before making contact with the board surface (Figure 7.21).

Figure 7.21: Maximum power is achieved when the punch penetrates the board.

The Power Side: The power arm or side is the arm or the side of the body that transmits the force of the attack into the opponent's body (Campbell, 1974; Weers, 1995, 2003). In most throwing and striking arts the power is necessarily transmitted by pushing into the opponent. The driving leg is aligned with the power arm and both are being employed in the same direction with an optimal angle of attack. It is important to recognize that it is **not** just the power hand that drives into the opponent during a committed throw or a committed punch, but the **entire arm and side of the body** (Campbell, 1974; Weers, 1995, 2003). It is equally important to remember that throwing and punching power comes out of the hips, not out of the hands or shoulders. The driving leg provides a pushing force into the planet; the reaction force from the planet is then transferred **through the hips** to the body parts that will make the action. The power of any technique is, therefore, effectively transmitted through the use of a complete hip rotation.

In most cases the maximum amount of force is delivered when two bodies are moving towards each other. It is therefore advisable to have your opponent moving **toward** your power side. One of the simplest examples of this type of action is when your opponent defender steps into a well-placed side kick (Figure 7.22). A corollary to the previous statement is that it is very difficult to push effectively against something that is moving away from you, unless you are moving faster than your opponent. Consider attempting to strike someone who is moving away from you. Even if you can make contact, the strike will not pack the power of a collision when your opponent is moving towards your striking weapon. Conversely though, throwing actions can, and do, happen under circumstances in which the defender is retreating and the attacker is bringing the force of the attack to bear upon the defender at a faster rate than s/he can retreat.

Figure 7.22: Maximum force can be delivered when an opponent is moving towards the power side as in this case, where one player is lured into leading with a punch, only to run on to the end of the 'defender's' waiting side kick.

Realignment and Redirection of Force: In a battle in which forces collide, the larger force will always emerge the victor. In the world of Judo, (Kano, 1986) spoke to us from the grave and reminded us that the essential truth is to use your opponent's force against him or her by adding it to your own force pushing in a particular direction. We have already discussed the application of realignment and redirection of force, several times in this section. As an instructor, one of your performance goals should be to bring your students to an appreciation that fighting strength for strength is a futile exercise. True mastery comes from a realization that it is better to redirect an opponent's force rather than try to match it and overcome it.

Support Foot: We have touched on this aspect of biomechanics when we discussed the concept of the hole. By definition, the support foot is the foot that bears your weight. It can also be referred to as the weighted leg. Understanding the principle of the support foot or weighted leg is essential to making the human structure collapse. Consequently, throwing actions should attack the support foot. Moreover, whether striking or throwing, the best time to attack is when the opponent's weight has been fully committed to a step or strike. In the moment in which an attacker has chosen to fully commit to a step or strike s/he is unable to change the course of action and is, therefore, vulnerable to counter attack. Any time you have more force available for use in a particular situation than your opponent, you have a tactical advantage. The essence of the matter then, is that once your opponent has committed to a course of action (making a step), the foot on which the weight is being placed becomes a target for attack. We should also be aware that in addition to the weighted foot, other are variables involved in movement, such as whether a player is moving towards or away from the attacker or whether a player is leaning towards or away from the attacker.

There is also a pair of warnings here:

i) Your opponent's support foot in Judo is also his or her driving leg for throwing actions and is, therefore, the support upon which the rest of the weaponry is arranged. Placing yourself between the opponent's support foot and **your** off-balance hole would not be wise!

ii) Your opponent's support foot in Karate and Taekwondo is also his or her driving leg for kicking and punching actions and is, therefore, the support upon which the rest of the weaponry is arranged. Notice, however, that placing yourself between the opponent's support foot and **their** off-balance hole would not be wise!

Timing: Learning to time the tactical use (application) of a skill is a lesson in precision. If the skill is the least bit too early or too late, the effectiveness will not be as great. A well-timed skill will, therefore, reach its power peak at the moment of greatest vulnerability of the opponent. Timing evolves from a thorough understanding of force lines, speed, direction, distance and range, combined with a knowledge of the possible outcomes of any given action by an opponent. Since there are a limited number of movement possibilities from any given originating position, it follows that a martial artist who can accurately predict the next move, will also have the edge for timing his or her next attack or defense (Figure 7.17). It is the clear understanding of the pre-incident indicators, therefore, that allows skilled players to arrive in a position and simply wait for their opponents to arrive at the moment of execution.

There is a relationship between the attacker and the opponent, which affects timing. The relationship is based upon the preparedness of the attacker and the vulnerability of the defender as follows:

i) When your opponent is about to attack, s/he is concentrating so hard on his or her own technique that s/he can be blind to the need for personal defense. (Sun Tzu tells us *"you are most vulnerable when you think you are invincible"*).

ii) When a player attacks and then withdraws s/he is extremely vulnerable to counter attack.

iii) When your opponent is blocking your first attack, s/he is vulnerable to combination techniques, because the defensive tools are already pre-occupied. Invariably, defensive tactics applied in one direction leave a player vulnerable to the application of a technique in exactly the opposite direction. An example here is the novice in sparring who is induced block a kick on one side of the body only to be set up for a punch on the other side of the body.

iv) When your opponent pushes in the same direction as your technique, s/he cannot offer any resistance to your attack (Kano's principle of realignment of force).

v) When the opponent has just finished breathing out, energy is at its lowest ebb. Breathing in is normally associated with increasing power and breathing out with dissipating power, therefore, the best time to attack is at the end of an exhale, when your opponent has dissipated all his or her energy.

vi) When your opponent changes stances, direction or is off-balance.

vii) When your opponent has committed to a stepping action.

viii) When your opponent loses concentration.

A Final Comment: When executing a technique of any kind, there are several steps that will lead to a successful outcome as follows (modified from Weers, 1995, 2003):

i) Make sure your opponent is moving toward your power side.

ii) Locate the support leg, and potential weapons.

iii) Decide upon a tactical solution (what skill to employ).

iv) Locate the hole into which you will push.

v) Assess your opponent's posture.

vi) Place your driver opposite the hole, center your weapons, adjust the angle of attack and execute.

Chapter 8

SAFETY AND LEGAL CONSIDERATIONS

In this section I will discuss two sets of related issues. The first will involve issues of safety during training and the second will involve some of your legal duties as a martial arts instructor. Some of these issues will naturally overlap. I will deal with safety first, because these are issues that evolve from the previous sections on pedagogy and physiology. The legal issues follow thereafter and may contain some repetition…the redundancy only underscores their importance.

General Safety Considerations: Almost all authorities recognize that the safety of people involved in sporting activities is the primary responsibility of the coach (Corcoran and Graden, 1998; Flegel, 1992; Judo Canada, 1983; Martens, 1990; Mitchell, 1988; NCCP, 1979). Much of the material in this section is gleaned from these sources. While it is true that it is the personal responsibility of the students to monitor their own performance, they rely upon the coach to tell them what new techniques they are capable of performing and what techniques they are ready to learn. If students are asked to learn something for which they do not feel ready, they will feel confused and frustrated. Their lack of preparedness and understanding will also lead to a higher risk of injury. Ultimately, if you ask your players to do something for which they do not feel prepared you will invite an erosion of trust and respect combined with a loss of confidence in your ability to teach or to understand their needs.

As a martial arts instructor you have several duties that deal with the safety of your students, many of which are self-evident, but it is good for you to keep them in the front of your mind. Your duties with respect to safety relate to the nature of teaching, the teaching environment and how you prepare yourself to fulfill the role of coach. So, let's look at the nature of the teaching first:

i) Teach from a lesson plan. Plan the activity and have written lesson plans as an integral part of the overall learning program (Appendix 2). Keep a record of all lesson plans.

ii) Provide clear and precise instruction using appropriate pedagogical methods for the age, maturity level, skill level, fitness level and rank of your classes.

iii) Make sure that your students are reasonably matched for experience, size, age, or gender as appropriate. The applications to age- and gender-appropriate training are obvious, but it also applies to training competitors versus non-competitors. If your students are unmatched for any reason, there is a much higher risk of injury. One place where mismatching your students can be particularly risky is when high-ranking students are doing free-practice (daeryun, kumite or sparring for Taekwondo and Karate stylists and randori or grappling for Judo and Jujutsu stylists) with lower ranked students or when smaller, weaker students are working with larger, stronger students (Figure 8.1). If your class is engaged in free-practice, make sure that you remind your students to watch their force, speed and control, be vigilant and have extra sets of eyes to help you patrol the training area. Additionally, make sure that you remind your students to "calibrate" when they move from one training partner to another.

Figure 8.1: A great example of mis-matched training partners. The woman is a little over five foot and weighs 100 pounds; the seven foot man weighs 300 pounds. The risk of injury and frustration for both players is high.

iv) Explain the appropriate levels of cooperation and contact and enforce them during class. As a coach you need to be ever-vigilant for the use of strength and ego in class practice. The inappropriate use of either is inevitably going to result in injury. Be willing to act swiftly to stop the overt use of strength in unwarranted situations and stop excesses of ego immediately.

v) We have already discussed typical martial arts injuries so I will simply refer back to what I consider to be one of the best books on the subject: Estwanik (1996), however, you still need to understand and recognize when injuries occur. Require that all members of your coaching staff take classes in both First Aid and CPR. Be vigilant during training. Know how to evaluate the level and severity of an injury, once it has occurred. There are many occasions when a student can shake off a slight physical trauma and can continue training. Understand when a band-aid or a few minutes to recover is a good answer, when sitting out for the rest of the class is a good answer, and when seeking immediate professional medical attention is the right choice. Clear and honest communication between coach and student are essential in the evaluation of an injury.

vi) A regularly scheduled class practice is never the time to ignore an injury. There are, in fact, very few settings in which inattention to an injury is the right course of action. We might argue that a medal match at the Olympics might qualify, but that is between the coach and the competitor. Certainly I have been involved in competition at the national level both as a competitor and a referee, where a player has been hurt, but deliberately chooses to continue the fight rather than lose the match and a possible medal. Personally, I have never fought at the national level with an injury, but I have fought at the regional level (which is arguably much less significant) with broken ribs sustained early in the day. There are any number of reasons why someone may choose this course of action, but if you are the player's coach, it makes good sense for you to have discussed what to do, and counseled your player about what choices to make, **before** your player sets foot in the competition arena.

vii) We can always recover if we are hurt and come back to class later, but if we ignore an injury and continue to train, we risk turning an acute injury into a chronic injury. Long-term damage and chronic injuries can be harder, or perhaps, impossible to repair.

viii) Evaluate students for inability to participate. Understand that signs of fatigue, injury, frustration, lack of concentration, or lack of control are pre-incident indicators of high-risk situations. Always act swiftly to reduce risk. Monitor in-class performance, checking for confusion, frustration and fatigue. Allow your students to rest when they need to and allow free access to water at any time during practice. Students who are experiencing both frustration and fatigue may need both a rest and a simpler task. In these circumstances it might not be appropriate to break down a drill for the whole class, but a single student might benefit from being given a simpler drill if s/he is experiencing frustration. Remember when you have a group of mixed ranks doing the same drill, that novice players with a lower level of fitness will be placing much more stress on their bodies than mid-ranked players who are beginning to make impressive gains in physical fitness. Make sure that your non-verbal and verbal expectations, as well as the use of appropriate positive and negative reinforcements, are consistent with encouraging your novice players to evaluate their own performance and to do their very best. Having said that, however, you should remind your novice players to live within their own limits. Seek clarification from your students, so as to lessen the likelihood of confusion and frustration.

ix) As an instructor you should remind your students of risks often. Warn of risks that are general in nature, but also warn of specific concerns when introducing new materials. Make sure that you tell the students about risks when using weapons, kicking and punching or when applying joint locks and chokes. Discuss the limits of "safe" play and discuss the ways in which risk factors may be reduced. Sometimes all that is needed is a gentle reminder to your students to maintain control and be considerate of their training partners.

x) Provide appropriate emergency supplies and assistance. Unless you are a medical professional, you are not qualified to provide medical assistance beyond following simple, expected first aid procedures.

xi) Avoid turning your back to the mat. Keep a clear view of as much of the training area as possible at all times.

xii) Never leave the training area without a certified, assistant instructor in your place who understands and can continue your lesson plan.

There are also safety factors that pertain to the environment in which you teach. We do not always get to control all aspects of our training facility, especially if we are renting space in some multi-purpose facility such as a church, or school. Having said that, however, you can ensure the following:

i) Provide a safe training environment. Check for hard objects, loose pictures, trophies that may fall on your players, or protruding objects with which your players may collide during practice. Make sure that there is an adequate safety area around the training area (Figure 8.2). Moreover, make sure that you provide adequate space so as to enable everyone to work with minimal risk of collision. Of equal importance is the unrestricted mingling of different weight groups during training. If your mat space is limited, you may need to put a cap on class size or use a practice rotation to control the number of students training at any one time.

Figure 8.2: The Training Deck. Note the following items:
A: The mat surface is made of carpet overlain by ethafoam overlain by Tatami.
B: The moveable padded targets were later moved to the far wall, where there was less traffic, but where they could still be moved into the training area for drills.
C: The electrical sockets were moved from the location shown to eight feet above the training deck (see other in-text figures).
D: The large crash pads line the wall to add protection (see other in-text figures).
E: The first aid kit is just inside the doorway and within easy reach of the deck.
F: The pictures were securely mounted to the wall, but storing the red padded targets against this wall added additional measure of safety.
G: A well-lit training area.
H: A rigid 2x4 wooden frame wrapped with ethafoam and upholstery fabric was placed around the mats to prevent them moving.
I: The metal poles were wrapped with custom-made foam pads and a vinyl cover, so that they became a training tool, rather than a risk factor.

ii) Provide and maintain adequate training equipment. Be particularly sensitive to the nature of the crash pads, flooring in general, striking targets and shields, sparring equipment and weapons (Figure 8.3). Paying attention to the surface upon which your players are moving jumping, and/or falling can prevent a lot of knee injuries and broken toes. If you are teaching a grappling or throwing style, make sure that there is adequate cushioning to prevent injuries to the shoulders, elbows and back when falling. If you are teaching a predominantly striking style then the floor must resilient enough to permit pivoting and sometimes jumping actions. Obviously, if your teaching involves both striking and throwing components, like some styles of Hapkido, Jujutsu or Kung Fu are apt to include, then it is important to make sure that your training surface meets the needs of both sets of skills, being neither too soft, nor too hard. Japanese tatami, with an underlay of ethafoam, can make a good working surface under these conditions.

Figure 8.3: A separate room for equipment storage allows all pads and training aids to be kept off the deck when not in use, and allows for easy inventory control and replacement. Having a separate closet with a door prevents children from helping themselves to 'toys.'

A distinctly separate group of safety considerations are those that occur during the enrollment conference, and should become part of your standard operating procedure. By taking some simple precautions before, and during the enrollment process, the instructor can do much to improve safety of the training environment. If you are a business owner as well as an instructor, attention to these details sends very clear messages to your students (a.k.a. clients) about your business values, such as long-term investment versus short-term gain. The students who feel that safety is a very real concern to the instructor will be much more apt to work harder and take appropriate levels of risk. The logic behind this statement is that the students know that they have entered a partnership with the instructor in which they are both cognizant of the levels of risk and safety of the training environment. Martial arts training is all about risk; there is no getting away from it. Anytime you give your body to someone else for them to throw, twist or hit, you are opening a trust account with your partner and you are taking a risk. Students who know that they are taking these risks in a safe environment are going to be more relaxed, calm and considerate of their fellows. Accordingly, the things that a martial arts instructor needs to do before any student/client begins his/her first class include:

i) Have every new student read and sign a "Warning, waiver, release of liability, assumption of risk and agreement to participate" form (written by Scott Conway for the American Council on the Martial Arts Instructors Course, used herein by permission. Appendix 5 & 6).

ii) Have every new student fill out a health history when s/he enrolls (Appendix 7).

iii) Give copies of the membership rules, class safety rules, and blood policy to every student when they enroll. If the student is a minor, go over the safety rules, etiquette and blood policy with the parent, and make sure they also go over the rules with the child.

iv) Give your students a copy of the training syllabus, and prepare lesson plans in advance.

v) Have a fully stocked first aid kit on hand (Flegel, 1992).

Most of these safety issues are straightforward and stem from a clear understanding of your primary responsibility as a coach. Never lose sight of the fact that what you do, how you do it, and where you do it, will always be measured against your obligation to ensure the safety of your players.

General Legal Considerations Most of us consider ourselves to be reasonable, prudent coaches who use common sense and who are concerned about the safety of our players. The information in this section is, therefore, provided to help you protect yourself. Much of what is written here comes from the ASEP Leader Course (Martens, 1990), the ACMA Coaching Course (Corcoran and Graden, 1998) and associated readings. The ASEP course was written for coaches of all sports and the ACMA manual was written for all martial artists.

As we have already said, the nature of practicing martial arts involves risk, and if we are honest, something about that appeals to those of us who are drawn to combat training environments. All the same, we can, and should, minimize risk as much as possible. What follows really comes down to only two things:

i) Reducing risks.

ii) Keeping records.

Beyond your simple obligations to ensure the safety of your students, there are also legal responsibilities, which you assume the moment you choose to become a martial arts instructor. Ignorance of your legal responsibilities is not an acceptable excuse, so it is a good idea to know what you are undertaking, from a legal perspective. It is also a good idea to have a working knowledge of the statutes that apply in your state, county or town. What I will discuss are generally accepted standards of legal responsibility, but do not consider them to be a replacement for knowing the statutes in your own area.

Our main considerations in this section revolve around "risk management", which is why this section follows the section on safety. Recall that your prime responsibility to your students is to keep them safe. Your prime responsibility to yourself, however, is to keep records that attest to the fact that you do indeed view your prime responsibility as a coach as being the safety of your students. Keep adequate records of lesson plans, student forms and records, health history, injury reports and equipment purchase invoices. These things are all part of being professional about what you do as a coach.

There are four main legal areas about which you need to be aware: Discrimination, harassment and abuse, and negligence.

Discrimination: Discrimination is related to three aspects of coaching.

i) How you recruit and accept students into your classes.

ii) How you promote your students.

iii) Requirements of training/participation.

If you refuse to accept a student for anything other than objective reasons, then you are leaving yourself open to accusations of discriminatory practices.

The process of promoting one student *over* another is in itself an act of a discriminatory nature, but that does not make it illegal. It is part of what you are expected to do as an instructor. The promotion of a student to a new rank at a faster/slower rate than another is a judgment issue based upon objective reasoning. Understand the flip side: If you hold a student back you'd better have a very good reason, because in all likelihood you will have a disgruntled student and/or parent with whom to deal. Again, maintaining clear and open communication with students (and parents), keeping excellent records (including attendance cards and time-in-grade dates), teaching from a syllabus, establishing testing dates and having clearly established minimum ages for promotion can help you.

The participation requirements of what we do in martial arts can sometimes be misconstrued and be taken out of context. For this reason, make it your responsibility to maintain open lines of communication with parents and participants, and offer the option of non-participation.

Harassment and abuse: The physical nature of martial arts raises the likelihood of inadvertent and accidental contact with sexually sensitive areas of the body, or areas of the body that might be considered to be culturally off-limits by members of some group. The possibility of perceived "inappropriate touching" that results in a charge of molestation (of a child) or harassment (of an adult, same gender or mixed gender) is, therefore, very real. It is important for you to realize as a business owner and/or instructor in a supervisory position, that you can be held liable for allowing a harassing or abusive environment to exist, even though you were not the person who was the alleged abuser. Harassment, however, is not simply confined to issues of sexual harassment through inappropriate physical touching. Harassment could be defined as anything that makes a person feel harassed. Be aware, therefore, that what you may view as normal, someone else might view as harassment. The point here is not what you think, but what the other person **feels**.

Any of the following might easily be considered harassment:

i) Making derogatory comments.

ii) Making jokes or using obscene language, slurs and demeaning or stereotypical stories.

iii) The use of physical gestures that demean, degrade or show hostility towards a person or group.

iv) Physical actions that might threaten or intimidate a person because of his or her membership in a particular group.

v) Staring at a person because of his or her membership in a particular group.

Tolerating any of the actions listed above could be a basis for legal action because you have an affirmative duty to address the issue. In addition, coaches are responsible for the education of their staff and the development of some reporting process whereby issues of harassment can be addressed.

The solution is simple and obvious: **As a business owner and/or instructor, be professional and enforce a similar level of performance from your students**.

Another aspect of harassment is the potential for abuse of the "power" position. As coach, you are in a position of power and under-ranking students will tend to obey your instructions because they trust and respect you and because they feel that it is a necessary part of obtaining the benefits they seek from your tutelage. You must discharge this office with complete professionalism at all times. Your students and assistants will model your example, and the risk of being accused of unwarranted activity will be lessened.

One last aspect of harassment is dealt with in the nature of the Risk Agreement (Appendix 5). The risk agreement was developed by Scott Conway, an attorney, writing in the American Council on Martial Arts Instructor Certification Manual for the National Association of Professional Martial Artists (Corcoran and Graden, 1998) and is used herein by permission. In the Risk Agreement, we are notifying our students of the types of physical contact that will be involved and obtaining their consent. We are also offering a non-participation clause as a way of further reducing risk. From this perspective you can see why it is so important to have written documentation of informed consent in every student's file. In the case of minors, have their parents sign the forms.

Child Abuse: Although martial arts practice (but not competition) is often a co-ed activity, mixing age groups (children and adults) together in the same class at the same time, with the same instructor and the same lesson plan is not a good idea. If your time/space constraints are such that you have different age populations are training at the same time, then use assistant instructors, keep your age groups separated from each other and provide age-appropriate instruction to each group. Understand that keeping children out of your adult classes is simply good risk management. As an adjunct to mixed age groups, do not permit adults and children to be changing in the same facility at the same time. Again, avoidance is simply good risk management. If there is no opportunity for child molestation, the problem will not arise. If you behave as a professional and expect your assistants to model your behavior and example, then risks in this area will be minimal.

It is a sad fact that child abuse occurs and as martial arts instructors we should be on the front line protecting the lives of our young students. Child abuse can take many forms extending from physical and emotional maltreatment to sexual abuse. Sexual abuse of a child involves activities, which are designed to give sexual gratification to an adult or someone who is four years older than the victim (Block and Reece, 2005). The Boy Scouts of America manual (1998), gives a succinct definition of child abuse or neglect as involving *"either the action or lack of action of a person who occupies a situation of responsibility for the care of the child."*

The sexual molestation of a child often involves bribery, threats or force to coerce a child into compliance with a sexual activity. Such activity might include exhibitionism (exposure of sexually sensitive areas of the body), voyeurism (watching sexual activity), fondling (inappropriate touching) and rape. It is important to recognize that boys and girls can be sexually abused by adults or by other children. Unfortunately, victims often feel shamed, humiliated, embarrassed and unable to talk about their experiences, sometimes because they fear the molester. Victims may also be reticent to speak of their experiences because they may assume a level of personal responsibility for the abuse or fear the repercussions or anger of their parents or teachers. Molestation occurs from the abuse of positions of trust and more than 80% of sexually abused boys get abused by people they trust outside of their immediate family. Again according to the Boy Scouts of America manual (1998), apart from the sexual abuse of boys, most abuse occurs within families. Recognizing the occurrence of sexual abuse can be difficult, especially if the child is unwilling to talk about his or her experiences.

As instructors, it is our responsibility to protect children and to teach them to "Recognize, Resist and Report" instances of abuse (Boy Scouts of America, 1998). Equally, it is incumbent upon the instructor to recognize signs of possible abuse and report such signs to the appropriate authorities. The hardest part of the 3R's is giving children the freedom to speak out when they feel they have been abused. As we have said, children are often reluctant to talk about their experience and instructors are not professional therapists. As martial arts instructors we should aim to be role models with whom the children should feel comfortable and safe. The implication is that children should feel that they might turn to their instructor for help and assistance if they are abused.

Young people are entitled to protection from abuse and martial arts instructors owe them a high level of duty in this regard. In order to protect the children in your classes I recommend the following practices that can be synthesized from several sources including Amateur Rowing Association (2002), Boy Scouts of America (1998), British Judo Association (National Governing Body for Judo in England) (2003), Bushido Zazen International Society (2003), English Karate Association (NGB for Karate in England) (2004), Football Association of the United Kingdom (2001), YMCA (2001):

i) Generate a child protection policy and hand it to every parent when a child enrolls in your program.

ii) Educate your instructors and all volunteers who come into contact with children in your classes concerning child safety policies.

iii) Instructors should communicate regularly with parents and involve them in decision-making processes that affect their children.

iv) Treat all children equally and with respect and dignity.

v) Exhibit the highest standards of professional behavior and care at all times.

vi) Respect all children's touch boundaries and their rights not to be touched in ways that make them feel uncomfortable. Instructors should respect the rights of children to say "no." The use of a risk agreement, (Appendix 5), which includes a non-participation clause is very helpful in creating an awareness of the expected range of physical contact involved both for the parents and the children, and clearly explains a participant's right to exclude him or herself for any activity with which s/he feels uncomfortable.

vii) Encourage children to take responsibility for their own actions and decision-making. Children who feel that they are able to make decisions for themselves are much more likely to actively resist abuse and report such events to responsible adults.

viii) Never leave children unsupervised.

ix) Instructors should not be alone with children and should endeavor to create settings where instructors are clearly visible to each other or other adults when they are working with children.

x) Instructors should be aware of situations that can be misconstrued or manipulated by others. Examples of such situations might include being alone with the children or the use of martial arts techniques that might be easily misconstrued by onlookers.

xi) Instructors should watch for, and be aware of, any sign of injury or abuse in a child and be ready to discuss their findings with a child's parents in a non-threatening manner.

xii) Instructors should not abuse children in any way, which includes all forms of physical (striking, shaking), verbal (humiliating, degrading), sexual (inappropriate touching or verbal exchange) or mental (shaming, being cruel) abuse.

xiii) Instructors should ensure that restroom facilities are unoccupied by suspicious or unknown people before allowing children to use the facilities and stand in the doorway while children are using the facilities.

xiv) If children must be supervised in restrooms or changing areas, always ensure that instructors, parents and or officials work in pairs.

xv) Instructors should use age-appropriate teaching methods and maintain reasonable child/adult ratios in class. The YMCA (2002) suggests that there should be a 1:8 instructor to child ratio for children between the ages of 6 and 18. This ratio is a guideline only, because each State will have its own guidelines for childcare.

xvi) Do not engage in horse play with children.

xvii) Instructors should not allow children to use inappropriate language or behaviors.

xviii) Instructors should not allow any child to leave class with anyone other than the child's parent, guardian or person for whom the parents have given express and written permission.

xix) Instructors should not take children alone in their personal vehicles, without the express permission of the child's parent.

xx) Never take children to your home without their parents or guardians present.

xxi) Instructors should avoid sharing a room with children when away from home on a tournament or clinic trip without another parent or adult being present.

xxii) Instructors should be ready to report any concerns that pertain to child protection to appropriate authorities. Appropriate authorities might include the management personnel of the church, school or YMCA facilities in which your club practices, the Social Services Department, and possibly, the police. It is paramount that the instructor keeps factual, written records of concern along with dates and times.

To help instructors recognize and act upon instances of potential physical and/or sexual abuse there are signs that can be helpful, such as:

i) An unwillingness of a child to interact with a particular person for no obvious reason.

ii) Unexplainable changes in behavior such as becoming very quiet or withdrawn.

iii) Sudden and unexplainable mistrust of adults.

iv) Body language involving shying away and cowering.

v) Exhibiting behaviors with sexual overtones that a child of his or her age would not normally exhibit.

vi) Physical evidence that sexual activity has occurred. Such evidence may include soreness, irritation or bruising of sexually sensitive areas of the body.

vii) Evidence that physical abuse has occurred such as bruising, scratching, cuts, burns and/or bite marks. Bruising in areas of the body that would not normally get bruised during accidental activity are warning signs.

viii) Evidence of an injury for which the explanation does not seem consistent.

Other evidence that indicate some form of psychological stress in a child's life can include:

i) Self-destructive behaviors including substance abuse, self-inflicted injury, depression, thoughts or actions pertaining to suicide.

ii) Raised levels of personal anxiety as indicated by loss of appetite or sleep.

iii) Regression to earlier levels of development such as thumb sucking or bed wetting.

iv) A sudden drop in academic performance, missing school or discipline problems in class.

If an instructor receives a report from a child or adult or sees clear evidence of child abuse there are several things that the instructor will need to do:

i) Remember that you are not a therapist.

ii) Stay calm.

iii) Talk to the child and emphasize that the child is not responsible or to blame for what happened.

iv) Reinforce the child's right to speak about what happened.

v) Take what the child says seriously. Listen.

vi) Do not badger the child for details.

vii) Do not ask any leading questions because they might contaminate the child's testimony at a later date.

viii) Keep a written record; including names of people involved, times, dates, locations, physical signs, dialog and other relevant information.

ix) Reassure the child, but do not promise to keep the matter secret. Explain to the child that it may be necessary to inform other people.

x) Report the event to the appropriate authorities.

Negligence: According to Corcoran and Graden, (1998), writing for the American Council on Martial Arts, under the auspices of the National Association of Professional Martial Artists, Layon (informally published data, 2003, 2004), writing as legal council for the United States Judo Association, and Martens (1990), writing for the American Coaching Effectiveness Program, coaches (regardless of sport) have nine legal duties. You will notice that many of these duties overlap with the items that we discussed earlier in the chapter, in the general safety section:

i) Plan the activity.

ii) Provide proper instruction.

iii) Provide a safe training environment.

iv) Provide and maintain adequate and appropriate training equipment.

v) Match your students appropriately for size, age and/or ability.

vi) Supervise your students.

vii) Evaluate your students for injury.

viii) Warn of risks.

ix) Provide appropriate levels of emergency assistance.

If you fail in any of these duties then you could be found negligent and subject to civil action. In general, for an instructor to be found negligent, it is normally necessary to demonstrate that the coach had a legal duty that was not performed, and which resulted in injury or loss to a player to whom the coach owed the duty (Martens, 1990). Although many of these issues were covered in earlier sections, it is good to remind ourselves of them again in this section.

I have already mentioned planning the activity through the use of lesson plans and the development of a syllabus. From the perspective of negligence, the most obvious aspect of proper planning involves the introduction of advanced drills to students who have not been adequately prepared. Consequently, if you do not consider the physical and mental preparedness of your players when introducing a drill you may be negligent in your duty to adequately plan the activity. As an example, let us say that you have an overweight person who joins the dojo to lose weight and in the first week you have that person doing vigorous calisthenics as part of the warm-up. There is a risk of negligence here, primarily because as a coach you should know better than to expect an overweight person to do vigorous calisthenics when his or her body is not yet ready for such activities. In this example, providing lower intensity activities and reminding that person to live within his or her limits would be all that is required to remove the risk entirely.

A final part of proper preparation involves record keeping. Keep a file of written lesson plans. If a player gets injured on your mat and then comes back several weeks, months or years later to seek compensation for his or her injuries, will you be able to remember your lesson plan for the night of the injury? If there is an injury, keep a record of the event and clip a copy of your lesson plan to the report. You will then have two copies of the lesson plan: One in your master file, and one in the student's file.

As we have said often in this text, you have a duty to provide appropriate instruction, which means that you must teach according to accepted practices of your martial arts style and you must teach using accepted practices for the age of your students. An example of not providing age-appropriate instruction is teaching full force joint locking techniques to a twelve year-old child because applying joint locks can cause damage to young, under-developed bones. As a final comment here, teaching according to accepted practices of your martial arts style simply means using common sense, protecting your players while they practice, not exposing them to unnecessary risks, and playing by the rules.

The next duties are related to each other, and include the obligation to provide a safe training environment and to provide and maintain equipment. You should make sure that your training surface is firm and yet can cushion a fall. If the floor is a wooden floor, then there should be no risk of splinters. If the training surface is covered, the cover should not be torn or have holes and/or wrinkles in it. Never practice on a concrete surface without some form of approved martial arts training surface above it. There should be an adequate safety area for traffic around the mats. The walls and floor of the dojo should be clear of objects such as nails, splinters, or objects that can become dislodged or fall. Ensure that there is adequate lighting in all areas of the training area including the restrooms and the changing areas. Keep chemicals out of reach of children.

If weapons are used as an integral component of the martial arts style that you teach, ensure that they are stored away from students who do not know how to use them and make sure that the weapons are safe to use. When using wooden sticks and knives make sure that they are free of splinters. Never practice with a live blade. Protective sparring equipment, striking targets and shields should be well-maintained and replaced when damaged.

Regardless of whether you own or rent the facility in which you train, do a regular check of the physical spaces (training floor, dressing rooms, restrooms, travel areas and equipment) before class. Remove and/or warn of potential environmental hazards. Like it or not, cleanliness is another aspect of a safe training environment and says a lot to your students about what things you value. An instructor who takes time to make sure the training facilities are clean, cared for and safe, is much more likely to teach in a similar fashion, than one who does not.

The next area of concern is matching your players for size, age and/or ability and then discharging your obligation to supervise the activities of your students closely. It is your duty to ensure that your players are not matched in such a way as to place one in a significantly disadvantageous position relative to the other. To do so increases the risk of injury and is cause for accusations of negligence. Consequently you must consider not just size, age or ability but level of physical conditioning, attitude, maturity and experience. It is your responsibility to intervene if your students are mismatched or are not adhering to the expected levels of cooperation or control, which brings us to the duty of supervision.

Supervision requires that the coach be on the mat while training takes place. Equally, the coach should maintain a position from which s/he can observe the entire mat. Turning your back on a group of students to offer specific supervision to a smaller group of students can be considered negligent. Look at it from this perspective: You have several pairs working together performing a drill. You go over to one particular pair to offer advice and then an injury occurs behind you. When the insurance adjusters call and ask you what you saw, you are obliged to tell them that you didn't see the incident because your back was inadvertently turned when the event occurred. It now moves into the realm of possible negligence. Supervision on its own is not enough. You must act swiftly to reduce risk or deal with an emergency.

The next duties involve evaluating your players for their ability to participate and for any possible injury. Go back to the chapter on physiology to see the recommendations about injury. Beyond dealing with injuries, as a coach, it is your responsibility to ensure that your players are healthy enough to take part in your classes. Be vigilant for signs of fatigue or loss of concentration, since both are pre-incident indicators and both raise your risk factors dramatically. Always allow free access to water and rest. Likewise, when frustration sets in, consider breaking down the drill in order to preserve a safe training environment and to raise the level of comprehension (Gleeson, 1967).

Since martial arts training involves close, personal activity, it is important to make sure that your players are not contagious in any way. If a student has a disability, health concern, or is recovering from an injury it is advisable to get a doctor's permission before returning to practice. When a student does return to training after an injury-induced lay-off, be cognizant that the psychological trauma may take longer to heal than the physiological injury. By way of illustration, students who suffer a knee injury may be reluctant to depend on the affected leg when they first return to class, even if their doctor has told them that the knee is now fine. It is the psychological fear of re-injury that holds the student back. Placing students in a situation they fear is an increased risk factor and requires wisdom and understanding on the part of the instructor.

Keep written records, including a health history on each of your students. How would you like to recruit an apparently healthy individual and then watch the student have a heart attack on your mat during the warm-up? Wouldn't you prefer to know that the student had a pre-existing heart condition and had obtained a doctor's permission to participate, rather than be unaware of it until the event transpires before your eyes? If you know ahead of time, then the pair of you can monitor what the student does and jointly develop a training program that is appropriate for the medical condition. Having developed a mutually agreed upon training program, you will have warned your student of the risks, obtained written consent and given written freedom to stop training whenever the student felt the need to do so. You are both now mutually aware of the training expectations and the medical situation.

We have said this often, but it bears repeating; you have a duty to provide an explanation of inherent risks and obtain an agreement to participate. It is your duty to warn of the risks inherent in the drills you teach. When you teach something new, warn of the risks and provide reminders often. Simply put, this means doing things like reminding students to strike with the correct weapon when hitting a training surface with hands, feet, knees or elbows, to turn the head when throwing forward, to fall safely and in accordance with established practices for the style you teach, to use appropriate force and levels of contact at all times, not to crank on joint locks and to tap out when it locks. It is for this reason that I have stressed the use of waivers and risk agreements (Appendix 5 and 6). Have your students sign a new waiver each year and for any special events and be prepared to discuss the risk agreement and the waiver with your students. Keep all student records, even the old waivers.

Lastly, I also want to touch on vicarious liability. If you have assistant coaches helping you teach, or even teaching for you when you are away, **you are still responsible for the results of the assistant's teaching**. Simply put, if you are the chief instructor you cannot delegate your legal duties. It is permissible to have assistants, but if they are working under your authority, you are legally bound for negligence as though you were teaching the students yourself.

Summary: Like it or not, litigation is a fact of our society. Ignorance of your duties is not an excuse and failure to ensure the safety of your players will lead you into legal hassles. To protect yourself:

i) Keep it professional.

ii) Keep written records.

iii) Remember that your prime responsibility is the safety of your players.

Chapter 9

FINAL THOUGHTS

So there it is. I have given to you the best of what I have currently learned; I give credit for the good bits to all my teachers, mentors, guides and students. For my errors, omissions and weaknesses, please forgive and remember that I too am just a student. As a book, I'm sure that there are places where, in later times, I will wince when I read what I have written, but that is as it should be. I have not yet learned all that I need to know. This is not the perfect book; nor are we perfect teachers. Despite the flaws and weaknesses in the text, remember that I have had only one goal throughout: to create opportunities for success. If by writing, I can make your road a little easier and increase the likelihood of your success, then my purpose will have been well served.

Those of us who like to call ourselves coaches, teachers, sensei's, sifu's, (or whatever title suits you) are probably called to that role because we have a burning desire to learn and want to pass on what we learn. That; and we get pleasure from seeing our students go on to their own successes. If we are honest, however, we know that the learning is a life-long journey and that every time that we step on the deck to teach, we step on as both teacher and student. It is yet another reason why we bow at the beginning of class.

It is my hope that this manual has been of use to you. I have poured into these pages nearly forty years of experience as a student in several martial arts, and as a coach, referee, and competitor at various levels from the local to the national. I have also mixed in the perspectives I have acquired from my life as a university professor and as an entrepreneur. My journey, much like yours I suspect, is one of learning and growing, falling and standing back up. Such is life. So from that perspective, Judo is both a metaphor and a way of life for me.

Finally, in drawing this thing to a close I thought that perhaps I should attempt to come up with some suitably wise and useful things to say…but all I have are my guiding thoughts, the thoughts that served as the undercurrent to the experience of writing.

If I could summarize the undercurrents that have weaved their way through this book, they would probably be something like this:

- Know that you are a work in progress.
- Remember always, that you too, are the student.
- Remember always, that your students can easily be your teachers.
- Show up to class with an empty cup.
- Maintain an attitude of gratitude.
- Look for the opportunity and the lesson in all situations.
- Care for your students, each of them is a precious gift.
- Know what you want to achieve as a martial artist.
- Know what you want to achieve as a coach.
- And, for the Boy or Girl Scout in each of us…Be prepared.
- Be organized, keep records and have a plan of where you are going
- Lastly, remember my initial quote at the beginning….excellence is a habit.

I wish you well and hope our time together has been of value to you. Thank you.

BIBLIOGRAPHY

Abernethy, B., et al., 1997. The Biophysical Foundations of Human Movement. Human Kinetics, Illinois, 425p.

American College of Sports Medicine, 1995. Guidelines for Exercise Testing and Prescription. 5th Edition, Williams and Wilkins, Maryland, 373p.

Alessandra, T., 1990, Relationship Strategies. Nightingale Conant, Illinois, 38p.

Amateur Rowing Association. 2004. Good Practice in Rowing. Participant welfare, good practice and child protection policy and procedures. 26p. Available at: www.ararowing.org/youth/childprotect.php

American Red Cross, 1993. Standard First Aid. Staywell, Boston, 231p.

Ames, R., 1993. Sun-Tzu: The Art of Warfare. Ballantine, New York, 321p.

Anderson, R.A., and Anderson, J.E., 2000. Stretching. Shelter Publications, Bolinas, California, 223p.

Bare-Grounds, T., 2001. The Bare Essentials Guide for Martial Arts Injury Care and Prevention. Turtle Press, Connecticut, 240p.

Block, R.W., and Reece, R.M., 2005. Maltreatment. In: Crosby, A. G., and others, editors. About Children: An authoritative resource on the state of childhood today. American Association of Pediatrics, 271p.

Boeckner, L., 1998. Nutrition and the Athlete: Fueling Your Sport.
http://www.ianr.unl.edu/pubs/foods/nf73.htm

Bompa, T.O., 1999. Periodization Training for Sports. Human Kinetics, Illinois, 239p

Boy Scouts of America. 1998. The Boy Scout Handbook, 11th Edition, B.S.A. Publications, Texas, 472p.

British Judo Association. 2003. Child Protection Policy, Procedures and Guidelines. 39p. Available at www.britishjudo.org.uk/childprotection/policy.php

Brown, L.R., 2009. Plan 4.0. Mobilizing to Save Civilization. Norton. New York, 368p

Burke, L., 1998. Carbohydrate Depletion – is it for you?
http://www.sportsci.org/news/compeat/deplete.html

Buckingham, M., and Clifton, D.O., 2001. Now, Discover Your Strengths. Free Press, New York, 260p.

Buckingham, M., and Coffman, C., 1999. First, Break All The Rules, Simon and Schuster, New York, 271p.

Bushido Zazen International Society. 2003. Child Protection Policy. Available at www.bushidozazen.dzaba.com

Byl, J., 2004. 101 Fun warm-up and cool-down games. Human Kinetics, Illinois, 187p

Campbell, B., 1974. Championship Judo Drill Training. Zenbei Publishing, California, 128p.

Canney, J., 1991. Martial Arts Injuries. A&C Black, London, England,112p

Carnegie, D., 1936. How to Win Friends and Influence People. Pocket Books, New York, 276p.

Chu, D.A., 1992. Jumping into Plyometrics. Leisure Press, Illinois. 80p.

Chun, R., 1982. Advancing in Taekwondo. Harper and Row, New York, 419p.

Cochran, S., 2001. Complete Conditioning for Martial Arts. Human Kinetics, Illinois, 174p.

Corcoran, J and Graden, J., eds. 1998. American Council on Martial Arts Instructor Certification Manual, Graden Media Group, Florida, 261p.

Cooper Institute for Aerobics Research. 1999. The American Council on Martial Arts Instructor Certification Manual. Supplement. Cooper Institute, Texas.

Covey, S.R., 1989.The Seven Habits of Highly Effective People. Fireside Press, New York, 358p.

Coyne, L.L., 2003. Carbohydrate Loading. Con in the "Carbo-loading" Argument.
http://www.centralhome.com/ballroomcountry/carbohydrate-loading.htm

Csikszentmihalyi, M., 1991. Flow: The Psychology of Optimal Experience, Harper Collins, New York 303p

Delavier, F., 2001. Strength Training Anatomy. Human Kinetics, Illinois, 124p.

Dewey, C.P., 2005a. United States Judo Association, Coach Education Program, Level I Manual, Fifth Estate, Alabama, 153p.

Dewey, C.P., 2005b. United States Judo Association, Coach Education Program, Level II Manual, Fifth Estate, Alabama, 156p.

Dewey, C.P., 2005c. United States Judo Association, Coach Education Program, Level III Manual, Fifth Estate, Alabama, 172p.

Dimitrius, J-E, and Mazzarella, M., 1999. Reading People. Random House, New York, 295p.

Dispenza, J., 2007. Evolve Your Brain: The Science of Changing Your Mind. Health Communications, Inc., Florida, 510p.

Doidge, N., 2007. The Brain that Changes itself, Penguin, New York, 427p.

Dominguez, R.H., 1979. The Complete Book of Sports Medicine. Warner Publishing, New York, 182p.

Duncan, J., 2002. Is there a secret to retaining teenage students? Martial Arts Professional Magazine, Vol. 7, no. 4, p.38.

English Karate Association, 2004. Child Protection Policy. Version 5, 15p. Available at www.EKGB.org.uk

Estwanik, J., 1996. Sports Medicine for the Combat Arts. Boxergenics Press, N. Carolina, 272p.

Faber, A., and Mazlish, E., 2002. How to talk so kids will listen and listen so kids will talk. Quill, New York, 286p.

Flegel, M.J., 1992. Sport First Aid. Human Kinetics, Illinois, 185p.

Football Association of the United Kingdom, 2001. Child Protection Procedures and Protection Handbook. London, England, 35p.

Fox, S.I., 1993. Human Physiology. Wm. C. Brown Publishers, Iowa, 671p.

Gagne, R.M., Briggs, L.J., and Wager, W.W., 1992. Principles of Instructional Design. Harcourt, Brace and Jovanovich, New York, 365p.

Gilbert, J.N and Beatie, B.R., 2003. Using reflective Tools to Enhance learning. Strategies. Vol. 16, number 5, pp.11-14.

Glazier, M., 2002a. Maximizing Student Results with Nutrition: Part 2: Pre-Training Supplementation. MA Success, July 2002, p58.

Glazier, M., 2002b. Defeating the Martial Arts' Age-Old Nemesis – Joint Injuries. MA Success, August, 2002, p.54.

Gleeson, G., 1967. Judo for the West. Barnes & Co., Cranbury, New Jersey, 207p.

Gleeson, G., 1983. Judo Inside Out. Lepus Books, Wakefield, England, 155p.

Gleeson, G., 1989. Judo Games. A & C Black, London, 72p.

Glover, B., 1996. The Runner's Handbook. Penguin Books, New York, 726p.

Goleman, D., 1995. Emotional Intelligence, Bantum Books, New York, 352p.

Graden, J., 1997. How to Open and Operate a Successful Martial Arts School. Florida, 177p.

Grisogono, V., 1984. Sports Injuries. John Murray, London, 294p.

Hall, S., and Brogniez, J., 2001. Attracting Perfect Customers. Berrett-Koehler Publishing, California. 204p.

Hamill, J., and Knutzen, K.M., 1995. Biomechanical Basis of Human Movement. Williams and Wilkins, Maryland, 532p.

Handal, K.A., 1992. The American Red Cross First Aid and Safety Handbook. Little, Brown and Company, Massachusetts, 321p.

Hawkins, D., 2002. Power vs. Force: The hidden determinants of Human Behavior. Hay House, California, 341p.

Haymes, E.M., and Wells, C.L., 1986. Environment and Human Performance. Human Kinetics, Illinois, 164p.

Headley, S., and Massad, S., 1999. Nutritional Supplements for Athletes. National Association for Sports and Physical Education, Maryland. 66p.

Hendricks, G., 2009. The Big Leap. Harper One, New York, 216p.

Henkel, N., 2002. Solutions for Problem Parents. MA Success, Vol 2, no.5, pp.56-63.

Herbert, R.D., and Gabriel, M., 2002. Effects of stretching before and after exercising on muscle soreness and risk of injury: systematic review. British Medical Journal. Vol. 325, p.468.

Herrigel, E., 1953. Zen in the Art of Archery. Pantheon Books, New York, 90p.

Hirsch, S., and Kummerow, J., Life Types. 1989. Warner Books, New York, 278p.

Huang, C.A., and Lynch, J., 1992. Thinking Body, Dancing Mind. Bantam Books, New York, 306p.

Janssen, J., 1996. The Mental Makings of Champions: How to Win the Mental Game. University of Arizona.

Judo Canada, 1983. Coaching Certification Program, Level II. Canada, 168p.

Kano, J., 1986. Kodokan Judo. Kodansha International, New York, 264p.

Keirsey, D., and Bates, M., 1984. Please Understand Me. Prometheus Books. California, 210p.

Kim, S.H., 1997. Teaching Martial Arts. Turtle Press, Connecticut, 207p.

Klein, S.B., 2002. Learning: Principles and Applications. Mc Graw Hill, New York, 564p.

Kreider, R.B., Fry, A.C., and O'Toole, M.L., 1998. Overtraining in Sport. Human Kinetics, Illinois, 403p.

Kujala, U.M., 1995. Acute injuries in soccer, ice hockey, volleyball, basketball, judo, and karate: analysis of national registry data. British Medical Journal. Vol. 311, pp.1465-1468.

Le Beouf, M., 1987. How to Win Customers and Keep Them for Life. Berkley, New York, 190p.

Leggett, T., 1978. Zen and the Ways. Charles E. Tuttle, Vermont, 258p.

Le Unes, A., and Nation, J.R., 2002. Sport Psychology. Third edition. Wadsworth Publishing, California, 498p.

Luttgens, K., and Wells, K. F., 1989. Kinesiology: Scientific Basis of Human Motion. Wm. C. Brown, Iowa, 656p.

Martens, R., 1990. Successful Coaching. Human Kinetics, Illinois, 237p.

Maltz, M., and Sommer, B., 2000. Psycho-Cybernetics. Revised Edition, MJF Books, New York, 353p.

Micheli, L., 1995. The Sports Medicine Bible. Harper, New York, 339p.

Mitchell, D., 1988. The Martial Arts Coaching Manual. A& C Black, London, 192p.

Mitchell, D., 1992. The Young Martial Artist. Overlook Press, New York, 128p.

Moore, W.S., 2000. Fundamental Considerations in Cerebrovascular Disease. In: Rutherford, R.B., Ed., Vascular Surgery, Fifth Edition, W.B. Saunders, Pennsylvania, pp.1713-1730.

Moran, G.T., and McGlynn, G.H., 1997. Cross-Training for Sports. Human Kinetics, Illinois, 232p.

Morgan, F.E., 1992. Living the Martial Way. Barricade Books, New Jersey, 312p.

Nakamura, K.T., 1992. One Day, One Lifetime. World Seido Karate Organization, New York, 196p.

Nakayama, M., 1978. Best Karate: Fundamentals. Kodansha International, New York, 144p.

National Coaching Certification Program. 1979. Coaching Theory: Level 2. Canada.

Nicholas Institute of Sports Medicine and Athletic Trauma, 2002. NISMAT Sports Nutrition Corner: Carbohydrate. http://www.nismat.org/nutricor/carbohydrate.html

Nishiyama, H., and Brown, R.C., 1960. Karate: The Art of "Empty Hand" Fighting. Charles E. Tuttle, Vermont. 251p.

Nurchis, R., 2002. Nutrition and the Role of Diet in Martial Arts Competition. Journal of Asian Martial Arts, Vol. 11, number 1, pp.29-51.

Ormond, J.E., 1999. Human Learning. Third edition, Prentice Hall, New Jersey, 557p.

Palmer, P.J., 1998. The Courage to Teach. John Wiley, San Francisco, California, 201p.

Peters, R., 1997. Don't Be Afraid To Discipline. Golden Books, New York, 205p.

Pitino, R., 1997. Success is a Choice. Broadway, New York, 275p.

Powers, S.K., and Howley, E.T., 1990. Exercise Physiology: Theory and application to fitness and performance. Wm. C. Brown., Iowa, 539p.

Rifkin, J., 2009. The Empathic Civilization. Penguin Books, New York, 674p.

Riso, D.R., and Hudson, R., 1996. Personality Types. Houghton Miflin, New York, 514p.

Riso, D.R., and Hudson, R., 1999. The Wisdom of the Enneagram. Bantam, New York, 389p.

Scott, S., 2005. Coaching on the Mat, Welcome Mat Books, Missouri, 141p.

Selye, H., 1978. The Stress of Life. 2nd Edition. Mc Graw-Hill, New York. 516p.

Siddle, B.K., 1995. Sharpening the Warrior's Edge. PPCT Research Publications, Illinois, 148p

Sternberg, R.J., 1997. Successful Intelligence, Plume Publications, New York, 303p.

Tedeschi, M., 2000. Hapkido: Traditions, Philosophy, Technique. Weatherhill, Connecticut, 1135p.

Temme, J., 1996. Team Power. SkillPath Publications, Kansas, 242p.

Thompson, G.J., and Jenkins, J.B., 1993. Verbal Judo: The gentle art of persuasion. Quill Publications, New York, 222p.

Tracy, B., and Rose, C., 1995. Accelerated Learning Techniques. Nightingale Conant, Illinois, 96p.

Watanabe, J., and Avakian, L., 1960. The Secrets of Judo. Charles E. Tuttle, Vermont, 186p

Weers, G., 1995. USJA Level I Coach Certification Course. United States Judo Association. Colorado, 89p.

Weers, G., 1996. USJA Level II Coach Certification Course. United States Judo Association, Colorado, 101p.

Weers, G., 2003. The Fundamental Skills of Judo. Weers Publication. Illinois, 122p.

Wilen, W., et al., 2000. Dynamics of Effective Teaching. Longman, New York, 397p.

Wiley, C.A., 1995. Martial Arts Teachers on Teaching. Frog Limited, California, 227p.

Willett, W.C., 2001., Eat, Drink and be Healthy. Simon and Schuster, New York, 299p.

YMCA – Ireland, 2002. 3.2 Child Protection Policy: Northern Ireland, 36p. Available at www.ymca-ireland.org

Appendices

Appendix 1: Sample Eight-Week Progression from White Belt to Yellow Belt

	Week 1	Week 1	Week 2	Week 2
Month 1	Falling ways I, body and foot movement, hand positions, basic punches (jab, cross, hook, uppercut)	Falling ways II, footwork, "the hole", gripping drills, foot sweeps (O and Ko Soto), scarf hold and escape options	Falling ways III, movement / footwork, front and round kicks	Falling ways IV, footwork review, the hole again, basic hip throw, hold-down and uphill escape
	Week 3	**Week 3**	**Week 4**	**Week 4**
Month 1	Falling ways V, creating a push, foot work, evasion and blocking (high, mid, low)	Falling ways VI, ranges of combat, closing distance, opening distance	Low level kicking escapes from punches and/or wrist grabs, introduce side kick, application of front and round kicks	Four basic ground hold positions, control principles, grips and no grips, escapes
	Week 5	**Week 5**	**Week 6**	**Week 6**
Month 2	Movement, pad and partner, kicking punching and blocking drills, weapon formation, target acquisition	Falling VII, making the transition from standing to ground	Review strikes, kicks and blocks, build into no contact free movement to end class "looking for opportunity"	Falling VIII, escapes from grabbing attacks, moving to the dead side, getting away
	Week 7	**Week 7**	**Week 8**	**Week 8**
Month 2	Falling IX, sleeve end clothes grabs, first set	Falling X, wrist grabs, first set	Review for test	Test for rank

Appendix 2: Sample Lesson Plan

In this example, we using a one-hour judo lesson for between fifteen to twenty boys and girls, aged 6 through 10, and ranging from white to green belts. The class is one month out from an in-house Judo tournament. The notes in red are for you, the reader; they would not normally be there.

INSTRUCTORS: _____

DATE: _____

TEACHING GOAL: Finding the right moment to throw (note: this is your reason for doing all the drills in class and something to keep in your mind all the way through)

1. Syllabus Rank Components taught: (note: in this class, the throws are not new, they are being worked on for the tournament)
    a. Beginning group - Hip throws
    b. Advanced group - Shoulder throws "pizza"
    c. Both groups - Finish in a hold

2. Terminology:
    a. Goshi - Hip
    b. Seoi – Shoulder
    c. Nage - Throw
    d. Hajime - Begin
    e. Matte – Stop
    f. Osaekomi – Hold down

3. ~10 minutes: Warm-up and what the children are supposed to learn from it:
    a. Freeze Tag but you can only unfreeze a player using a hip throw. Learn to throw quickly
    b. Rolling break falls with different challenges to make sure they know how to roll, fall, and adapt to being thrown (note: we emphasize relaxing and not holding the breath).

4. ~45 minutes: Main Class Components:
    a. 25 to 30 minutes: (Split the class) beg.- hip throws with partners, adv.- shoulder throws with partners. (go over terminology with both). Start static (note: to get the throws right first), then get them moving, then get them exchanging grips and moving and throwing
    b. 10 to 15 minutes: One or two-minute judo matches to get ready for tournament (environmental application for techniques) (note: we would also talk to the children about each match as needed and explain what happened and why it happened)

5. Biomechanical Principles Exposed: (note: we wouldn't tell the children all of this, but we would keep these in mind and emphasize correct posture and position in reinforcement. We might ask the children to tell us what they think are important aspects of making the throw work)
    a. Getting the right grip
    b. Getting the hips across
    c. Bending the knees
    d. Keeping the back straight
    e. Body rotations
    f. Pushing into the ground, chest forward, "put a lid on it!"

6. 5 minutes: Discussion Topic: 3 Rules of Self Control
    a. Focus the eyes, Focus the mind, Focus the body
    b. Why? What's the benefit? In the dojo? At school? At home? How does it apply to the tournament we have coming next month?

Appendix 3: Sample Goals and Progress Questionnaire

NAME: _____

DATE: _____

CURRENT RANK & STYLE: _____

Section 1: Progress

Please answer the following questions. As you progress in the martial arts, you will find that your goals and reasons for training will change. This is entirely natural, and we admire your courage in setting goals and working towards them.

1. Why did you originally start martial arts?

2. What do you find interesting about your lessons?

3. What do you like most about the classes?

4. In what ways do you feel our program has helped you thus far?

5. What is your main long term goal within our program?

6. What could we do to help you achieve your goal?

7. What is the main reason that you are still training?

/OVER

Section 2: Goals

Studies show that the act of writing down your goals is a powerful motivator in the achievement of success. Please write five goals below with a reason for each and a deadline. Be sure to distinguish between your short term goals and long term goals. Remember that goals without deadlines and action plans are only dreams. For goals to be of use in your life, they must be accompanied with a series of steps and a time line for completion of the steps. The goals do not have to be martial arts related.

1.

2.

3.

4.

5.

Section 3: Comments

_____ is a place where we all grow together. As such, the instructors would value any positive feedback that you may have concerning our programs and services. If you have any comments please feel free to comment below.

Appendix 4: How Can Parents Help?

1. Bring child to the dojo between _____ and _____
2. Adult classes begin at _____ and the adults need time to change and start warming up, so please pick up your child before _____ at the latest. We understand if there are extenuating circumstances that might make picking up a child difficult occasionally, but please respect all of our clients by collecting your child on time.
3. Make sure your child arrives and leaves with their own uniform, clothes, shoes, books and school pack.
4. Encourage children to follow and respect the Dojo rules and the instructor's instructions
5. Leave the instructors in charge of the class. You are encouraged to watch, but please do not coach, or otherwise distract the children.
6. Encourage your child to practice for 15 minutes every day and show you what he/she is learning.
7. Download the lesson plan for the week and ask your child to show you the material that was supposed to be covered in class.
8. Watch a class once or twice per month
9. Be sure child is well-rested and eating nutritious foods. While your child's diet is your concern, his/her behavior on the mat is ours. Please, no caffeine, candy, sweets or junk food before class.
10. While it is their responsibility to fill in their own black belt kid's sheets, you can remind your children to do so and to bring them to class.
11. Also check the Black Belt Kid's Sheet roster by the main office, it will tell you whether we actually received your child's sheet for the week.
12. Periodically review the Children's Manual and Rank Requirement with your child, so that both of you know what to expect.
13. Talk to your child about qualities emphasized for stripes. Notice and encourage these behaviors at home.
14. Talk to an instructor at least once a month about your child's progress. Maintain a dialogue with the instructors regarding challenges your child may have here or elsewhere, any information which may help us better instruct your child, or any other interests or concerns you may have.
15. If you have any questions, concerns, or suggestions, we want to hear them, so please feel free to chat with _____. _____ are assistant instructors in the children's class and will be happy to chat with you, but any issue you raise with them, will be passed onward through the management line for the dojo.

Appendix 5: Sample Warning, Waiver, Release of Liability, Assumption of Risk and Agreement to Participate

THIS AGREEMENT MUST BE SIGNED BY ALL MEMBERS WHO WISH TO PARTICIPATE IN ANY _____ SANCTIONED EVENT.

In consideration of being allowed to participate in any way in the sanctioned events of the _____, I, _____:

1. Recognize and understand that martial arts training is a physical contact activity and that my participation might result in serious injury, including permanent disability or death, and severe social and economic loss.
2. Recognize and understand that such risk may be due to not only my own actions, but also the action, inaction or negligence of others, the regulations of participation, or the conditions of the premises, or of any of the equipment used.
3. Recognize that there may be other risks that are not known to me or to others or not reasonably foreseeable at this time.
4. Agree to inspect the facilities, equipment and pairings prior to participation. I will immediately inform an instructor if I believe that anything is unsafe or beyond my capability and refuse to participate.
5. Assume all the foregoing risks and accept personal responsibility for any damages that may result from injury, permanent disability or death.
6. Enter martial arts training and/or competition entirely of my own free will and understand the importance of following the rules of training and competition. I have been given a copy of the rules and regulations of the _____ and agree to abide by the instructions given therein.
7. I certify that I am in good physical condition, and have no disease, injury or other condition that would either impair my performance or physical and mental well-being during intense training practice and/or competition, or pose a risk to others.
8. Grant permission in case of injury to have a doctor, nurse, athletic training or other emergency medical personnel provide me with medical assistance or treatment for such injury.
9. Release, waive, discharge and covenant not to sue, _____, its affiliated organizations and national governing bodies, their officers, instructors and personnel, other members of the organizations, participants, supervisors, coaches, sponsoring organizations or their agents, and if applicable, owners and leasers of the premises from any and all liability to the undersigned, his or her heirs and next of kin for any and all claims, demands, losses and damages which may be sustained and suffered on account of injury, including death or damage to property, caused or alleged to be caused in whole or in part by the negligence of the releasees or otherwise.

I HAVE READ THE ABOVE WARNING, WAIVER, RELEASE AND AGREEMENT TO PARTICIPATE. I UNDERSTAND ITS CONTENTS AND DO HEREBY SIGN IT VOLUNTARILY.

_____ _____ _____
Printed Name   Signature   Date

_____ _____ _____
Printed Name of Parent or Signature   Date
Guardian if under ____

_____ _____ _____
Printed Name of Parent or Signature   Date
Guardian if under ____

Appendix 6: Risk Agreement

AUTHORITY TO TREAT

I, the undersigned, give the instructors, staff and responsible adults the power to authorize medical or other treatment of the student named _____, subject to the limitations listed below, if any. If I am not the named student, I am the parent, guardian or responsible adult for the named student, and I have legal right to grant this power. Treatment may be made without regard to whether I or any other parent, guardian or responsible adult has been contacted or has consented to the specific treatment, provided it does not conflict with the limitations outlined below. This authority begins on the date signed and continues indefinitely.
Limitations to treatment:

_____

Information of Medical Significance:

_____

By granting my authorization, I assume responsibilities for all decisions made, provided they are reasonable decisions under the circumstances based on the knowledge and understanding of the person making the decisions, and I trust their judgment and offer the benefit of the doubt to them in any claim or legal proceeding. This presumption may only be overcome by clear and convincing evidence that they acted with malice or willful gross negligence, and if so they may still be liable
Signature and Date:_____

Print Name and Relationship (if other than self): _____

I understand that the instructors, senior students, or others may have some skills in first aid, CPR, and, at their discretion, I authorize them to use those skills and techniques to assist in any circumstance in which they judge their skills would be necessary or helpful.

Initials: _____

ADVISORY OF RIGHTS AND RESPONSIBILITIES

Safety is not the sole responsibility of instructors and staff. Everyone in class is responsible for their own safety and the safety of those around them.
All students have the right and responsibility to excuse themselves from any exercise they believe will be harmful to them. All students must evaluate each situation in the context of their skill and current physical condition, and conduct each drill in a manner that is safe. If an instructor gives an instruction that is unsafe for the student, it is the student's responsibility to inform the instructor that the activity may be unsafe. The instructor will routinely excuse the student from unsafe exercises and drills. The instructor may ask or an explanation, and the student is expected to provide one.
All students have the responsibility to train and conduct themselves in a manner that helps all students and instructors remain safe. Students must give those who are training enough room to avoid interfering and avoid being accidentally struck by someone else practicing, which is especially important when others are practicing with weapons.
In the event of an injury, students have the right and responsibility to evaluate the extent of harm, stopping what they are doing even if it includes a partner, and determining if it is safe to continue. Unless a student is certain that further practice will not create or worsen a problem, all students are encouraged to stop what they are doing and inform the instructor. In the event of a serious injury or the appearance of a serious injury, all students, instructors, staff and visitors, notably parents, have the right to call a stop to a particular training exercise.

If a student notes an unsafe training situation, which may include a student performing a skill incorrectly, a student not showing due regard for the safety of others, a defective piece of training equipment, a potentially dangerous obstacle or condition on the floor, or anything else that may cause or lead to harm of students, instructors, visitors or guests, then the student is expected to correct the situation if it is within his ability or to notify an instructor or staff member immediately. If something is simple to correct, such as removing an obstacle from the floor, the student should correct the situation. If the situation may require the authority of the instructor or staff, or if it is not a simple matter, then an instructor or staff member should be notified immediately.

Initials: _____

ASSUMPTION OF RESPONSIBILITIES AND RISK

Martial arts training is a potentially dangerous activity. Bumps, bruises, scrapes, scratches and soreness are commonplace, and most students will encounter this sort of minor injury from time to time in their training. More serious injuries are possible, including sprains, strains, twists, cramps, and injuries of similar magnitude, and the student can be expected to encounter these injuries infrequently. The possibility of more serious injury exists, including fractured bones, broken bones, torn ligaments, though not all students encounter such serious injuries. There remains, despite safety precautions, the remote possibility of crippling or death, though this is certainly not expected in this martial arts class.

I understand the above statement of risk, and I understand the rights and responsibilities of students. I assume responsibility for my own safety (or the safety of my child), understanding and accepting the risks involved with martial arts training. Even if the instructor has informed me that no serious injuries have ever happened in this school or with any of the instructors, I understand that this does not mean that there is no possibility of harm. By assuming this risk, I completely absolve all instructors, staff, guests, students, landlords, management companies and any and all other parties of liability for my harm, unless intentionally caused in criminal conduct.

Initials: _____

NOTICE AND CONSENT TO INSTRUCTORS

This school seeks to make use of highly trained professional instructors, with both expertise and experience both in the art(s) that we teach and in teaching. Classes may be taught by the head instructor or any other qualified instructor. Should an instructor be unavailable for a given class, a junior instructor, senior student or guest instructor may teach. The choice of the instructor is left to the discretion of the school.

I understand that I may not always have the instructor I desire, but I shall seek to learn from whomever is teaching, to show the respect due the position of teacher to whomever is teaching, and to conduct myself in accordance with the etiquette established at this school. I understand that I have the responsibility for my own safety without regard to who may be teaching the class. I specifically consent to any instructor the school, instructors or staff feel are sufficiently qualified by standards they set to teach the class. I specifically understand and agree that the full force of this document applies no matter who is teaching.

Initials: _____

NOTICE OF PHYSICAL CONTACT

Complete martial arts training involves a wide variety of skills. While practicing these skills, students may have contact with any portion of the body. The groin may be the target of kicks, strikes or grabs. The chest, buttocks, groin or any part of the body may be contacted by any part of the training partner's body during training with martial arts techniques, or incidentally contacted while performing a martial arts technique which targets another portion of the body.

When male and female students train together, or when adult and minor students train together, and in any other training combination, the purpose and intent of the school, instructors and staff is to provide an environment for all students to learn and practice martial arts and self-defense. Students are expected to conduct themselves appropriately at all times to ensure the best training results for everyone.

Should any student feel that a training partner is engaging in contact beyond the scope of training, or a training partner is taking undue and unacceptable advantage of training contact, or if a student is made uncomfortable by any training exercise or partner, then that student has the right to withdraw from the exercise or drill. If the contact of a training partner appears inappropriate, the student should inform the instructor privately. If the conduct of the training partner or any training partner appears criminal, then the instructor should be informed and the authorities may be notified either by the student or the instructor, or both.

Initials: _____

CONSENT TO PHYSICAL CONTACT

I understand the nature of physical contact in martial arts training, and I understand that I have the right to immediately withdraw from any exercise or drill in which the contact of any party seems beyond the scope of training and makes me uncomfortable. I agree to abide by school etiquette in all matters pertaining to training, and I shall not in any way conduct myself inappropriately or take inappropriate advantage of the contact martial arts training involves.

Initials: _____

INDEMNIFICATION BY PARENTS

Applicable only to parents enrolling a minor child.

I agree not to bring any claim or suit against the school, instructors, staff, guests, students, landlord, or any other parties on behalf of my child for any injury or harm sustained by any event short of a criminal act, and then only the criminal shall be the subject of such a suit. I further agree that I will not cause to be brought, nor encourage a claim or suit. I also agree not to cooperate in the bringing of such a suit or claim except insofar as I may be legally required to do so. Finally, I shall indemnify the school, instructors, staff, guests, students, and any and all additional defendants covered by this agreement for all judgments, costs, attorney fees and other expenses incurred as a result of a breach of this agreement.

Initials: _____

ARBITRATION CLAUSE

Should any dispute arise between me, my child, or anyone acting on behalf of my child, regarding this school, then I specifically agree that the dispute shall be resolved in binding arbitration. Should a suit be filed in Court, I specifically authorize the Court to order the case to binding arbitration.

SEVERABILITY

If any clause, sentence, phrase or statement is found unenforceable or invalid by any Court of Law, the remainder of the document shall remain valid enforceable and the invalid clause, sentence, phrase or statement shall be considered struck from the document.

DURABILITY

This document is effective from the date signed with no expiration. Furthermore, the terms of this document are retroactive to the beginning of training and visiting this school if this document was signed after that date.

I have read this document, and I understand its content. I agree to abide by the terms stated herein.

Student Signature and Date: _____

For minor students:

Parent Signature and Date: _____

Parent Signature and Date: _____

Witness Signature and Date: _____

Appendix 7: Sample Health History Form

Name:_____ Age: _____

Birth Date: _____

Past and Present Health History (check all that apply)
- _____ Diseases of the heart and arteries
- _____ Abnormal electrocardiogram ECG
- _____ High Blood pressure
- _____ Angina pectoris (chest pain)
- _____ Epilepsy
- _____ Stroke
- _____ Anemia
- _____ Abnormal Chest X-ray
- _____ Cancer
- _____ Asthma or other lung disease
- _____ Orthopedic or musculo-skeletal problems
- _____ Diabetes

If any of the above are checked, please explain and indicate any recommendations your doctor has made regarding exercise:

_____

_____

_____

Is there a family history of heart disease, hypertension, stroke, diabetes, lung disease or epilepsy?

_____ Yes _____ No

Level of Physical Activity:

Yes ____ No ____ Are you currently involved in a REGULAR aerobic exercise program?

Yes ____ No ____ Are you currently involved in a weight training program?

Yes ____ No ____ Do you regularly perform stretching exercises?

What best describes your level of physical activity during the last 4-6 weeks
- _____ Very Active
- _____ Moderately Active
- _____ Occasionally Active
- _____ Inactive